# The Royal Road Of the INCA

## ABOUT THE BOOK

One of the major discoveries of our times is the network of highways built by the Inca nation. These helped to create a civilisation of unparalleled wealth.

Victor von Hagen has spent half a lifetime unearthing these routes and the various civilisations which travelled them. The Incas built them to conquer and occupy their neighbouring tribes and united a vast geographical area into the Inca Empire. The Spanish used the same roads to conquer the Incas and expand their own empire.

Thousands of miles of graded, levelled, terraced, paved highway soaring among the highest peaks of the Andes, cascading and twisting down to the white sands of the Pacific – they are an unparalleled engineering feat.

An unrivalled story teller, von Hagen brings together the great human stories and historical events which have been played out on these roads – the Inca conquest, the Spanish conquest, the Civil War, the last Inca uprising, the great age of Scientific exploration and his own and others' archaeological discoveries.

## ABOUT THE AUTHOR

The last one of the great figures of contemporary archaeology, Victor von Hagen has devoted the past 40 years to archaeological and ethnographical adventure. He has led countless expeditions: to study the Jivaros Indians in the Amazon jungle, to unearth the Maya civilisation in Guatemala and Mexico, to study the Chibcha in Colombia, apart from his research in Chile, Bolivia, Peru and Ecuador on Inca roads. Author of more than 56 books, his best known are *The Realm Of the Incas*, *The Ancient Sun Kingdoms of the Americas*, *The World Of the Maya*, *The Golden Man* and *Search For the Maya*. Most recently he has led an expedition through Turkey and Iran to rediscover the roads which the Ancient Persians built to conquer Greece.

# The Royal Road

# Of the INCA

VICTOR WOLFGANG VON HAGEN

# GORDON & CREMONESI

Designed by Heather Gordon-Cremonesi
Set in 'Monotype' Bell and printed in Great Britain
by W & J Mackay Limited, Chatham

ISBN 0-86033-009-5

Gordon Cremonesi Ltd
New River House
34 Seymour Road
London N8 0BE

# Contents

## PART V   CONTI-SUYU: THE FOURTH QUARTER

## Maps and Plans in text

# List of Illustrations

4

# Chronology

1526    *March*. Contract between Pizarro, Almagro and Fernando de Luque for the search for Peru

*January*. Treaty between Spain and France: Francis I freed.

1527    Pizarro on the isle of Gallo

Medici driven from Florence

Pizarro lands at Tumbes for the first time

1529    Pizarro granted a royal contract for the conquest of Peru

Cardinal Wolsey deprived of his office as Lord Chancellor of England

Sultan Solyman attacks Vienna

1532    *16th May*. Pizarro lands at Tumbes and marches inland towards Cajamarca

Hernando de Soto becomes the first European to see the royal Andean road

*16th November*. Atahuallpa captured

1533    *April–January*. Hernando Pizarro journeys over the Inca roads to Pachacamac

Henry VIII divorces Catherine of Aragon, marries Anne Boleyn

*July*. Distribution of Atahuallpa's ransom: Atahuallpa put to death

*August*. The conquistadors move south toward Cuzco

*December*. Pizarro enters Cuzco. Manco Capac becomes puppet Inca

1534    *23rd March*. Cuzco refounded as a Spanish city

*June*. Sebastián Benalcázar conquers Quito

Order of Jesuits founded

1535    *5th January*. Lima founded as the colonial capital of Peru

Sir Thomas More beheaded

Felipe Huamán Poma de Ayalá born in Cuzco

Pizarro and Almagro sign a new agreement on the division of Peru

*3rd July*. Diego de Almagro begins the march to Chile

1536    *6th May*. Manco Capac in revolt, Cuzco besieged

Henry VIII orders the death of Anne Boleyn

1537 Almagro returns from his epic journey, raises the siege of Cuzco

1538 Almagro and the Men of Chile are defeated by Pizarro's forces at the battle of Las Salinas; Almagro garrotted on the orders of Hernando Pizarro

1539 Francisco de Orellana discovers the Amazon

*17th April.* Garcilaso de la Vega, "El Inca", born in Cuzco

1540 Pedro de Valdivia leaves for the reconquest of Chile

Henry VIII has Thomas Cromwell beheaded

1541 *26th July.* Francisco Pizarro murdered by the Men of Chile

*August.* Padre Vicente de Valverde killed and eaten by natives on the Isle of Puna

Hungary overrun by the Turks

1542 *16th September.* Battle of Chupas

Francisco de Carbajal arrives in Peru

*20th November.* Charles V issues the New Laws for the protection of the Indians

Manco Capac establishes the last Inca capital at Vilcabamba

Mary Stuart becomes Queen of Scotland

Copernicus publishes his work on the solar system

1543 *30th June.* Vaca de Castro issues the *Ordenanzas de Tambos*, regulating the maintenance of the Inca roads and *tampus*

1544 The first Viceroy of Peru, Blasco Núñez, arrives

*October.* Gonzalo Pizarro declares war against the Viceroy, pursues him to Quito

1545 Discovery in Potosí, Bolivia, of the richest silver mine in the world

Council of Trent

1546 Blasco Nuñez, Viceroy, defeated and beheaded

1547 Battle of Huarina, Carbajal victorious

Pedro de Cieza de León arrives in Peru

Henry VIII dies, his son crowned Edward VI

Birth of Cervantes

1548 Civil war between the Spanish Crown and the forces of Gonzalo Pizarro

*9th April.* La Gasca defeats and executes Pizarro and Carbajal

Pedro de Cieza made "First Chronicler of the Indies"

*August.* Redistribution of *encomiendas* by La Gasca

1552 Antonio de Mendoza, second Viceroy of Peru, arrives

1553 Cieza publishes his *Parte prima de la Cronica del Peru*

1554 Cieza dies

1617 Vásquez de Espinosa travels in Peru

1799–1802  Alexander von Humboldt travels in Ecuador and Peru

1848 William H. Prescott publishes his *Conquest of Peru*

1852–80   Sir Clements Markham travels in Peru
1877   E. George Squier publishes his *Peru* (important source material for the study of the Inca roads)
1911   Hiram Bingham discovers Machu Picchu
1931   Robert Shippee and Lt. Johnson pioneer the study of the Inca roads by aerial photography, discover the "great wall of Peru"
1938   Alberto Regal, *Los Caminos del Inca en el Antiguo Peru*, Lima
1947   Victor W. von Hagen begins study of Inca roads
1952–60   Von Hagen systematically explores Inca roads
1967   Gene Savoy discovers the last Inca capital, at Vilcabamba

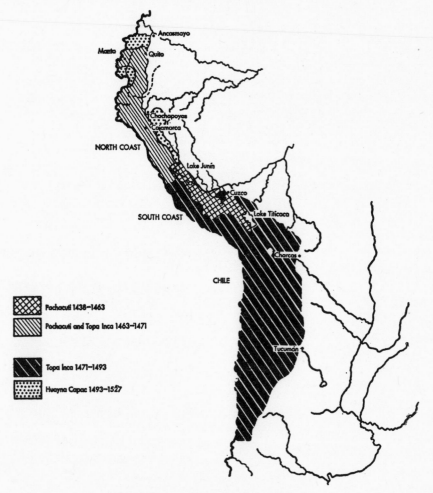

Pachacuti 1438–1463

Pachacuti and Topa Inca 1463–1471

Topa Inca 1471–1493

Huayna Capac 1493–1527

The chronology of the Inca expansion.

An Inca courier or *chasqui*, trained from youth to run at high altitudes. By a series of relays, each running two miles, a verbal message could be carried 1250 miles in 5 days. (*Courtesy Royal Library, Copenhagen*).

An Inca *quipu*, a series of strings hung from a base cord. Half-hitch knots tied in the strings represented decimal units and served as a reader and rememberer for records and *chasquis*. (*Courtesy Royal Library, Copenhagen*).

## CHAPTER ONE

# Capac Ñan: The Beautiful Road

This is the story of a road—not of any ordinary road, but of the Royal Highway of the Incas, which was thought by the first Spaniards to see and travel along it to be "the longest and grandest in the world", while the Incas themselves called it Capac Ñan—the "beautiful road".

It was built at a time when men in the far different world of Europe sought to discourage land communications, which they viewed as a risk to security. In Peru the reverse was the case: the road was conceived and constructed as a way of uniting politically a vast and heterogeneous area, including such geographical extremes as mountain and jungle.

On the desert-bound coasts of Peru and Chile, each riverine oasis was separated from its neighbours by a wide stretch of fierce and uninhabitable desert, which acted not only as a geographical, but also as a cultural, barrier. The Inca highway united these oases. In the Andes there were, until the advent of the Incas, an almost incredible number of distinct tribes, each one cut off from contact with the others by what were often insurmountable obstacles—rivers, chasms and awesome gorges. Once these had all been bridged and connected, over a distance of 3,000 miles, by the all-weather, all-pervading highways (for there was not just one road, but a whole road system), there was no longer any impediment to unity. Lateral roads branching out from the primary routes were pushed into the jungles, and a comprehensive network of communications took shape.

In this way, the Incas overcame geographical differences and integrated the many and varied tribes into a political whole that became Tihuanti-suyu: the empire of the four quarters.

However, unfortunately for the Incas, their road-building programme also provided the prelude to their oblivion; for, when a new people with new weapons arrived from the Old World, the very efficiency of the road system —with its well-serviced bridges, its many regularly maintained wayside stations, and its courier system—contributed more than any other single element to the final destruction of the Inca empire. So well thought out was it, and so well had it been adapted to the geography of the country, that the conqueror had no option but to use it. Indeed, the wayside stations, the *tampus*, grew into villages, the villages into cities, and, beginning in the eighteenth century, developed into metropolises. Without exception every large city in the western part of South America—Quito, Cajamarca, Juaja, Cuzco and Arequipa, and, on the coast, Trujillo, Lima, Ica and, 2,000 miles to the south, Concepcion in Chile—had its origins in the Inca past.

This "longest and grandest road in the world", the main arteries of which went from Quito, in Ecuador, to Cuzco, in Peru, to Chuquisaca, in Bolivia, then deep into Chile and back along the coast to Ecuador (a total distance of over 5,000 miles), provided the stage on which over a thousand years of history was acted out.

In fact, the route followed by the road was in use a thousand years before the advent of the Incas. Then, beginning in about A.D. 1100, the Incas began the series of conquests that led them to absorb into their empire tribes that had preceded them in the area by many centuries, and were in many instances even more culturally advanced than they were themselves.

As the Incas advanced so did the roads, following or often proceeding with the armies. By the year 1493—the same year, it will be recalled, as Christopher Columbus, on his third voyage to the New World, appeared on the Atlantic coast of South America—the whole of the empire from Chile to Quito had been linked up by a network of all-weather roads.

In 1532, Francisco Pizarro and his small band of myrmidons appeared in Peru. From the very moment that they set foot in Tumbes, a coastal town at the extreme northern end of the empire, they were made aware of the roads, which proved decisive in advancing their conquests. "We marched along a broad road," wrote the official scrivener, "made by manual labour and traversing the whole land. By the side of the road flow channels of water . . . at the end of each day's journey there is a *tampu* like an inn. Parts of the road are paved and bounded on each side by a wall. Two carts could be driven abreast upon it . . . in many parts of it, rows of trees for shade were planted on either side." In the Andes "the road is level and the part that goes through the mountains is paved, being broad enough for six men on horseback to ride abreast."

The initial impact that these roads had on the Spaniards was too strong to be dissipated by time. By following the zigzagging step road up into the cordilleras, it took them only two days of travel to ascend from the coast to a height of 11,000 feet above sea level. This road took the form of a vast flight of drylaid stone steps, with turn-offs and resting places. The scrivener observed, "The road . . . was very steep, but there was no other place to ascend but by this road."

How it must have contrasted with the roads in Europe, which they had so recently left! There, as a sixteenth-century traveller said, one had need of "a falcon's eye, an ass's ear, a monkey's face, a merchant's word, a camel's back, a dog's mouth, a deer's foot" to arrive at one's destination.

The Inca road was constantly in Pizarro's mind as he dictated the letter that would carry to the King of Spain the first news of the conquest. Known as the *Letter from Pizarro*, the copies of this epistle were so eagerly read when printed that, in passing from hand to hand, they were actually thumbed into extinction. However, it seems reasonable to assume that the essence of Pizarro's letter is contained in a small pamphlet published in Lyons in 1534 under the curious title of *Nouvelles de certaines Isles de Perou*. This mentions the Inca road (*chemin*) fifteen times in its fifteen small sextodecimo printed pages: "*les chemins du pays sont fort beaux et larges*". In the same year, the book entitled *The True History of the Conquest . . .*, written by Pizarro's secretary, Francisco de Xeréz, appeared. Its only illustration shows Atahuallpa sitting in his litter facing the Spaniards, while in the foreground, prominently delineated, is the paved Inca road, kerbing and all.

The Inca road led directly to the lair of the Lord-Inca Atahuallpa, who, as every Indian soon learned, was trapped and held there. He sought to escape by offering to fill his prison room twice with gold and once with silver. Hernando Pizarro, the brother of the conquistador, rushed off to hurry up the flow of the Inca's ransom from coastal shrines hundreds of miles distant. Even while bent on this single-minded purpose, the ways of the Inca so impressed Hernando Pizarro that he exclaimed, while on his gold-gathering journey, "The royal road over the mountains is a thing worthy of being seen, because the ground is so rugged. Such beautiful roads could not, in truth, be found anywhere in Christendom. For the most part, they are paved. There are bridges over every stream . . . there are numerous suspension bridges, which are marvellous to see . . .".

It was not until 1547 that Pedro de Cieza de León, the first historian of the Inca empire and its roads, arrived in Peru. By that time—fourteen years after the conquest—the empire was dismembered, the two principal conquistadors, Almagro and Pizarro, were both dead, and civil wars between the survivors had further reduced their numbers.

Gonzalo Pizarro, the last of the four Pizarros to be both alive and in Peru, was then lord of the lands. He had raised arms against his liege, Charles V, and a bishop, Pedro de la Gasca, had arrived to put down the rebellion, armed with nothing more than a sheath of royal decrees in *carte blanche*, each one bearing the signature, rubric and seal of the King of Spain. The bishop could thus pardon or condemn simply by the strokes of a pen.

Never has the pen proved so much more effective as a weapon than the sword: men were won over by the stratagem, and among them was Pedro de Cieza de León, who was then following his *capitán* "without plaint." In his inimitable histories of the period, Pedro de Cieza has left us a fascinating picture of the last vestiges of the Inca empire, and, naturally, much detail about their roads.

In 1550 the conquistador was replaced by the settler, and with the settlers came a small company of padres, whose purpose, beyond carrying out the rites of marriage and burial, was to see to the conversion of the Indians. Among this group was the learned Jesuit José de Acosta: observant and tolerant, he is included among the chroniclers of the Inca road. Other padres followed: the frail Cristóbal de Molina, whose frailty was accentuated by the effort of travelling with Diego de Almagro "to the ends of the earth", that is Chile; Antonio Vásquez de Espinosa, who was sent in 1617 to count the heads of the Indians who had embraced the cross of his God; and many more.

The Age of Reason brought French and Spanish natural philosophers to the ancient realm of the Incas. Lt. Jorge Juan, and others like him, were amazed by the sections of Inca road that they found still crossing the scarred Andean earth. They noted down their impressions and helped fill the record. So too did Baron Alexander von Humboldt, who travelled for the "acquisition of knowledge". After journeying along the Inca roads for hundreds of miles, he thought them "the most useful and stupendous works ever executed by man". His many writings contain abundant references to them.

Although he did not see the roads himself, since he was partially blind and never travelled to South America, William Prescott drew the information for his *Conquest of Peru* from original Spanish sources. He told how "the road was conducted over pathless sierras buried in snow; galleries cut for leagues (perhaps "yards" would have been a better word) through living rock; rivers were crossed by means of bridges that swung suspended in the air; precipices were scaled by stairways hewn out of the native bed-rock . . . difficulties which might appal the most courageous engineer of modern times."

Prescott inspired a new generation of travellers, who now came armed with measuring tape and camera lucida, to make scientific observations of what they found. Then the daguerrotype appeared: Léonce Angrand, who started his diplomatic career under Louis-Philippe, often left his post as Consul General in Lima to ride about Peru and Bolivia, recording ruins and roads with the aid of his trained and talented pencil. Sir Clements Markham, who had been told by Prescott himself that he must see the Inca ruins with his own eyes, took up the suggestion and added generously to the archaeological literature on the subject. Ephraim George Squier, a New Yorker who triumphed over dire poverty to win a technical education, and included among his many talents one as a surveyor, used this to bring a new scientific accuracy to the study of Peruvian archaeology. It is to Squier that we owe the only authentic, accurate illustrations of Inca suspension bridges, which survived until his time.

CAPAC ÑAN: THE BEAUTIFUL ROAD                    15

Hiram Bingham, the famed discoverer of Machu Picchu, was led to Peru "by seeing a picture of the Bridge across the Apurimac" in Squier's book. Once there, he followed the ancient roads to the edge of the last capital of the Incas.

During the first four decades of the twentieth century, scholars, travellers, and archaeologists continued to nibble away at what was left of the once-great road system. In 1931, Robert Shippee, as pilot, with Lt. Johnson, as aerial photographer, again and again noticed evidence of the Inca roads in the photographs they took, but since the roads were not their prime concern and they lacked the ground contacts to act on what they had filmed, their discoveries remained partial. A Peruvian scholar then tried to retrace the road system through a close reading of ancient and modern literature on the subject, but his attempts were in vain as it was the very earth upon which the roads were written that had to be scoured and searched.

In 1934, the present author arrived in Ecuador to undertake this task. The search, still fragmentary, was continued in a desultory fashion until 1952, when, under the aegis of the American Georgaphical Society, an expedition equipped for a complete investigation into the nature, construction and physical history of the Inca highway system was put down in Peru.

This field research continued until 1958 and resulted in the first mapping of the road system. Many of the *tampus* were located, and the manner in which the system functioned was thoroughly explored. This work opened up the entire southern part of Peru to archaeologists, who before that had scarcely touched on the area. New archaeological regions were opened up in the north, and the efforts of the expedition to find the roads that led to the last capital of the Incas in Vilcabamba, buried in the forests of the Upper Amazon, inspired the 1965 expedition led by Gene Savoy, who finally found it.

This then is the story of that road, "the longest and grandest in the world".

The first and the only authentic picture of Atahuallpa's meeting with the Spaniards. He is shown holding a bible in his hand while Padre Valverde speaks to him. Behind Valverde the Pizarros. In the foreground the curbing of the Inca road. (*From* La Historia Verdadera . . . *by Francixco de Xeres, Seville 1535*).

# PART I

# CHINCHA-SUYU:
# THE FIRST QUARTER

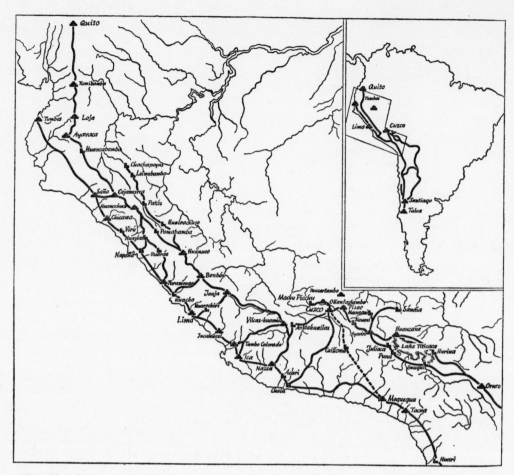

The Chincha-suyu roads: the important cities in Peru and Ecuador on the Inca road.

## CHAPTER TWO

# The Kingdom of the Quitus

The royal road of the Chincha-suyu (the Lynx Quarter—one of the four quarters of the Inca empire) was thought by the first Europeans to see it, in 1533, to be the longest continuous road in the world. From its beginning at the holy shrine in Cuczo, where the traveller made a *mocha*, a bow of reverence to ensure that he had a safe journey, the road ran all the way to Quito and beyond, a total distance of 1,230 miles. It was at the northern end of this road that, in the notable year of 1547, the warrior-chronicler Pedro de Cieza de León began his journey across the Inca empire.

There was little about the circumstances of his birth that would have led one to expect that Cieza, as he is commonly called, would become the first great chronicler of the Incas. Born in Villa de Llerena, Spain, not very far from the great Roman road that ran between Salamanca and Seville, he was the son of Lope de León, who kept a small shop.

Before leaving for the New World "at an age so tender that I hardly rounded out thirteen years", Cieza somehow managed to obtain an education, though he obviously did not attend a university. He freely admits that his attempts at writing histories "was a temerity on the part of one of so few letters", but he nevertheless acquired a gracious literary style and a penetrating sense of inquiry. Moreover, like many others of his time, he attained intellectual maturity early.

It was the arrival in Seville, on 9th January 1534, of the Peruvian treasure ship *Santa Maria del Campo* that inflamed his mind with the desire to seek his fortune in the New World. "I remember the rich pieces of gold that I saw in Seville, brought back from Cassamarca where the treasure of Atahuallpa, promised to the Spaniards, was collected", and he doubtless read—for who then did not?—the little tract called *La Conquista del Perú*, written anonymously by a soldier on his return to Spain.

In 1535, with his father's consent, Cieza left on the vessel *Cifuentes* and disembarked at Cartagena "in the Indies"—to distinguish it from the two other towns with the same name in Africa and in Spain. Immediately he joined a company of explorers setting out for the Sinú, and for eleven years he served as common soldier in various companies, exploring and conquering the tribes of Colombia. By the time he entered Peru, as one of a group answering the royal summons to put down the rebellions there, he was twenty-six and had for some time been carefully noting down the things he had seen. Indeed, his notes were already so bulky that he was forced to walk so that his horse could carry them.

Once the military attachment to which he belonged had crossed the natural bridge of Rumichaca (now the border between Colombia and Ecuador, and then the northern frontier of the Incas), Cieza put down in his notebook, "The time has come to give my quill to the great things that are to be recounted of Peru." The first and most impressive of the "great things" was the highway: "One of the first things that claimed my attention . . . was how the great and splendid highways we see throughout their realm could have been built; the number of men that must have been required; what sort of tools and methods they used to level the mountains and cut roads through the rock to make the roads as broad and useful as they are and as we see them now."

Though they had roamed far and wide, the Spaniards knew of no other land whose physical features even remotely resembled those they encountered in the Inca empire. Its coast, where rain never fell, was a desert, over 3,000 miles in length. Along it were dotted forty or more riverine oases, where tribes lived and developed agriculture. Between the oases was a lifeless void of desert. Since trees were relatively rare, the idols of these coast-dwellers were of wood. As the menacing sun was always there and could not be appeased, their principal deity, which controlled the sea, was the moon. The main building material was mud—hence their attention to pottery, the finest known. Houses and temples were built of sun-dried brick —adobe—so that their most fabulous cities were, in truth, constructed of nothing more than plastic mud. That was one Peru.

In the high sierras the Spaniards found a completely different environment, which we call the second Peru. This area was more or less a treeless tableland covered with long grass, and exposed to extreme heat at midday and extreme cold at night. Rain was seasonal, the soil fertile and the air rarefied, and the area was relatively densely populated. There were enormous valleys (quebradas) and canyons that, had there not been any roads and bridges, would effectively have isolated each tribe from the others, as was indeed the case before the Incas arrived.

East of the cordilleras lay the montaña—the third Peru. The incessant rains brought by the eastern trade winds made this an area of luxuriant vegetation with dense forest, composed of scrub and gnarled, delicately flowered trees, at an altitude of over 8,000 feet, and tropical jungle below this level. The Inca roads even penetrated this inhospitable area.

There were thus three very different Perus, and similar conditions prevailed elsewhere in the Inca empire, which, beside Peru, comprised what are now Ecuador and Bolivia, together with part of Paraguay, the mountainous area of Argentina, and almost the whole of Chile. As Piedro de Cieza followed the banner of his king down the royal road, he became aware of and commented on the magnificence of the Incas' achievement in building the roads that bound this vast area together.

Proceeding southwards from Rumichaca, at the northern extremity of the Inca empire, the first tribe that the party reached were the *Cara*, in what is now Ecuador. Before they were conquered and absorbed into the Inca empire, the Cara had been one of the many independent tribes inhabiting the Andes. Their houses were earth-walled and circular, and their agriculture was Andean in pattern: they cultivated maize, quinoa and potatoes; the *cui* (guinea-pigs) they raised in their houses were a readily available source of protein; and they, too, had domesticated the llama. The Cara buried their chieftains in pits; and worshipped the sky and the snow-capped peaks surrounding them. Among these peaks were Cayambe (19,258 feet high) and Cotopaxi (19,347 feet), a volcano that was almost continuously in eruption.

In 1493, when Columbus was enjoying his first triumph in Spain after the discovery of the New World, Huayna Capac, the eleventh Inca, began his conquest of the Cara. This required long and costly battles. The tribe's resistance so enraged Huayna Capac that he ordered all their chieftains to be beheaded at the edge of a lake. So much blood flowed that it reddened the waters, and from that day onwards the lake was called Yahuarcocha—the Lake of Blood. Caranqui was made the provincial capital. All the Inca structures erected there were built between 1493 and 1527. These were the buildings that Pedro de Cieza saw as he marched through it with his company in the summer of 1547.

"From the Mira river," Cieza noted, "over which suspension bridges were hung, one descends, by the royal road, to the large and sumptuous lodgings of Caranqui, whence one can see the Lake of Blood. These lodgings . . . are in a small square. Inside there is a beautifully built stone pool. The palaces and the houses of the Incas are also made of fine, great stones skilfully joined without mortar—a sight to see. . . . There was even a sun temple where the walls were once covered with hammered sheets of gold and silver. . . . It has now fallen into ruins."

Now there is not even the semblance of a stone wall there, though as late as 1735 one building was still standing. This we know from the members of the French Academy who arrived that year in Ecuador to measure the arc of three degrees latitude of the earth's surface. They found the ground pocked with burial mounds and the bare mountains dotted with defensive *pucarás*— fortresses.

From Caranqui, Pedro de Cieza went "along the famous road of the Incas . . . to the settlement of Otavalo". There had long been tribal enmity between the Otavalo and the Caranqui, but somehow the Otavalo had managed to survive as a tribal entity. Indeed, even now the Otavalo Indian follows the track of the Inca highway, though the road itself has long disappeared. Continuing south, the road then crosses a snow-bound pass to Cochasqui, where, to confirm the presence of the road, Inca ruins have been found.

After Cochasqui, the volcanoes begin. The snow-covered, serrated peak of Cayambe is the first in a chain of thirty that the traveller encounters on the way south; many of these are active and most are permanently snow-capped. Volcanic activity has gone on for centuries. Cotopaxi erupted during the Spanish conquest of 1534. It was due to the violence of one of its eruptions that the deep canyon of Guallabamba was opened up between Quito and Otavalo.

Pedro de Cieza found Quito, a principal stop on the Inca highway, and situated fifteen miles south of the equator, "healthy and cold rather than warm". With an altitude of 9,300 feet, it "lay in a plain like a hollow formed by the high surrounding sierras". In the decade since its conquest by the Spaniards, wheat, brought there in 1540 by a Flemish priest, Jodôco Ricke, had been planted, barley had been introduced and the colonists had filled the warmer valleys with European fruit trees, such as the orange and the lime, and had even begun cultivating grapes. Cieza found the Quiteños "of medium stature, fine yeomen, still living in the ways established by the Inca Lords".

The contingent of the King's men to which Cieza belonged, one of many groups on their way along the road in answer to the royal summons, were well received in Quito, and for good reason: the conqueror of Quito, Sebastián Benalcázar, who owned the whole land in fief, was personally leading the contingent.

Although a quarter of his life was a blank (he could not recall his last name, and the one he bore was simply that of the Moorish town where he was born), Don Sebastián was formidable and efficient: a predatory sort of man. He said that at sixteen he had killed a mule with a blow of his fist on its snout because of the beast's failure to extricate itself from a quagmire. Then, fearing his father's wrath, he had made his way to Seville and signed on a ship to Panama. There he had exhibited an energy that few could equal: he could out-walk, out-fight and perhaps even out-love any of his command. He stook part in the Inca conquest, shared handsomely in the ransom of Atahuallpa, receiving 9,909 pesos of gold and 407 marcos of silver, and in 1534 was sent in pursuit of the last Inca general, Rumiñahui—"Old Stony Eye", since he had but one. Retreating northwards, the Incas fell back on Quito, set light to the grass thatch of the town's fine buildings, and retreated further. On Whit Sunday 1534, Quito fell to Benalcázar. He became the founder of San Francisco de Quito.

It was this Benalcázar that Pedro de Cieza followed to Quito in answer to the call for men to quell the revolt of Gonzalo Pizarro.

Gonzalo was the last of the four Pizarro brothers to be left alive in Peru. In 1542, on his return from an epic expedition into the jungle around the upper reaches of the Amazon (which he discovered), he found that his brother Francisco was dead and that the realm of the Incas had been divided between the partisans of Francisco and of Diego de Almagro (by then also dead), who had been the two original conquistadors. The Council of the Indies had introduced the "New Laws", which, among other things, proclaimed the freedom of the Indians. The conquistador–settler, who had previously controlled the Indians by means of his *encomienda* (his allotted area, the inhabitants of which had to pay him tribute) now found himself deprived of a labour force, with the result that all material progress was brought to a halt. Gonzalo Pizarro, at the urging of most of the settlers, assumed the title of *procurador* of Peru and led the troops that killed Peru's first viceroy.

In 1546, a new force was sent against him under the command of the bishop Pedro de la Gasca, who had been given the title of "President", and who moved, appropriately enough, just like the bishop on a chess board— obliquely. At this, Gonzalo Pizarro tried to rally his old *capitanes* to his side. On 8th April 1547, he wrote to Benalcázar, and, after informing him of all that had taken place, continued, "If you should be tempted by La Gasca . . . remember what is of interest to one, affects the other. . . . Do not fail to notify me of all you know . . . for what is yours is mine and what is mine yours."

The tribes about Quito, like almost all others in the Inca realms, were all anti-Inca, and in the early fifteenth century they had formed a defence league against Inca encroachment. However, by 1463 the Inca army coming from the south had conquered the whole of the north Peruvian coast and extended the empire as far as Quito itself. Roads were extended, courier (*chasqui*) posts set up, and the moment came for the final Inca conquest. Huayna Capac, the "young chief rich in virtues", conquered Quito and, by 1493, extended the empire's borders to the natural bridge of Rumichaca.

It was Inca policy, when faced with a recalcitrant people, to resettle dissidents among seasoned tribes and to repopulate the area with loyal subjects. These Quechua-speaking colonists, called *mitimaes*, accelerated the process of effective integration by bringing with them many aspects of Inca civilisation: the tripartite division of land between people, religion and state; the *mita* labour tax; the use of storehouses, and other new methods of organisation; and, finally, an extension of the road network, with its postal and courier systems and its many *tampus*.

It is said that Huayna Capac grew fond of Quito. The usual well-constructed

Inca buildings were erected there: a temple of the sun, houses for nobles, and a superb one for Huayna Capac. In this part of the empire he fathered yet another son, whom he called Atahuallpa ("heroic turkey"). It was he who was to bring disaster to the Inca empire.

The royal road began in Quito. "Despite the great distance, [1,230 miles] from Quito to Cuzco, which is more than the distance from Seville to Rome," says Pedro de Cieza, "the road is as busy as the one from Seville to Triana, which is the most that can be said." The Roman road to which he alludes here is the Via Argenta, which was built by the Emperor Tiberius after A.D. 24 and ran from Salamanca to Seville. Cieza would have travelled over it as a boy, before coming to the New World. It was only by comparing the Inca with the Roman roads that Cieza could convey to his readers the extent and the structure of Peruvian highways, since there was no other such road system in Europe.

"Upon leaving Quito, one comes first to the village of Panzaleo. The people here differ from their neighbours especially as regards their headbands, for that is the way different tribes are known. They wear a sort of woollen poncho, without sleeves or collar. For footgear they wear sandals made from the fibre of a plant they call *cabuya*, which grows long-spined pads which yield the hempen fibres used for the sandals, the headbands that they wear about their hair, and also the thick ropes used for the cables from which they hang their hanging bridges. Some of the women dress after the fashion of Cuzco, very handsomely with a long blanket that covers them from neck to feet. At the waist they tie it round with a beautiful woven *chumpi* belt."

The next village the party reached was Mulahalo (the present-day Mulalo), where there were "great lodgings and storehouses of supplies for the Incas and their *capitanes* when they came this way". The village lay to the east of the river San Felipe, the banks of which the royal road followed. Nearby, the snow-capped dome of the Cotopaxi thrust into the azure sky. The natives were, as was to be expected, full of tales of its fiery outbursts. It was this volcano that was in eruption when the Spaniards made their conquest in 1534, "and then it seemed to be raining ashes for several days".

Tacunga, properly Llactacunga, followed after a further four leagues (fourteen miles)—the ideal distance between halts. "Of all the towns that we passed where there were residences for the Inca or lodging places, nowhere were they so magnificent as in Llactacunga. Although now in ruins, they reveal their former grandeur, for on certain walls it can plainly be seen where the figures of llamas were encrusted with gold. This magnificence was especially to be found in the apartments reserved for the Inca."

Parts of these buildings remained above the surface when Antonio de Ulloa appeared on the scene two centuries later, in 1735. His interest in antiquities was such that he had the remains sketched and the sketches published in his book. A young mathematician born in Madrid, and future

Governor of Louisiana, Antonio de Ulloa was twenty years old when he set out for South America with the French Academicians on their way to measure the arc of the equator.

Less than fifty years after, Alexander von Humboldt, later the celebrated geographer, followed him to the area, and it is to Humboldt that archaeology is indebted for the only technical description of Llactacunga and, with it, a splendid drawing. In 1801, while following the route of the Inca road to Peru, during the third year of his five-year expedition "for the acquisition of knowledge", Humboldt came upon Llactacunga. He found that the structure formed a square, the sides of which were thirty-seven yards long. Four great trapezoidal doors were distinguishable. There were eight apartments; the walls were over five yards high and just over one yard thick. There were eighteen niches (the *leitmotiv* of Inca architecture), distributed, wrote Humboldt, "with the greatest symmetry".

Cieza found that "the people of Llactacunga all go about dressed in woollen ponchos, well made and handsome. Their houses are of stone and grass-thatched. They drink *chica*, a corn liquor, like all the rest of the Indians. . . . The women are affectionate and some of them very good looking."

Ambato was the next *tampu* (hispanicised as *tambo*) reached after leaving "Tacunga, by the highway". The Ambato river, flowing in an easterly direction, was crossed by a suspension bridge the apparent fragility of which much disturbed one of the padres. Cieza wrote, "below Ambato there is a rope bridge to cross the river, which is rather swift and swollen".

After another ten miles over the same high, cold land, the road led to Mocha (altitude 10,708 feet) and its "sumptuous lodgings", as Cieza described them, "so many and so large that I was amazed . . . since the Lord Incas lost their power after 1533, all the palaces and dwellings have fallen into ruin and in their present state only their general outlines can be seen . . . but as they were of beautiful stone and finely constructed, they will endure for ages without wholly disappearing." Were it not for this description and those that followed it in the next century, it would be difficult to believe that the Ecuadorian highlands had really been occupied by the Incas, for barely a trace of them remains.

The Inca highway, which, in the absence of any other road, continued to be used until the nineteenth century, also disappeared in the stream of progress, although, as late as 1870, an American naturalist wrote of "travelling over a portion of this ancient road going toward Riobamba . . . well paved with cut blocks of dark porphyry. It is not graded but partakes of the irregularity of the country."

For the next few days, the land over which Cieza and his fellow soldiers travelled was dominated by the extinct snow-covered volcano Chimborazo. At 20,561 feet high, it was famed for centuries as the highest mountain in the world, and Elizabeth Barrett Browning sang of "by how many feet Mount

Chimborazo outsoars Himmeleh". Alexander von Humboldt climbed it in 1801 and considered it "the grandest mountain in the world . . . I had all my life imagined that of all mortals I was the one who had risen highest in all the world . . .". It was painted fifty years later by Frederick E. Church, the great landscape painter of the Hudson River School.

Near Chimborazo lay Riobamba (Lirepampa), the chief city of the Puruhá tribe. The area was densely populated, with many villages, and, although very high up, the land was extensively cultivated: maize, beans, squash, potatoes and quinoa were grown there. The Puruhá language has long since been lost, but such place-names and patronymics as survive show that the tribe occupied a very extensive area. The Puruhá wore sleeveless woollen ponchos, but were most clearly identified by their custom of wearing their hair long, piled up in a circle around the head and tied with a string made from the fibres of the cabuya; this was also used as a sling. Cieza noted that "they speak the common language of Cuzco [Quechua] although they have their own. To the west lies the snow-covered extinct volcano called Urcolazo [Chimborazo], where there are few inhabitants. Skirting this sierra runs the road that leads to the coastal city of Guayaquil . . .".

From this point south, the royal road, for lack of any alternative route, crossed the high and frigid *puna*—the name given to the dry desert-like steppes found above 13,000 feet, a vast, bleak area with great stretches of tall coarse *ichu*-grass, meagre pasture for the wild huanaco. The volcanoes having been left behind, the land now became a monotonous series of ridges and depressions over which ran the royal road: nearly nine yards wide, cleared of grass, but without a road bed, since the hard surface was sufficient base for the traffic of a culture that did not have wheeled vehicles. However, the road was edged by a small wall built of field stone and held together by mud-cement.

On its way through this area, the road circled an ice-fringed tarn, the Colta. Around its edge were rocks covered with mosses and lichens, and brightly flowered lupins rose out of a mass of woolly leaves. Near to the lake were the little rills that formed the headwaters of the river Guamote, which gave its name to the Tambo de Guamote, and this area Cieza found "all level land and very cold".

At this point just the track of the Inca road can be seen, for what had remained of it was incorporated into the modern road that negotiates the near arctic conditions of the geographical knot of Tiocajas. Now, as in the time of Cieza, the remains of a fortress (*pucará*) can be seen here. The Indians of the region, the Cañari, were forced to build the fortress in order to defend the area, which had only recently been conquered by the Incas, from any opposition coming from the north.

Benalcázar, riding at the head of the column, was anxious to point out that here, on this barren and uninhabited *puna*, he had in 1534 won a battle against the fortress's Inca defenders and their general, Rumiñahui.

Ticsán, where even now there remain the ruins of a *tampu* and a small fortress, is situated 12,000 feet up on a *páramo*, or wind-swept plain. Nearby is the city now known as Alausi. Once, in Inca times, Ticsán had been where the highway met a road to the coast. Now, however, the scattered ruins are as vague as the unwritten history of the pre-Inca inhabitants of the district, though Cieza confirmed their existence.

It was here in 1492 that Huayna Capac, who was simultaneously carrying on invasions of both the coastal region and the sierra, heard that certain of his chieftains had been killed on the island of Puna close to Guayaquil, the main port of entry to Ecuador. Although it is a mere seventy-five miles from this point to Guayaquil, one must cross the high cordillera and descend through the densely forested *montaña*, for here the western mountains are in the tropical zone. Still, the Inca engineers forced a road through it, along the higher reaches of the river Alausi .The road emerged at the headwaters of the Guayaquil river. In the words of Pedro de Cieza, "Huayna Capac ordered a highway to be built along the Guayaquil river, which is very large. The highway, if one judges it by certain sections of it that remain, was a magnificent thing. . . . It is known as the Pass of Huayna Capac." This description was confirmed by the discoveries of modern engineers when they began the construction of the new road linking the seaport with the sierra, and following the same route as the old Inca road.

Continuing on his way south, Cieza noted, "To the right and left of the highway I am travelling, there are quite a few settlements and *tampus* . . ." The first of these was Pomallacta (Achupallas), where there are the remains of a *tampu* and where the small temple of the sun was incorporated into the parish church. Next came Sinazahuán, which Alexander von Humboldt said was dangerous for travellers. It was immensely cold and barren, and the *tampu* was over 11,000 feet above sea level.

By this time the highway had come to Cañari territory. To reach it the Inca highway went over its highest point (over 14,800 feet) and passed over a hail-swept *páramo*, to arrive at the *tampu* and lodgings of the Inca. In July 1801 Humboldt wrote, "One crossed the pass of the Andes called the parama de Azuay, at an altitude of 4,372 metres [approximately 14,344 feet]. It is almost the same elevation as Mont Blanc. While it was only with great effort that our mules were able to progress over the swampy ground, for the space of 7,500 metres [nearly 5 miles], we could see the remains of the grandiose road of the Incas, approximately seven metres wide and resting on foundations sunk deep into the earth. . . . The surface of the road was paved in blocks of porphyry of a blackish colour."

Next, the road turned south to Inga Pirca, on which were lodgings and a palace. This was built near a small stream and above the gorge of Intihuaynca, on which is carved an image of the sun (*inti*), while nearby there is a stone bench cut out of the living rock in Inca fashion and known locally as Inca *chugana*—the sport of the Inca. The ruin, the only Inca building to be seen above ground in the whole of Ecuador, is a many-chambered structure. There is also an oval section, in the best late Inca style, on which once rested a two-roomed gabled house, which fortunately Humboldt sketched, since it is now no more. It was listed by an Inca–Spanish chronicler as a royal resting place.

Henceforth, the road to Tumpipampa went downwards. The mountains receded, the air became soft, almost bland. The fields were purple with potato blossoms and for mile upon mile the road was lined with cabuya, a succulent cactus. At 8,500 feet, the land breaks out in riotous fertility. In the "flowering plain" lay Tumpipampa. The land was that of the Cañari.

The Cañari, who controlled the uplands from Chimborazo southwards to Loja, were certainly "a very large, powerful tribe that ruled over a great many others". Like all other tribes, they were farmers first and soldiers second; agriculture, despite the unfavourable climate, was widespread. The Cañari Federation, well aware of its neighbours, kept on good terms with most. Their allies included the Jivaros, who inhabited the region of the upper Amazon, which, though high up, could be reached in two days' walk. The Jivaros practised a ritual of head shrinking on their enemies. When threatened, they allied themselves with the Cañari, with whom they also traded, obtaining from them such goods as chonta wood, parrot feathers, arrow poison, and various tropical food stuffs, including earth nuts, sweet potatoes, and manioc. The Cañari were such excellent metalworkers, and the gold, silver and copper artefacts that they produced were so plenteous and so finely worked, that the gold pieces that escaped the conquistadors' crucible amazed the European goldsmiths of the sixteenth century. Copper was so common among the Cañari that, in just one large collective burial, more than a ton of bronze axe-heads were discovered.

Even before the advent of the Incas, they husbanded herds of llama and spun the fibres of the alpaca into fine cloth, which was much appreciated for trade. Their currency was salt and copper. "They wear their hair long", said Pedro de Cieza, "and coil it around their heads in a knotted crown and on it wear a round wooden ring as fine as sieve wire (tied occasionally with ribbons). They can be recognised as Cañari wherever they go. All Indians wear different insignia on their heads to distinguish one tribe from another, just as the Emperor Charles V has an army of Spaniards, Germans, Flemings and Burgundians, all with their own dress and particular headgear."

The royal road then continued to Tumpipampa, or Tomebamba (now Cuenca), which is situated above a plain where two rivers meet. "The Temple of the Sun," said Pedro de Cieza, "was stone built and set together without mortar and with the most subtle skill. The façades of the buildings were beautiful and highly decorated, some of them set with precious stones. The walls of the temple and the palaces of the Incas were covered with sheets

1. The ideal Inca as he was characterized by a European artist in the period of the Noble Savage. He is dressed in Classical attire, as was then the European fashion in painting. The umbrella is authentically Inca. (*Frazier*, Voyage de . . . Pérou, *Paris 1750*)

2–6. The landscapes and Inca stonework on the Chincha-suyu road: (*top*) the terraces around Tarma with the Inca road above the terracing; (*bottom left*) Wiener's drawing of Huanuco, a fortified tampo on the main road; (*centre*) the reviewing stand of Vilcas-huamán carved from a single block of stone; (*bottom right*) another carving from a single stone block, the altar to Inti, the Sun God, at Cañar; (*bottom centre*) a wayside marker found on all roads, an *apacheta*, placed at the highest point of the road where each passer-by placed a stone, a symbol of burden, in order to lighten his load.

7. The execution of Atahualpa as shown by a 17th-century *mestizo* (Indian–Spanish) artist of Cuzco. Atahualpa is shown beheaded, while Spanish soldiers below attack Atahualpa's Inca retinue.

8. A Spanish 18th-century illustration of Ecuadorian landscape with three types of bridge (*left to right*): a suspension bridge, an *aroyo* (pulley system) for conveying animals, and an *aroyo* for people. In the foreground, three strata of society (*left to right*): a woman in Spanish dress, an Inca noblewoman, mestizos of Spanish and Indian origin, the middle cast of the 18th century, and on the right the ordinary Indian. (*Juan and Ulloa*, Voyage, *vol. 1, Madrid 1746.*)

9–15. The characteristic hallmark of Inca architecture was the trapezoidal niche, window and door: (*top*) the *tampu* of Limatambo (Pimac-Tampu) on the approach to the Bridge of San Luis Rey; (*far left*) the temple or Osno at Vilcas-huamán; (*left*) a window niche at Ollantaytambo; (*centre left*) a doorway at Machu Picchu; (*centre right*) drainage outlets in the walls of Sacsahuamán in Cuzco; (*right above*) windows at Machu Picchu; (*bottom right*) open window niches, still trapezoidal, looking across the Urubamba at Machu Picchu.

16–21. The eternal Inca road mastered every variety of landscape: (*left*) the steproad soaring to the peaks of the Andes; (*top centre*) the walled coastal road across the Pacific coastal desert; (*centre*) the causeway across the marshes north of Cuzco; (*bottom centre*) the walled road across the Altiplano towards Puno and Titicaca; (*right*) the tortuous hill road entering Cuzco from the northwest; (*bottom left*) the cascading mountain road scores the hills before it joins the coast road near Pisco, where the modern road has been laid parallel with or on the very foundations of the old Inca lateral.

22. A descendant of the Indians called Inca beside the walls of the palace of the Lord-Inca Roca in Cuzco. The stones are characteristically set in the Inca fashion without the use of mortar.

of the finest gold. The roofs of these buildings are of a grass thatch so well laid that, barring a fire, it should last for ages. . . . I would say that these lodgings of Tombebamba were a remarkable thing. Today [1547] all is cast down and in ruins, but still it can be seen how great they were."

Topa, the tenth Inca, appeared here with his hosts in 1463, followed by his son Huayna Capac. After he had subjugated the redoubtable Cañari (in 1480) he later made them into a *corps d'élite*. It was at Tumpipampa, while the Inca engineers were completing a road from this newly-won city to the gold mines of Zaruma, that Huayna Capac learned of the first landing of Francisco Pizarro and his "thirteen men of Gallo" at Tumbes. When Pizarro sailed away in 1527, leaving behind two men, Alonso de Molina and a negro called Gines, Huayna Capac is said to have asked that they be brought to him, for, having heard of other *suncasapa* ("bearded ones") who had appeared in Bolivia on the borders of his empire several years before, he wished to question these new arrivals. It is impossible to be sure what happened to them: a mystery surrounds their fate.

Sometime after 1527 Huayna Capac died. Since there was no clear line of succession under the Inca political system, one of the many sons of the reigning Inca had to be selected, following the advice of a Council of Elders. The one chosen was then groomed to be the *Sapa Inca*. Thus, after Huayna Capac's death, his son Huascar, born in Cuzco, was selected. This happened despite the fact that Huayna Capac, sensing, as he lay dying, that the empire had grown too large and unwieldy, had contemplated breaking it up into two administrative units: Cuzco to the south and Quito to the north.

Atahuallpa, one of his other sons, who was five years older than Huascar, held the *de facto* office of vice-ruler of the north, with the formidable title of *Incap ranti* ("one who stands for the Inca"). He refused to accompany the cortège bearing the mummy of his father back to Cuzco or to pay homage to his brother Huascar as Inca. His excuses were specious enough, but in the eyes of his brother this was *lèse majesté*. "Huascar," said a Peruvian–Spanish chronicler whose family was of this line, "was beloved in Cuzco: although he was clement and pious, he was also presumptuous and devil-may-care courageous. He was about twenty-five."

Atahuallpa was made of sterner stuff. He had travelled widely with his father, taken part in the subjugation of Quito, and was known to the best generals. "He was ruthless and vengeful: a man of great determination."

In 1530, the Cañaris at Tumpipampa were asked by Huascar to honour their pledges of friendship and to aid him as Inca—whereupon, by a ruse, the Cañari captured Atahuallpa, with the intention of bringing him forcibly to Huascar. However, Atahuallpa escaped to the north, raised his armies, and defeated Huascar in one battle after another. On entering Tumpipampa, he ordered a fearful slaughter of the Cañaris for having aided Huascar. After that the Cañari became the enemies of Atahuallpa, so that when the Spaniards arrived they became their most faithful Indian allies.

"Leaving Tumpipampa," Cieza continues, "by the great highway leading to the city of Cuzco, one crosses the entire province of the Cañari . . . everywhere there are many settlements. . . ." The level of the land rose again, and the road passed through Cumbe, on the *páramo*, and Nabon, on the heights overlooking the Leonquiacu river. Next came Ona, which was reached after crossing the *páramo* and then the bridge of Alpachaca, a suspension bridge made of rope-cables. This part of the road was at an altitude of about 11,000 feet. In July 1801, Alexander von Humboldt, following the track of both the royal road and Pedro de Cieza, was able to glimpse from here the Pacific Ocean, sixty miles to the west.

The next stop on the royal road was Saraguru. "One comes here," noted Cieza, "to the province of the Paltas, who go about dressed like the others. They wear their hair long, and, besides their own language, speak that of Cuzco. . . . The Paltas have the same living habits as the Cañaris and wear ribbon fillets for headbands. The fruit *palta* grows in great abundance in their lands." *Palta* was the Peruvian word for avocado, a fruit that here grew as large as a melon.

It was the custom among the Paltas to compress the fronto-occipital part of the skull, causing deformation. According to the Cuzco born Garcilaso de la Vega, "They pressed the head of each newly-born child between two boards, thus transforming it into a long skull. Such children were derisively known as *palta uma* ["palta heads"], which is what they looked like."

Saraguru still has the remains of a *tampu* and, at a place called Paquishapa, a *pucará*, confirming Cieza's statement that "this province of Paltas was considered important and these lodgings were fine and spacious".

After Saraguru, the road continued to climb, crossing the Alto de Pullal, a barren area covered with stunted, small-leafed and brilliantly flowering trees. The land was shared equally by brilliant, shimmering green humming-birds and condors, which fed on the carcasses of animals and men who had died in this remote region. Alexander von Humbolt remembered "the solemn impression" he felt on beholding the complete uninhabitableness of the cordilleras side by side with the still-surviving wonderful remains of the great road of the Incas—a stupendous work.

After Tambo Blanco, so called because the first Spaniards to come this way saw it covered in deep snow, the land suddenly dropped away and the road zigzagged down, crossed the Catamayu (*mayu* being Quechua for "river"), and entered Loja.

Pedro de Cieza was amazed, as were the others on the way to Cuzco, to see the number of Spaniards who had already settled around Loja. As the land was at a low altitude for the Andes, only 7,500 feet, there were many villages of Palta Indians: "very large villages with natives who observe and hold the same customs as their neighbours". The Indians, parcelled out to the conquistadors by means of the *encomienda* system, were cultivating both native fruits and the fruits introduced by the Spaniards: grapes, figs, oranges and apples. There were also large herds of swine. Loja lay in an intermediate zone between the evergreen and deciduous forests. In the deeper, lush valleys, tall tree-ferns flourished luxuriantly, together with many plants of the genus *Ficus*—strangler fig-trees, for instance—and the immense ceiba, producer of tree-cotton, the capoc fibres used by the Indians for weaving. In the following century Loja was to become famous for the discovery of the cinchona tree, the bark of which yielded quinine—a specific for tertiary malaria.

Loja had been founded in 1549, the year before Cieza arrived there. Close by was the royal *tampu* of Cusipampa. The buildings, as well as the well-used highway, were still there in 1560, when padre Salinas Loyola travelled there.

There were "ancient buildings all along the *camino real*, *tampus* or lodgings of the natives, very well built of stone masonry and appearing regularly every twelve to fifteen miles . . . the good roads that the Indians made are the most noteworthy in the world and the finest made, even though placed in difficult and rugged country. Attempts are made to keep them in repair, although it has not been done with the same care and efficiency as under the Inca rulers."

Alonso Mercadillo, the founder of the new settlement of Loja, rode out to meet the detachment. A friend of Gonzalo Pizarro, who was now in open rebellion against the Crown, Mercadillo had been given a contract to found the new city and, to help him do this, allotted huge grants (or *repartimientos*, as they were called) of Indians. Before the arrival of the royal army, he had written to Gonzalo Pizarro saying, "I will order the plains to be depopulated", so that the royal armies would be deprived of food and of any natives who might assist them; but this had not yet occurred. When Pizarro wrote to him at Loja a month later, Mercadillo had gone over to La Gasca. He clearly saw the signs, so, when Benalcázar appeared with his well-armed detachment, he hesitated no longer, but declared for the King against Gonzalo Pizarro and went over with all his men. A few months later Charles V of Spain learned in an official report that "Mercadillo has joined with his troops at Loja."

## CHAPTER THREE

## The Road to Cajamarca

At a place called Colampó, a few leagues south of Loja, the royal road divided into three parts. The first, not a main route and very infrequently used, descended to the desert coast and the city of Piura, one of the first cities established by the Spanish, who founded it in 1533 on the ruins of an Inca halting place. The second road went through Malacato, and proceeded down the verdured, tropical valley created by the Chinchipe river, which less than 100 miles away flowed into the Marañon, one of the largest tributaries of the Amazon. The Chinchipe was a highly auriferous river and the cultures about it were very advanced; they traded with the highland-dwelling Incas. The third road, the royal road proper, went directly south and crossed the suspension bridge over the river Calvas.

After the next *tampu*, Cariamanga, the road crossed the *altos*, that is the heights, of Ayahuaca, and then descended into Ayahuaca itself, the name of which means "the shrine of the corpse". It was then engineered to follow the valley created by the Quiroz river, which rose in these mountains and flowed through the desert coastal region to the sea. In following this valley, the road had to cross seven small rivers—bridged where necessary by the usual suspension bridges constructed of rope-cables—before reaching the important fortress-city of Cajas (Chulucanas).

The conquest of Peru had begun here at Cajas. Here the Europeans had come, for the first time, to the Highway of the Sun; and, from the well-constructed roadway and the things they noted in the city of Cajas, they had gauged the greatness of the empire they were about to assault. Hernando de Soto, the future discoverer of the lower Mississippi river, led the sortie of forty horsemen from the coast. This marks his first significant appearance in history.

In 1533, in answer to Francisco Pizarro's appeal for conquistadors, Hernando de Soto had come to the isle of Puna, situated off the coast of what is now Ecuador, bringing with him a number of mounted soldiers. For this, and on account of his person and calling, he was given a captaincy. De Soto, described as "a man full of good impulses, a gentleman and a soldier" was born in about 1500 of a noble, albeit impoverished, family; indeed, so well descended was he, that he qualified as a gentleman "on all four sides"— *hidalgo de los cuatro costados*. In the usage of the time this meant that he was of unmixed blood, neither Moor nor Jew, and so eligible to be a Knight of Santiago. Yet, when he first appeared in the ranks of soldiers fighting in Nicaragua, "he had nothing more than his sword and buckler for his fortune". On his arrival in Peru, he was about thirty years of age, had wavy hair, a pointed beard, and moustaches that were rather long and drooping. "Above middle height, he was graceful and looked well either on foot or upon horseback."

On landing in Peru, Francisco Pizarro became instantly aware that the country had changed since he was last there in 1527. The beautiful buildings he had seen at Tumbes in 1527 lay in ruins; the Indians were far less friendly. He then discovered that there had been a civil war, and the name of Atahuallpa (the Spaniards wrote it "Atabilpa") was heard all over the land. The conquistadores had an interpreter, a native of Puna whom they called "Felipillo". They had taken him back to Spain in 1527, and there he had learned such Spanish as he knew. But he was of limited usefulness, for he had never been to the mountains, had no idea of the extent of the empire, and was deficient in the subtleties of the Quechua language—added to which, he was of such spurious snobbery that, despite the suffocating heat, he continued to wear the high Spanish ruff!

The Spaniards, then, did not even know the name of the adversary of Atahuallpa, so they called him "Cuzco", confusing the capital with the Inca. Soon they realised that their every movement was being watched, and that there was an efficient messenger service, operated by couriers called *chasquis*, who came and went with a frequency that was frightening. In time the Spaniards came to the conclusion that there had been a final battle and that the victor, Atahuallpa, was now in the high sierras not too far distant. Indeed, one of the Incas' *curacas* was waiting to see if and where the "bearded ones" would ascend the Andes.

Francisco Pizarro led his 167 soldiers, foot and mounted, along the coastal road to Serran, where the desert gives way to the foothills of the Andes. At Serran (now a large hacienda) there was an Inca-constructed fortress and a wayside station for authorised users of the road. Pizarro, by close questioning (involving a small amount of applied physics—that is, torture) of the couriers who plied between mountain and desert, learned that about sixty miles away, and almost in a direct line from where they were, there was a place called Cajas, of some importance. He therefore decided to send a highly mobile force up the stone-laid lateral road to the sierras, to see what could be learned of the whereabouts of this Atahuallpa.

"Hernando de Soto went with forty men," an old soldier called Diego Trujillo wrote in 1571 (by which time he was one of the last survivors of the expedition), "and I went with him. We went up the step road with our forty men. It took us two days and one night to cover the twenty leagues [sixty miles], before gaining the royal road."

Hernando de Soto was the first European to look upon and comment on the Inca highway. As reported, he put his men into battle order and then followed the road until he came to the first buildings. There before them, dangling from the large-limbed trees, were several dead Indians hanging by their feet. This was Cajas, which, he reported, was a village in a small valley surrounded by mountains.

The people there were fearfully agitated, particularly when they saw the horses the Spaniards had with them, and they did not calm down until it was explained to them that de Soto had come only to have their submission as vassals to his Emperor. A *curaca* came forward to explain that he was Atahuallpa's vassal and was there arranging contributions from all the tributary cities. He told the party that the city of Cuzco was thirty days' journey away, that in Cuzco one of the Inca's houses was four crossbow shots (400 feet) in length, and that there was a hall there that contained the mummified body of Old Cuzco (Huayna Capac, who had died in 1527). The floor was covered with silver plate and the walls with gold and silver plate, while gold strands were twined into the grass thatched roof. He also told them that only a year had passed since Huascar, the son of Old Cuzco, had lost all these cities to Atahuallpa.

At Cajas, in addition to the Temple of the Sun and a fortress, whose thick walls were made of adobe, there was a house of the sun virgins. These were *ñustas*, "chosen women", selected each year throughout the lands for their comeliness and dexterity; their duties were to weave garments for the attending priests, prepare a liquor fermented from corn (*accha*), and take part in the rituals surrounding the religion of the sun. Their persons were considered inviolable. Indians who attempted to enter the house were hanged.

Diego Trujillo stated that Hernando de Soto, that "man full of good impulses", ordered "from their house the Virgins of the Sun, who excited the soldiers like the fruits of paradise. They numbered 500. He then gave to each of us the women we liked best."

Such an action might well have destroyed the mission of conquest, yet the *curaca* either was so frightened or had so little option that he offered himself as a guide. So, with the head-man in tow—that is, chained—de Soto marched south towards Huancabamba, a larger city. "A wide road", Hernando de Soto reported in the first historical description of the royal way, "connects these two towns, and the same road traverses, they say, all the land from Cuzco to Quito, a distance of more than 300 leagues. The road is level. The part that goes over the mountains is well constructed. It is broad enough for six mounted men to ride abreast. By the side of the road water is channelled, with which travellers can slake their thirst. At the end of each day's journey there is a house like an inn [a *tampu*]. At Cajas there is a toll-house at the bridgehead, where a guard is always stationed to receive tolls in kind [that is, beans, corn, chilli-peppers] from those who use the road and bridge. No one can come out of or into the town without paying a toll. No traveller can enter or depart with a load by any other road than that one on which guards are stationed, or he does so on pain of death."

"Huancabama was larger than Cajas . . . containing finer edifices and a fortress built entirely of cut stone . . .", said Pedro de Cieza, who arrived there fourteen years later. Of its Temple of the Sun he reported that "From all the regions round about, the Indians came to worship in this temple and bring their offerings. . . ."

In 1802, Humboldt found the "great Inca road was still well preserved between Cajas and Huancabama, and the remains of great constructions can be distinguished, nine of which I found between Cajas and Huancabama, most of them probably *tampus* or *caravanserais* . . .". 150 years later, the von Hagen expedition, making the first systematic survey of the Inca road system, found large sections of the road intact, including parts of the eastern lateral that led towards the jungle and the area inhabited by the Aguarunas, a Jivaro sub-tribe who, in the fifteenth century, defeated an army of the Inca.

Continuing on its way towards the historic city of Cajamarca, 100 miles to the south, the royal road now followed the valley gouged out by the Huancabama river, though first it rose to cross the high, cold *puna*. By the beginning of the nineteenth century, the mule path that had once followed the original royal road had been forced lower, and Humboldt remembered that he "had to ford the river twenty-seven times, due to the sinuosity of its course, while above we could see, at the edge of the valley's precipice, the vestiges of the straight Inca road. . . ".

At Pomahuaca the road crossed the river by a large suspension bridge, then went on to Ingatambo, where parts of the road are still visible. Working its way through the troubled terrain of the region, it continued to Huambos, which had a royal *tampu*, and then to the ancient silver-producing region of Chota, before coming at last to Cajamarca.

By the time that Pedro de Cieza reached Cajamarca, after having ridden over 800 miles of Inca highway, he had a good grasp of how the empire functioned.

The word "Inca", now used as both noun and adjective, was then (and still is) mistakenly applied to the people over whom the Incas ruled. They were *runa-simi*. The term "Inca", properly used, refers only to the ruler—the Sapa Inca—and, as a title, to members of his family and its branches, and to those who were Incas by privilege.

The Incas, speaking of them now as a tribe, intruded into the valley of Cuzco in about A.D. 1000. After this, they slowly and inexorably engulfed all the other tribes in the area. As these tribes were conquered, either by exhortation or force, they were incorporated into the empire.

The *runa-simi*—the people, that is—were the base of the Inca social pyramid. Each tax-paying Indian, or *puric*, belonged to a community (*ayllu*) based on the division of land; he was a unit in the decimal social pattern of the Inca empire. The *ayllu*, in turn, was the basic social unit. It was less a clan than a great patrilinear group, owning a definite region of arable land, or *marka*. This held the community together. It was reinforced by mutual obligations, traditions and religious beliefs, and was protected by the same "upstairs gods". In short, it was a group of people living together, sharing land, animals, and, to a certain extent, the usufruct of the land. Everyone belonged to an *ayllu*. Indeed, all were born into it, for the principle itself was ancient and had developed over a long period in primitive Andean societies; the Incas merely systematised it.

The political and, hence, economic system of the Incas was thus built up pyramidally, and organised according to the decimal system. At the bottom was the able-bodied tax-paying worker. The workers were controlled by a straw-boss, the straw-bosses by a foreman, and the foremen by a supervisor. So it went on, the decimal pattern persisting to the level of *curaca*, an official who ruled over 10,000 workers. He in turn was responsible to the governor of the province, who was subject to the ruler of one of the four quarters of the empire. Finally there was the *Sapa Inca*, the apex of the social pyramid.

The Incas were an agricultural society. All were farmers. They had no plough as the Spaniards knew it, and had no draught animals. Instead they used the footplough (*taclla*), which the men operated, working backwards across the soil, while the women followed, breaking up the heavy clods of earth. People tilled the soil communally, chanting rhythmically as they worked. Primitive methods indeed; yet these people made the Andes, the desert and the Upper Amazon into a great centre of plant domestication. More than half the basic foods that feed the world today were developed here—potatoes, beans, maize, sweet potatoes, yuca (manioc, tapioca), earth-nuts, cashews, red peppers and cayenne, tomatoes, pineapples, papaya, chocolate, and so on.

Agriculture was bound up with irrigation, and, by applying what they had learned from those they had conquered, the Incas developed irrigation systems that were equal to any found in Mesopotamia. The lands from the sea to the high Andes were terraced after ecologically sound methods, which contributed to soil preservation and to soil creation as well.

Since their foodstuffs could be stored dry for considerable periods of time, and since there existed both public and private systems of storage, the dire threat of famine, which hung over every Neolithic society, was obviated.

This also allowed leisure time.

However, this is not to say that the Incas were idle when they were not working on the land. In every house there was at least one loom, and this was used to produce a variety of woven goods. The wool of the llama, too heavy and greasy for finer weaving, was used to make sacks and coarser blankets. The alpaca yielded the wool used for most other purposes; when spun, dyed and woven it became ponchos, blankets, headpieces or stoles. The wool of the vicuña was generally reserved for the Inca caste.

All, more or less, were potters. Everyday utensils such as pots, dishes and bowls were made by the people who intended to use them, as was also the case with woven goods; this meant that each household within the *ayllu* was self-contained. All were craftsmen; and craftsmanship brings a certain psychological fulfilment. Societies of craftsmen are often stable societies composed of satisfied individuals, a situation that has a great deal to do with the fact that such societies are based on manual work and therefore less liable to fluctuation than those based on mass production.

Taxation presented no problem under the Inca system, with each tax-payer paying his *mita* (tax) in kind or as services rendered, but when the Spanish overlords arrived and demanded tax money, a thing completely missing in all primitive American societies, the whole basis of the craft culture was undermined.

There were frequent holidays: public festivals related to the agricultural year. The barbaric pageantry of the journey to market, where surplus produce was bartered, can only be dimly surmised. "In all parts of this kingdom", observed Pedro de Cieza, "there are the greatest markets. In one market the traffic was so great that among Indians alone, without including the Christians, a value of twenty-five or thirty thousand pesos changed hands daily. This is truly wonderful. . . ."

Now, in order to understand what happened in Cajamarca on that day in November 1532 when, in less than an hour, the empire disintegrated, and in order to understand its consequences, the nature of the structure of the Inca caste system and the way it operated have first to be made clear. At the pinnacle of the social pyramid was the Sapa Inca, who both believed himself and was believed by the people to be directly descended from Inti, the sun god, whose divinity he shared. The divine right of Inca kings was never questioned. The very land, the earth, the people all belonged to him; gold, the sweat of the sun, and silver, the unshed tears of the moon, were his property. The Inca was absolute; he was god. He was the final court of appeal, so that he and the others of his caste were plenary rulers, their absolute powers held in check only by ancient customs and their fear of revolt.

Yet the Inca's concern for his people was also very real. Position, power and wealth came from the well-being of the people, and thus the good of society was his primary concern. The state had only one group of entrepreneurs, the Inca caste. They alone controlled the administrative and, in turn, the statistical services (which determined the work to be carried out and the number of taxable individuals), together with the legal system and discipline; and they were thus able to organise society in such a way as would allow them to satisfy their imperialistic urge to conquer and control. Since there was no money, contributions to the state (the tax or *mita*) were based on services rendered and the produce of the tilled land. The entire concept of the cash-nexus was missing. Everyone worked, everyone produced. All employment was productive. Since laziness deprived the state of tax, it was a capital crime; bachelors, since they were non-productive as regards children, were outlawed, as were homosexuals, who "wasted human seed". Under this system the distinction between economic, political and technical activities did not exist: they were all one. The land was owned by the state—that is, the Inca. The lesser man, through the medium of his *ayllu*, which was a kind of holding company, had only the use of his land, not ownership; and his share of that land increased or decreased with the size of his family.

The Indian's orbit was restricted. He travelled, as the first Spaniards in the realm were quick to note, only at the pleasure of the state; and even his leisure activities were ritualistically regimented. Never in history has there been so perfect a womb-to-tomb society as this, though, for all these restrictions, there were definite advantages to the system. For one thing, the storage of produce lessened the chance of famine, for, in times of crop failure, the royal storehouses were open to all. Then, animals—llamas, vicuñas, alpacas—were, like the soil, conserved. Roads were maintained and the realm made secure. Yet it would be a mistake to call this collective principle "socialism": the empire was not for the people; equality was not even an ideal. On the contrary, the state existed for the Inca and his caste.

This, in effect, was the socio-economic background for the meeting of Spaniard with Inca.

"Cassamarca [that is, Cajamarca, the 'town in a ravine'] was known throughout the kingdom because of its size and wealth." Situated at 9,200 feet above sea level, it is surrounded on all sides by mountains. These are lower to the north and south, the route followed by the royal road. Francisco de Xeréz, the royal scrivener, described the town in a minimum of words: "Two rivers flow through the valley. It is level, well peopled, and surrounded by mountains. The town has 2,000 inhabitants. The plaza is larger than any that I have seen in Spain. The whole of it is surrunded by a wall. There are two gateways. . . In front of the plaza is a stone fortress. . . ."

Cajamarca controlled lands of considerable diversity. Silver, copper and even tin ore were worked in the vicinity. Cultivation was intensive and irrigation highly developed. Channels and tunnels were constructed to bring down water from the mountains, and often these had been bored through the living rock. One such channel, cut through the rock by pre-Inca engineers, was over a mile long, and followed a zigzag course to slow down the flow of water. The inhabitants had also built dams and sluice gates, thereby gaining control over the upper reaches of rivers—a matter of life and death to the desert coastal regions.

Thus it is not surprising that Cajamarca formed an alliance with the great desert kingdom of the Chimú. In 1461 though, the Incas appeared on their borders, and, after defeating a combined Andean–coastal contingent, absorbed the whole area into the Inca empire.

This Inca domination proved to be short-lived; and it was here in Cajamarca, as the triumphant Atahuallpa was "taking the waters" in the first week of November 1532 that he learned of the Spanish invasion.

Atahuallpa had been kept well informed. He knew about the arrival and departure of the "bearded men" in 1527, and also knew of their return, on 13th May 1532: "People have arrived by a big ship out of the *hatun-cocha*." But at that moment he was engaged in a life-and-death struggle with his brother Huascar for possession of the empire. His couriers, the *chasquis*, who were able to convey a message from Quito to Cuzco in five days, kept him informed daily. Then, with the help of the *quipu*, a mnemonic device, he determined that the invaders numbered a mere 177, together with animals like hornless deer, which they mounted. He knew all about their arms, horses, guns and swords. It was an illogical interpretation of the intelligence he received that proved fatal.

Atahuallpa's reaction to the invasion remains even today an enigma. Why did he allow this small contingent of Spaniards to cross the country and enter the passes? With reference to their ascent, a Spaniard reported, "The road was so bad [it was a stepped road and difficult for horses] that they could easily have taken us there, or at another pass that we found between here and Cajamarca. . . ."

Why did he permit them to disrupt and despoil, when this would have been instantly punishable by death had any of his own subjects been the offenders? By what aberration did he allow himself to fall into one trap after another?

Atahuallpa did not regard the strange newcomers as gods, or even supermen. It is true that horses, arquebuses and writing made a great impression on him, but he knew that the Spaniards were human—all too human—and that they were vulnerable. His spies had assured him that once the horses were unsaddled they were not dangerous, and that the arquebuses, once fired, took a long time to reload, during which time the arquebusier was very vulnerable (which was true). But he also became aware that the Spaniards knew about the civil war then in progress, and that they were making a marked effort to dispose his governors in favour of those who supported Huascar.

Whatever the complex reasons—and we do not know them all—the Spaniards were allowed to proceed over the well-organised Inca road system; and it was this that betrayed Atahuallpa, just as the straight Persian roads betrayed the Persians to Alexander.

Ascending by way of a steep, stone-laid lateral road, Pizarro's men gained the wide highway, a continuation of the road that Hernando de Soto had seen earlier. The royal highway led them to Cajamarca, which they entered at the hour of vespers on 15th November 1532. Hernando de Soto was despatched with fifteen horsemen to "ascertain the disposition of the Inca". He was followed by Hernando Pizarro, one of the four brothers of doom, and they were directed to Atahuallpa.

The Spaniards remained mounted during their dialogue with the Inca. Felipillo, the Indian from Tumbes who had been taken to Spain in 1527, acted as translator. Atahuallpa said, "Inform your captain that I will visit him tomorrow with my chieftains . . . he is to occupy the public buildings in the square and no others till I arrive. Then I will order what shall be done."

That night the soldiers looked upon the Inca's watchfires. These seemed to light up the whole side of the mountain, glittering in the darkness. "They seemed," said one who was there, "as thick as the stars of heaven."

The entrance of Atahuallpa the following day and the subsequent events of his fall were related in newsletters of the period. The first to circulate in Europe was the famous *Letter from Pizarro*, which was so fascinating that all copies of it have disappeared. Another newsletter, a copy of which is now in the British Museum, is the *Nouvelles certaines Isles du Perou*, mentioned earlier. It describes the events of 16th November 1532 as follows.

"The same day Atahuallpa directed his course toward the city of Cajamarca and arrived there in the evening, being carried in his litter all decorated with plaques of the finest gold. Several Indians went before him to clean the road, although it was already clean and there was nothing to clear away. After him followed others, some of whom danced while others sang. Many Indians guarded him, some carrying battle-axes and others halberds made of silver; also gib clubs hung from their belts. Francisco Pizarro, seeing that Atahuallpa was arriving at the city, prepared all his men—both foot and mounted—for the assault, and hid them in two parties behind the *galpones*. A gentle father, called Valverde and belonging to the Dominican order, went out alone [apart from an interpreter] carrying a Bible in his hand, and spoke to Atahuallpa. He told Atahuallpa the things that were written in the book that God had ordered them to do. Then Atahuallpa demanded to see this book, and, as soon as he had it in his hand, threw it to the ground. The said gentle father picked it off the ground and

ran screaming towards Pizarro, crying aloud that the faith of Jesus Christ
must be heard.

"At this point Pizarro came out fully armed, along with all the people that
he had, both on foot and mounted. Reaching the said Atahuallpa, he laid his
hand on him and pulled him down from the litter, while the others strenu-
ously put to death all those who carried him, and then went bravely into the
midst of Atahuallpa's army, a large number of whom they stabbed to death.
The battle lasted from vespers until it was night. They took as prisoners
many of the principal Indians. . . . The said Atahuallpa, seeing himself
prisoner and fearing to be put to death, promised to give the Christians a
room filled with gold, twenty feet high and eighteen in width . . . and he
furthermore promised more silver than could be counted. . . ."

The ruins of Huanuco (Viejo), drawn from an aerial photograph.

## CHAPTER FOUR

## Hernando Pizarro's Golden Journey

Atahuallpa, held in "protective custody" attended by his *ñustas*, and some of his council, attempting to learn chess and cards and to understand the language and ways of his captors, waited just as impatiently as the Spaniards for the arrival of his ransom. However, after two months, the soldiers were not only becoming restless and bored, but also fearful of what might happen: "The Governor Pizarro and all of us saw ourselves in great danger every day. . . ." If it took much longer for the gold and silver to arrive, they reasoned, the Inca might raise his armies, and then they would never be permitted to depart with the treasure.

It was then decided to hurry up the flow of the ransom. Atahuallpa himself suggested it, proposing that a detachment of Spaniards, accompanied by his chieftains and a convoy of his people, go down to Pachacamac, the most sacred of all the shrines on the coast of Peru, to ensure that it yielded up its gold and silver. The Governor immediately acted on the suggestion, and selected his brother, Hernando Pizarro, to lead the gold-gathering journey to Pachacamac.

Hernando, who boasted that he was the only one of the Pizarros that was legitimate, was a tall man, with a coarse, pock-marked face, thick tongue and lips, and small eyes, but he was nevertheless a fine horseman and a good soldier, and had a commanding presence. He was very sensitive to the slightest social cut, not being too sure of himself and in consequence arrogant; yet he was capable and highly literate. He survived all his brothers, living to be exactly 100, and proved to be the only one to die in his bed.

A royal inspector, Miguel Estete, was selected to accompany Hernando Pizarro's expedition and to make a report of all minutiae. Don Miguel was to profit handsomely from the Inca's ransom, for he was the one who had pulled the royal fringe or *llautu* from the head of Atahuallpa when he was captured.

Estete began his report thus: "On Wednesday, the day of Epiphany (which is vulgarly called the Festival of the Three Kings, 5th January 1533), Hernando Pizarro set out from the town of Cajamarca with twenty horsemen and a few arquebusiers. . . ." When one considers that these few men, and several chieftains who went along at Atahuallpa's bidding, made up the total strength of the party, it can be seen just how daring Hernando Pizarro's trip was. To reach his destination, he had to travel over 600 miles of Inca highways, passing through territory inhabited by innumerable potentially hostile people.

Beginning their journey, Hernando Pizarro and his "twenty" followed the royal road of Chincha-suyu from Cajamarca to Baños, the next town to the south. There, a sumptuous building housed the hot sulphur baths that gave the town its name. Keeping to the royal road, the party then proceeded through Namora, Ichocán and Cajambamba, towns that still bear the same names and are located on or near the ancient highway. By 13th January the expedition had reached a small village called Tambo, which was subject to Huamachuco.

A chronicler who passed the same way as Hernando Pizarro noticed that the style of architecture in the area, which had been conquered by the Incas less than 100 years before the arrival of the Spaniards, was not Inca. This applied to the wayside known as Virachoca-tambo, which ". . . was twenty-two feet wide and about 100 feet long, all of stone and roofed with long thick beams covered with *ichu* [grass] thatch, which they employed very skilfully."

Hernando Pizarro, then only twenty-six years of age, was, considering the lowly circumstances of his birth and his sparse education, a most literate man—his illiterate brother Francisco was, in fact, an exception. As the party moved over high, unknown ground, the chance of ambush threatening at every turn, still he managed to keep a record of the Inca roads and stations that he came across. Indeed, his reporting was of such quality that the places he described can be determined to this day.

At Andamarca, now called Mollebamba, the royal road divided: to the left it went straight towards Cuzco; to the right, it descended towards the coast by way of a narrow corridor between the massive Black and White Cordilleras—this branch led to Pachacamac.

At the next place, Yomabamba, Pizarro and his minions rode along a road eighteen feet wide; this can still be seen and is well-preserved. They took the road leading down through the towering Cordillera Blanca, a succession of gigantic, snow-covered peaks, culminating in Huascarán, the summit of which is 22,205 feet above sea level.

As Pizarro followed his guides down a steep road constructed as a series of steps, and with supporting walls and terraces, he could no longer contain his admiration: "Nothing equals the magnificence of this road across the sierra. . . ."

The party continued to descend for almost forty miles, following the stairway of the *pata-pata*, as the road was called. A few days later, Hernando de Soto, travelling along the same road with another scouting party, met the deposed and captured Huascar, who was trussed up like a felon. He was being brought to Atahuallpa for justice. It was here that Huascar offered de Soto more gold and silver than had been promised the invaders by his half-brother. That hastened his end. After de Soto had left, Huascar was garrotted and tossed into a river near Andamarca.

By 15th January 1533, Hernando Pizarro, having negotiated the great snow-filled passes, had reached Corongo, which is still known by the same name and is situated at an altitude of 10,472 feet. The ransom mission now had to descend by the difficult, tortuous road leading through the canyon of the río Santa, a magnificent, foaming, turbulent river fed by the melting snows of the Cordillera Blanca.

At Yurmarca there was a halting station, guardian of two great suspension bridges. As the suspension bridge was unknown in Europe, had never been used by the Romans, and was not thought out by the Europeans until 1810, Estete lacked words to describe it. What follows, however, is the first published description of an Inca suspension bridge: "Next day [Hernando Pizarro] reached a large village in a valley, and a very rapid river [the Santa] intercepted the road. It was spanned by two bridges close together, made of network in the following manner. They build a foundation [the towers] near the water and raise it to a great height; and, from one side of the river to the other, there are cables [made of twisted cabuya fibres] as thick as a man's thigh. They are held up by the towers and the ends buried in the ground with great stones. The width is that of a cart's width."

The remains of the towers that held the hanging bridges are still there, confirming that there were (as in many places) two bridges: one for the lowly *puric*; the other for the Inca caste. "One," the Spaniards explained, "is for the common people . . . while the lords and *capitanes* used the other."

The Inca road now ran along the west bank of the canyon, since the other side was so sheer, and avalanches so frequent, that it was impossible to build a road there.

At Huaylas, Hernando Pizarro "rested his company for two days". The ruins of the *tampu* and ancient city are still visible there.

From this point south, Hernando Pizarro had to his left a magnificent panorama of the Callejón de Huaylas. The snow-capped peaks, only twenty miles to the east, all rose higher than Mont Blanc and the Matterhorn, the highest being Huascarán, Peru's highest mountain.

After Mato, the official report stated, there was "a small village where all [the party's] needs—food, thirst and sleep—were satisfied". The road then crossed the río Santa again by another suspension bridge, for, as the east side of the valley here broadened out, it now allowed the Inca road undisputed passage. Continuing through Caras, then Yungay, "where the people came out as friends, gave food and offered Indians to act as relay carriers for [the contingent's] goods", the road reached Ranrahirca, a place to be avoided due to its history of avalanches. The latest of these took place on 10th January 1962, when 3 million tons of snow, rock and water broke loose from the peak of Huascarán and permanently buried 3,500 villagers.

As the valley continued to broaden out, the danger of avalanches lessened so much that the Inca road could keep to the east bank on its way through Huaras, where "Pumacallai [the *curaca*] met us to arrange a new relay of Indian porters". In the twenty-two miles between Huaras and Olleros, the road had to cross twenty-two rivers, large and small, all of which were bridged. "There is a bridge of stone or wood over every stream. . . ."

On 24th January, "after marching through the valley, where there was much tilled land and many flocks of llamas, we stopped for the night two leagues away from a small village called Pachicoto. . . ." A large hacienda of the same name now occupies the area where the *tampu* used to be. Despite the fact that it is 13,205 feet up on the bare puna, it was once an important junction, as walls, ruins and the tracks of roads testify. On reaching this junction, Hernando Pizarro "left the royal road that leads to Cuzco . . . and took the lateral road leading westwards to the coast."

At the next *tampu*, Marca, where the Inca road can still be plainly seen, the expedition turned west, passed over the lower parts of an *abra*, an opening of the Cordillera Negra, and began their descent. Reaching the coast at the great fortress of Paramonga, they joined the well-kept coastal road and followed it for the remaining 109 miles to Pachacamac. There, with a boldness that is understandable only because it was backed by the weight of Atahuallpa's command, Pizarro had gold and silver stripped from the holy shrine. Then, on 13th February 1533, with his work completed and hundreds of Indian porters loaded down with gold and silver, he ordered the return.

Somewhere on his return journey, he learned from his guides, who had heard it through the *chasquis*, who were continually coming and going along the roads, that one of Atahuallpa's greatest generals, Chalcu-chima, was at a place called Jauja in the high sierras. Yet where exactly was Jauja? Pizarro was informed that it was buried in the Andes, but that there was a more or less direct route there from Pachacamac. Having discovered that, he headed there.

As the convoy proceeded north along the coastal road, Hernando's guides pointed out to him a feeder road that connected the coastal and the royal Andean roads. This feeder, which ran from Huara up to the royal road, by way of Sayan, Churin and Oyon, was a mere sixty miles measured on the map, but it was uphill all the way. The remains of this road can still be seen clinging perilously to the sides of the Oyon canyon.

On their way along the road, the convoy "had to cross a pass where the snow was so deep that it came up to the girths of the horses". They emerged at Cajatambo, a town of some importance, with many mountain roads converging there. It has an arctic climate, exacerbated by the freezing winds that blow down from the snow-capped peak of Yanahuanca, which, at a height of 18,757 feet, dominates the area. Pizarro changed course, making for the main royal highway that he had earlier left in order to descend to the coast. The way south now lay along a well-walled road and past the ice-rimmed lake of Punrrún; two days later, on 11th March, the party reached the great flat plain of Pumpu (Bonbón).

To the Spaniards, Pumpu "was a large village". On their arrival there, the lords of the place "came out to meet Hernando Pizarro. We found here 150 *arrobas* [254 pounds] of gold . . . on its way to Cajamarca as part of Atahuallpa's ransom." The travellers noted that a river (the Mantaro) flowed out of the large lake they found there and that around the edges of the lake there were many villages and great flocks of birds, including pink flamingoes, which had a nesting place there. The river Mantaro was crossed by a bridge, the piers of which can still be seen when the water level is low. The Inca village of Pumpu is still visible. The lake, then called Chincha, is thirty-six miles long by six broad, and, at an altitude of 12,490 feet, is higher than the great Lake Titicaca. Its name, "Chincha", was given to one of the quarters of the Inca world—the Chincha-suyu.

Six leagues from Pumpu the convoy came to Xacamalca, and, after the next day's march, reached Tarma, which is located on a bald mountain, above the modern city of the same name. Hernando Pizarro "passed that night . . . at . . . Tarma, which is on the slope of a mountain. Here he was lodged in a painted house. . . ." The remains of fortifications, houses and *tampu* belonging to the old city are still extant, and are known locally as the "houses of Pizarro". Here the expedition stayed to reorganise for its march on Jauja. The local chieftain "behaved well" and supplied them with food and carriers. On Sunday 23rd March, Hernando Pizarro drew his party into battle order and led them out onto the road over the *puna*.

The sides of the road were then, as now, banked with local stone cemented with adobe mud to form a small wall, twenty inches high. The road, ten yards wide, encountered few obstacles in crossing the treeless *puna*, and was for the most part unpaved, as was usual with roads crossing this type of terrain. However, where the road had to negotiate a steep gradient, engineers had constructed wide steps, the treads of which were stone-lined. In addition, where the road passed over a marsh it was raised on a causeway, usually with a stone foundation; and if it traversed a region of constant rainfall, it was necessary to pave it there as well. Generally, though, the hard, well-drained *puna*, and also the land along the desert coast, provided the road with a bed that was sound enough without any need for paving. At intervals of twenty feet, there was stone-laid drainage, canals cutting across the road and effectively draining rain off the earth-surfaced highway. These features can now be seen as plainly as when Hernando Pizarro passed over this section of the royal way some 450 years ago.

"The town of Jauja," went Hernando Pizarro's terse report, "is very large. It is situated in a beautiful valley. It enjoys a temperate climate. A very large river—the Mantaro—flows near the town. The land is fertile. . . ."

The town was also of strategic importance: whoever held Jauja could control movement to the north. It dominated the Mantaro valley and also controlled one of the most important and most direct routes to the coast. The original inhabitants were the Wankas, "Field Guardians". They were a fierce people whose houses were built "as rounded fortresses of stone, like small castles". To defend their extensive, well-planted fields, the Wankas used the sling as their weapon, and many a re-exhumed skull shows the accuracy of their slinging, as can be seen from the many trepanned skulls discovered nearby. In the early fifteenth century, the Wankas effectively blocked the Inca's victorious progress north. Although the tenth Inca, Topa, sought through his ambassadors to induce them to "embrace his friendship . . . without having to get it by making war", the Wankas refused. Faced with integration or extinction, they chose extinction. The battle that followed was short, fierce and conclusive: the Wankas were absorbed into the empire. The Incas imposed on them their political system and religion, but allowed them to retain their rites, language and customs.

In the five days that Hernando Pizarro spent there, "he saw 100,000 people assemble every day in the principal square for the market". But the Spaniards were not there to count people but to take General Chalcu-chima, the conqueror of Huascar and a potential source of resistance, back to Cajamarca. It was the first time that the Inca general had had personal contact with the "bearded ones", and for the first time in his long military career Chalcu-chima did not know how to act. Strange people had come out of the sea, captured and held Atahuallpa for ransom, and he did not know whether to fight or flee. Hernando Pizarro made his decision for him: his place was beside Atahuallpa. So, carried in his litter with a vast concourse of blue-clad Rucanas, who alternately carried him and rested, Chalcu-chima followed the conquerors along the royal road back to Cajamarca.

The great city of Huánuco (elevation 12,156 feet) was reached on the last day of March, after the convoy had marched over five leagues of "roads . . . paved on account of the snow". Pedro de Cieza first saw it in 1547, thirteen years after Hernando Pizarro had been there. He acknowledged that it had "an admirably built royal palace, made of very large stones, artfully joined . . . beside it is the Temple of the Sun. . . . The stewards of the Incas were in charge of collecting tributes from the region that served this palace."

Huánuco, the chief city of the province of the Huamilies, was the largest city between Cuzco and Tomebamba. The enormous plaza alone held eight large buildings, of which the largest, called El Castillo, measured 675 feet by 950. Approached by three flights of steps, the doorways were ornamented with sculpted crouching puma figures. On the hills were located the houses of the inhabitants, and some 3,000 storehouses, or colcas. Pedro de Cieza's estimate of 30,000 inhabitants seems reasonably accurate. The habit of paying tribute became so ingrained that, fifty years after the conquest, the descendants of those who had been subject to Huanuco and gave tribute to the Incas were still doing so to the Spanish Viceroy of Peru. When these tributes began to decline, the Viceroy sent one Iñigo de Zuñiga (in 1562) to determine the reason why. The Indians were questioned in detail about their origins and the type of and quantity of tribute they had paid to the Inca. A typical extract from Zuñiga's report reads, "House 35. In this house an Indian woman called Ana Colque. Widow, about seventy years of age, without sons or daughters. She does not now remember the tribute given to the Inca. Her tribute is a ball of spun-wool thread every four months and one chicken every year with some eggs."

The original inhabitants in pre-Inca times were called Machas. They were conquered by Topa Inca in 1462. A population of *mitimaes* were moved in to ensure the land's allegiance to the Inca. Tribute was levied from everyone. In the valley of the Marañon, an important tributary of the Amazon, the tribute was coca leaf, fish, corn and gold dust; in the cooler regions, potatoes, salt, and cabuya fibres.

The venerable Carmelite friar Vásquez de Espinosa, who travelled extensively by foot and mule throughout Peru, in order to estimate the number of people he must convert, rode into Huánuco in 1564. He found it "situated on a wide and attractive plain with a beautiful, albeit stark, landscape without one tree. . . ." He spoke too of the excellent stone construction of the royal palaces, "and many buildings large enough to contain a racecourse; and of the warm baths. . . ." The hot water from the sulphur streams was conveyed some distance in closed stone conduits; the ancient baths in Huánuco itself are still preserved.

A twelve-mile segment of the royal road from Huánuco to Cajamarca has been closely studied. The outline of the symmetrical buildings that formed the *tampu* of Tarapaco—the first halting station outside Huánuco, and a place where Hernando Pizarro halted briefly—is still visible. On the flat level *puna*, the road is often as much as thirteen yards wide, suggesting that it was constructed to accommodate quite a formidable force. On the downhill sections the road is enclosed by retaining walls and drained by stone-lined conduits of careful workmanship. Excessively sharp descents were accomplished by means of stone steps with a tread no more than four inches high. The steps gave trouble to the Spaniards, with their horses, but not to the

Incas, who almost always travelled on foot. Despite centuries of climatic pressures—the daily extremes of temperature, and continual rain, snow and frost—this section of the road is still in a usable condition.

The step road led down to the Viscarra river, which it crossed by way of a bridge described by Hernando Pizarro's scrivener as "the most necessary bridge in the province". This was not a suspension bridge, but a wooden one, as was usual with rivers narrow enough to be bridged by a single span. It was built "of seven tree trunks twelve yards long, covered with lesser branches and surfaced with rock-mud".

After crossing several rivers, large and small, the road led them "to a good village called Huari, where there is a large and deep river [Quebrada Huaritambo] over which there is another bridge. This position is very strong, there being deep ravines on either flank". Here Chalcu-chima broke his silence to point out to a fellow-warrior that he had fought a battle here against Huascar and his troops, who had been guarding the pass.

Within five leagues (fifteen miles) the convoy reached Huacabamba, where two streams flow into a large river. Here they found "another deep river with *two* bridges, suspension bridges of network close together, the cables resting on stone towers set close by the river's edge . . . the rope cables stretching from one side to another are as thick as a man's thigh and hanging between them are stout cords of the same material, which hold up the bridge's platform. The horses crossed over without trouble. . . ."

The wayside station of Piscobamba followed. "It is built on the side of a mountain. The chieftain is called Taukuame. The Indians wore on their heads a kind of skein of red-dyed wool."

"The road is a sight to see," wrote Pedro de Cieza, who passed over the same road fourteen years later, ". . . how well built it is, laid out level and wide. It runs across mountains, part of it being dug out of the living rock, where there are stairways and resting places. . . ." Hernando Pizarro reached Conduco by this road. After continuing a short way further, he and his expedition reached Andamarca, now called Mollebamba. It was here, earlier in the year, that they had turned off the mountain road onto the road down to Pachacamac and the hot desert coast. "At this point the two royal roads to Cuzco unite."

By the time that Hernando Pizarro arrived back in Cajamarca, on 25th May 1533, he and his "twenty" had travelled over 1,120 miles of Inca roads. He had crossed over many Inca bridges, and his—the first—descriptions of them were made while the original system of maintenance was still operative. On his gold-gathering, iconoclastic journey to Pachacamac, he had traversed an immense stretch of hostile territory, with only Atahuallpa's verbal pledge to ensure his safe conduct. He had seen and described more of the Inca road in its pristine condition than any other European, and, although the thought of gold was his driving force, the thought that a people deemed primitive could have built and maintained such roads, and over such an inhospitable terrain, was overwhelming. He had returned with a precise knowledge of communications and a pattern for future conquest.

In November 1533, six months after completing his report, he submitted it to the royal historiographer, Oviedo, on the island of Santo Domingo. A witty cosmopolitan, Oviedo was the historian of the conquest—at once its Pliny and its Tacitus—and it was his task to ferret out the details of the new discoveries and to produce from them a coherent picture for the Crown.

Hernando Pizarro reported, "I received permission from the Governor, Francisco Pizarro, to go to a mosque of which he had intelligence. Located a hundred leagues away on the sea coast in a town called Pachacamac, it took us twenty-two days to reach it. The road over the mountains is a thing worth seeing because, despite the ruggedness of the ground, such beautifully made roads could not, in truth, be found anywhere in Christendom. The greater part of them are paved. There is a bridge of stone, hemp or wood across every stream. We found suspension bridges over a very large and powerful river [the Santa], which we crossed twice, and these bridges were marvellous things to see. They are so strongly made that the horses passed over them. At each passage they have two bridges, one used by the common people, the other by the lords and *capitanes* of their lands. The approaches to the bridges are kept closed and there are guards over them. The country is populous. There are gold mines in many parts of it. It has a cold climate. It snows and there is much rain. There are no swamps. Fuel is scarce. . . . All the people from the surrounding countryside come to the *tampu* towns to perform their duties when the army passes through the territory. They have, in these *tampus*, stores of fuel and maize and all other necessities. They count by certain knots and cords [*quipus*] and so record what each chieftain has brought. When they have to bring loads of fuel, maize, *chicha* or meat, they take off the knots [on one *quipu*] or make a new knot on the other strings, so that those who have charge of the stores keep an exact account. . . . When we arrived on the desert plains of the sea coast, we met with people who were less civilised, but the country was equally populous. . . . The road is very wide, with an earthern [adobe] wall on either side and houses [*tampus*] for resting at intervals. There are very large villages, the house of the Indians being built of canes and earth. For in this land it never rains. The walled road traverses the whole of this country. . . ."

Thus Hernando Pizarro gave the first and last glimpse of a barbaric empire that was shortly to be irrevocably destroyed.

## CHAPTER FIVE

## Tampus, Chasquis and Quipus

The room had been measured. The secretary, Francisco de Xeréz (whose namesakes came from Jeréz, the city that gave its name to that fortified wine, "sherry") had used the mathematical ability on which he prided himself to calculate that the room Atahuallpa had indicated was seventeen feet wide by twenty-two feet long, by eight feet high, and had a total volume of 2,992 cubic feet. This Atahuallpa had promised to fill once with gold, and twice with silver. Francisco Pizarro was so amazed by this ransom offer that he had summoned Xeréz himself to record it "as a formal pledge". It was then late November 1532.

Pizarro then asked Atahuallpa how long it would take his messengers to cover the 900 miles to the city of Cuzco, and how long it would be before the promised ransom was fulfilled. Atahuallpa, answering through a triple flow of translators, replied, "When the *chasquis* are sent . . . they run from post to post, village to village; fifty in relays, it will take five days. . . ." All of which was true.

So the royal road became a golden road. Long lines of Indians arrived laden with gold and silver in various forms, yet, since gold is heavier than iron, and a heavily laden man can cover, at best, only fifteen miles a day, the flow of treasure into Cajamarca was necessarily slow. Two, three, even four months passed, and still the room was not filled; not even the handsome amounts heaped up as a result of Hernando Pizarro's gold-gathering journey could fill the void, "Although I collected 85,000 castellanos of gold, 3,000 marcos of silver." (A castellano or peso de oro equals sixteen ounces and a marco of silver slightly over an ounce).

The ransom room was being filled, but not at the speed both conqueror and conquered wished. Time now became the enemy for both factions. In February, Diego de Almagro, the original partner of Pizarro in the conquest, arrived with reinforcements, thereby hurrying up the process not of filling the room with gold and silver, which continued to arrive, but of the departure from this earth of the Lord-Inca Atahuallpa. The transport of gold over such great distances—from Quito (800 miles away), Cuzco (900 miles away), and Chile (2,500 miles away)—was time-consuming; and all the while the seconds were ticking away to Atahuallpa's downfall.

Humboldt, while in Cajamarca in 1801, was "shown the room in which the unfortunate Atahuallpa was confined for nine months". The room was seen and photographed in 1945 by the present author, who noted it as a typical late Inca structure made of well-laid ashlars, with several niches, the hallmark of Inca architecture. The building is the only known survival from the time, at least above ground.

Pizarro suddenly declared that the ransom promise had been completed, even though the 2,992 cubic feet had not yet been filled to full capacity. His announcement came from no deep-seated humane instinct, but because the soldiers were restless, feared a gathering of forces, and, after waiting two years, demanded their share of the takings.

On 3rd May 1533, the goldsmiths began melting down the gold into sugar-loaf-shaped ingots, and soon after that the process leading to the legal murder of Atahuallpa began. On 18th June 1533 the distribution of Atahuallpa's ransom was effected. On Saturday, 26th July 1533, "as night was falling, the Inca was brought out of his prison and led to the middle of the square at Cajamarca; to the sound of trumpets his intended treason and treachery were proclaimed and he was tied to a stake". While in prison, he had been promised that if he agreed to become a Christian not a drop of his blood would be shed. The Christians kept their promise: Atahuallpa had a cord tied round his neck, and was garrotted. There was a protest from several of the conquistadors, who even drew up a memorial to that effect and signed their names to it, revolted that this judicial murder had been done in the name of God and justice. The Spaniards' missionary zeal had pushed faith to the verge of madness: love of God and love of gold had become so inextricably interwoven that it was impossible to say where one ended and the other began.

The distinction was no problem for Michel de Montaigne, the celebrated essayist, humanist and Lord Mayor of Bordeaux: "They trumped up against Atahuallpa a false accusation with false evidence. . . . The Inca had given signs of a frank, liberal and steadfast spirit . . . the conquerors, after having extracted 1,000,325 ounces of gold, besides silver, from him for his ransom . . . then treacherously had him publicly strangled, a horrible and unheard of calamity . . ." (quoted from p. 696 of the translation by Donald M. Frame, Stanford, California, 1948).

Yet all the king's horses and all the king's men could not put Atahuallpa back together again. He was given a sumptuous funeral, following which his people then spirited away his body, a puppet Inca was chosen, and the conquerors took the road to Cuzco.

Due to the detailed information about the Inca road between Cajamarca and Jauja that Hernando Pizarro and his "twenty" gave them, the army of conquest were able to plot in advance their arrival at and departure from the various stations along the Inca way.

Pedro Sancho de la Hoz, the royal notary, kept the record. Although only twenty-three when the conquest began, it was he who made the record of the distribution of Atahuallpa's ransom, noting down most carefully each share including his own, which was ninety-four marks of silver and 2,220 pesos of gold. He was by his own account a "gentleman on all four sides", and in this quality personally witnessed all the events between 1531 and 1534. He was to return to Spain, marry well, and leave again four years later. In the conquest of Chile he was to lose his head. Pedro Sancho recorded all the events that took place on the Inca highway up to Jauja.

The strategic importance of Jauja was instantly grasped by Francisco Pizarro, who made it the first capital of the newly conquered territories. Situated at 8,500 feet above sea level, in the valley gouged out by the Mantaro river, which flowed by the city, it both commanded the valley and controlled four roads. The verdant valleys surrounding it were extensively planted, and the hills above it were alive with domesticated llamas and alpacas, while all around there were circular stone storage *colcas*. From Jauja westward ran the most direct route to the coast—the road Hernando Pizarro had taken from the shrine of Pachacamac.

Pedro de Cieza arrived in Jauja in December 1547, thirteen years after the Pizarro brothers had passed through it on their way to the final conquest of Cuzco. It was then, as it had been in 1533, a rallying place for armies, but this time the action was directed against Gonzalo Pizarro.

The youngest of the four Pizarros, Gonzalo was born in the poverty-stricken province of Estremadura, that breeding ground of conquistadors. According to Augustín de Zárate he was (in 1545, when he was forty years old), "tall and well-proportioned; his complexion was dark, his beard black and very long. He was a lover of warfare and very patient of hardship. He was a good rider in both styles and a good shot with an arquebus. Considering his poverty of language, he expressed himself well, though very coarsely. He was unable to keep a secret . . . and immoderate in his pursuit of women, both Indian and Spanish." Gonzalo endeared himself to his men. He was considered "the best lance to come out to Peru". "The Pizarros", wrote a contemporary, "were all reared in penury, as proud as they were poor; thus their eagerness for monetary gain was in direct proportion to their poverty." Gonzalo had shared in Atahuallpa's ransom, receiving 384 marks of silver and 9,909 pesos of gold, and had taken a conspicuous part in the conquest as well as in the civil wars that followed. His Quixote-like expedition to find the source of cinnamon—an expedition that "cost 50,000 castellanos, mostly borrowed" and led to the discovery of the Amazon—was as heroic as any of the exploits described in the *Iliad*. On his return, in September 1542, after the expenditure of 210 Spaniards, 4,000 Indians, 5,000 swine, 1,001 dogs and huge flocks of burden-bearing llamas, he did not find the Peruvian world as he had known it: Francisco Pizarro had been murdered; his brother Hernando, who had gone to Spain to justify his legal execution of Diego de Almagro, was imprisoned for life; and the "New Laws" were being heralded about the land.

For, in that same year of 1542, on the basis of many complaints reaching the Crown of the cruel treatment of the Indians, the Council of the Indies had promulgated the "New Laws for the Good Treatment and Preservation of the Natives". These laws abolished Indian chattel slavery and freed them from forced labour. All colonists who held Indians as part of their property under the *encomienda* system would be accountable for their stewardship.

Since the main source of revenue a settler had was from forced labour, the New Laws aroused violent opposition. In Peru it brought about open rebellion, and Gonzalo Pizarro became its acknowledged leader, with the assumed title of *procurador*. Since he had at his command the fathomless revenues of the recently discovered silver mines of Potosí, Gonzalo Pizarro had "more income than is possessed in Spain by the Archbishop of Toledo and the Count of Benavento". It was he who directed the opposition to the new Viceroy, Blasco Núñez, who had come out on 18th January 1546 to enforce the New Laws.

When he found himself opposed, the Viceroy exclaimed, "Is it possible that our Emperor Charles, who is feared by all in Europe, should be disobeyed here by this bastard Gonzalo Pizarro, who refuses to comply with the laws?" The Viceroy had his answer in battle: he was pursued, defeated and beheaded. After that, Gonzalo Pizarro was the undisputed master of Peru, and, in addition possessed the silver mines of Potosí and a large fleet, which controlled the Pacific from Peru to Panama. Assuming the role of Governor, he extended his hand to be kissed, surrounded himself with a bodyguard, and used the royal "we".

"Why don't you now declare yourself king of Peru?" asked Francisco de Carbajal, his master-at-arms. "For in fact you have already done so. You have raised arms against the Viceroy and killed him in battle. You have now gone too far either to halt or to retreat. Proclaim yourself king, marry an Inca *coya*, a direct descendant of the Incas, *unite the two races* so that they may henceforth repose in peace under a common sceptre." This Falstaffian octogenarian, Carbajal, was always so ready with sagacious advice that people thought him to have had a "familiar spirit"; on the other hand, however, his sharp tongue, crafty mind, and long sword arm earned him the name of "Demon of the Andes". He seemed indifferent to danger in battle, was cool, watchful and cautious. When victorious he meted out justice in so light a manner that people almost seemed to enjoy being hanged by him.

He festooned the trees of Peru with men who ran counter to Pizarro's policy. "Never", wrote Pedro de Cieza, moralising on Carbajal faults, "has there been anyone to compare with him for cruelty, neither Marius nor Sulla, Dionysus or Phalaris; for in every phase of cruelty he showed himself a past master . . . the trees from Quito to the hills of Potosí from which he hung his victims bear witness to this."

Though clearly a man of his time—predatory, of course—Carbajal was more far-sighted than most and saw, four centuries ahead of his time, how the social structure of Latin America would develop. He was an extraordinary man living in extraordinary times.

Beyond the plain fact that he was born about 1460 in Ragama, Arevalo, in Old Castile, nothing is known of his youth or origins, though his phrasing and the quality of his writing lead one to think that he must have been well educated. By 1500, he was a soldier, and became one of the celebrated Spanish *tercios*, the finest infantry in Europe. At the sack of Rome (1527), he appropriated a library of notarial records which its owner was so anxious to recover that he paid him 1,000 ducats for its return. With this money Carbajal (already seventy or more) financed his way to America, and, after a sojourn in Mexico, arrived in Peru. This was in 1536, during one of the uprisings.

His first appearance in Peru was at the Battle of Chupas, near the great Inca city of Vilcas-huamán. He was then one of the "King's men", as he had been for sixty years. An experienced war-horse, he was named Sergeant-Major. While out scouting positions, he saw how the enemy—the "Men of Chile"—had placed their artillery. "So he ordered his men to move, saying many witty things. Forward good cavaliers, forward, advance without fear. Look at me, how fat I am. I go forward without feeling any fear of them."

After, he took part in various campaigns and so acquired wealth, but when he heard of the New Laws, which he suspected would bring on internecine strife, he converted his wealth into silver bullion and applied to the Council in Lima for permission to leave. It was denied, and, since he was thereby prevented from avoiding the coming troubles, he reluctantly joined Pizarro's rebellion. "I was unwilling", he explained, "to put my hand to the warp of this cloth, but, things being as they are, I promise to be the principal weaver." Which he was, the dominant warp in the weaving being blood-red.

In between fighting and pursuing the King's men who refused to accept Gonzalo Pizarro, he worked the silver mines discovered in 1545 near Potosí, and foresaw that the "mines would be more valuable than the whole of Old Castile in Spain". In time, they were found to be the richest source of silver in the world. Another of Carbajal's occupations was extracting confessions: "I had Diego Maldonado stripped and placed upon the *burro* [an instrument of torture]. 'Mother of God,' he screamed, 'do not kill me . . .'." Even when far into his eighties Carbajal's energy did not fail him: at one time he rode along the Inca roads from Chuquisaca to Quito, a distance of 2,000 miles; then returned to Lima; and then left yet again for a battle that was shaping up near Lake Titicaca, at the *tampu* of Huarina.

In 1547, however, his chief headache was Pedro de la Gasca.

La Gasca arrived in Panama in July 1546, with neither arms nor entourage. "Sire," he said to his king, "this enterprise seems to me troublesome and dangerous. . . ." He therefore asked for and was granted plenary authority. He also asked for and was given a quire of royal decrees in *carte blanche*, the contents of which he was to fill out at his discretion. La Gasca, who had studied law and theology at Salamanca, had already shown himself adept in other negotiations undertaken on behalf of the Crown. Frail in body, with little knowledge of military affairs, he nevertheless had this to recommend him: he was very wealthy, and so consequently impervious to bribery. From Panama he began to send letters to all the commanders based in South America, enjoining them to rally to the King's side. "Crafty letters," raged Francisco de Carbajal. It was one of these letters that won over to La Gasca's side that redoubtable warrior Sebastián Benalcázar, and, in turn, the young soldier–historian Pedro de Cieza.

First the Armada, the navy of Gonzalo Pizarro, defected to La Gasca, who thus gained control over the sea. Still Pizarro turned down an offer of clemency. "We do not want pardon for what we have done," he said, "we want approbation. I will die governing." So he retired with his forces to Cuzco to await La Gasca. While he waited, he put into effect a scorched-earth policy. All along the desert coast from Tumbes to Lima, *tampus*, bridges and llamas were destroyed wholesale: "I want not a single thing to fall into La Gasca's hands." This scorched-earth policy so completely wiped out all the breeding stocks of llamas acclimatised to the hot coastal region that the llama was never re-established there as a domestic animal. In addition, the Inca communication system suffered more destruction at this time than it had throughout the previous ten years.

As Gonzalo Pizarro controlled the high sierras, Pedro de la Gasca broke up his invading armies into various contingents so that Pizarro would not know where the main thrust would fall.

From Jauja, on 27th December 1547, Pedro de la Gasca wrote a twenty-three-page report to the King. He told how he had divided his troops into four sections, so that they could not all be ambushed at once, and how all had travelled along the Inca roads, arterial or lateral, some going along "the Huayna Capac [he writes it Guaynacava] road, which leads from Huánuco to Bonbón [Pumpu]." In December, with all four sections having safely made the rendezvous in Jauja, he prepared the final march along the Inca highway to do battle with Gonzalo Pizarro. It was at this moment that Carbajal wrote to La Gasca, in a very truculent tone, asking to see "the Holy Writ by which you find it permissible to proclaim with your fox's conscience that the Emperor has given you secret instructions to give battle to our Governor, Gonzalo Pizarro." He insisted that it was a waste of time and lives to send further messengers offering pardon, "for on their arrival here I hanged two of them. . . . May the Lord preserve your reverend personality . . . and may your sins bring you into my hands. . . ."

P E D R O  D E  C I E Z A arrived in Jauja sometime in December 1547, as a member of one of the four detachments. By that time he had travelled over a thousand miles of Inca highways, coastal and highland, and had had ample time, as he said, "to turn aside everywhere to see what I could of the regions in order to learn and set down what they contained." His notes burgeoned, for it was no small task for a young soldier on active service to take care of his developing manuscripts. In addition, writing was then extraordinarily costly, for a single sheet of foolscap then cost as much as a horse would fifty years later. "Often," he said, modestly enough, "when the other soldiers were resting, I wearied myself writing. Neither this, however, nor the difficulties of the land, mountains and rivers to be crossed, nor the intolerable hungers and the rugged roads ever stood in the way of my two callings: those of writing history as it occurred, and of following with unabated honour the standard of my *capitán*."

No sooner had he set foot in Peru, than Pedro de Cieza observed that the Incas operated a courier service over the royal roads. "News was carried by *chasquis* from Quito to Cuzco. The Incas invented a system of courier posts. . . . Every half-league [one and a half miles] there was a small house where two Indians always resided with their wives." Each courier ran his half-league until he came up to the other and shouted his message or, if it was complicated, gave over to him a knot-string record [*quipu*] with an oral message. So it continued from post to post, so that, by running in relays, *chasquis* could convey a message from Quito to Cuzco, a distance of 1,250 miles, in five days! The existence of these posts was confirmed by the von Hagen expedition (1952–60), which found a series of *o'kla* (*chasqui* shelter huts) between Jauja and Bonbón. The expedition proved that even modern, untrained Indians, running marked distances at altitudes of between 8,000 and 16,000 feet along the still extant highway, could run about one and a half miles, and that, if organised, their speed would be sufficient for them to cover 1,250 miles in five days.

Athletes train to overcome anoxemia (lack of oxygen in the blood, causing shortness of breath), but Indians living at high altitudes have become acclimatised to the lack of oxygen in the atmosphere by developing abnormally large lungs. Athleticism was here a matter of survival. One chronicler noted that *chasquis*, "who served the mails, were trained from boyhood in the art of running . . . and among Indians, running has always been practised." The result was acclimatisation. In the Andes, lack of oxygen is a fact of life, and, due to this, wrote Carlos Monge, "the human organism must surpass itself in the complicated adjustment of the physiological mechanisms."

The *chasquis* were changed every fifteen days so that the running would not be too arduous. Each province or *ayllu* through which the road passed was responsible for the *chasquis* within that area. In addition, Cieza observed, "The *chasquis* who carried these messages observed such secrecy that neither plea nor threat could make them reveal the message they were carrying. . . ." The system was so well organised that any invasion or insurrection occurring within the Inca empire was known within hours. The Spaniards were so impressed that they adopted the system themselves, and, in modified form, it survived until quite modern times.

In addition to the verbal message, the *chasquis* often carried and passed on a knotted string, the *quipu*, which served as a mnemonic device. The *quipu* had a base cord with a series of strings on which half-hitch knots, representing decimal units, were tied. With the aid of these, numbers running into thousands could be registered. The colour of a string denoted a specific subject—llamas, gold, people, arms, or whatever—but each *quipu* had to be accompanied by a verbal message. With the aid of this and information given by the *quipu*, the *quipu-camayoc*, the official rememberer, was able to commit to memory countless statistics and much specific information. While in Jauja, Pedro de Cieza asked the *curaca* Huacara Pora "to explain the system to me in such a way that I would understand it." On the *quipus* that he had stored away, he told Pedro de Cieza, there was recorded everything that had been given to the Spaniards from the time of the entry of Governor Francisco Pizarro in 1531 till 1533. "All was recorded without a single omission. And in this account, I saw the gold, silver and clothing that had been given, and even the llamas and other things. . . . I was amazed."

A vital part of the road system was the *tampu*. Since roads without inns are like a year without holidays, so communications cannot exist without there being halting stations. Those of the Incas were one of the first things that the Spaniards noted as they travelled along the roads, and they were quick to note their efficacy. The Spaniards at first referred to them as "lodgings of the Inca", but in time they recognised and began to use the native word *tampu*, which was hispanicised as *tambo*. Pedro de Cieza was the first to observe their form and function. "So that there would be adequate supplies for their armies, every four leagues [twelve miles] there were lodgings and storehouses abundantly supplied with everything found in these regions. Even in the uninhabited areas and deserts, there were such." *Curacas* (Cieza called them "stewards") of each tribe or province took great care to see that the Indians kept these *tampus* well supplied "and they kept accounts with *quipus* to see that there had been no fraud".

The frequency of *tampus* was determined by two factors: distance and terrain. Twelve miles was approximately the distance that a heavily-burdened man—for man was the first carrier—could cover in a single day. Llamas, when burdened, move at a leisurely pace, and thus take roughly the same time to cover the same distance. As new areas and tribes were conquered, the highways were, where possible, directed via established settlements, for these were ready sources of staple foods and of people for *corvée*. Where no such settlement existed, whole communities were moved to build, supply and serve a *tampu*. There are many examples of this.

*Tampus* varied in size. Some were no bigger than a house with a corral for llamas added; others were large, between 100 and 300 feet in length. The remains of many such can still be seen along the routes followed by the royal roads between Quito to Chile.

Road distances were measured in *topos*. "In many places," Cieza remembered, "there were markers like those of Spain [Roman milestones]. . . . They are known as *topos*, and each of them represents a league and a half [four and a half miles] by Castilian measure."

In the early years of the conquest, the Spaniards were full of praises for the *tampu* system, but when the conquest was complete and the civil war was over, much of the land was depopulated and laid waste, and many *tampus* destroyed. At first the Spaniards were unaware of what they were destroying. "For whenever the Spaniards passed," said Pedro de Cieza, "conquering and discovering, it is as though a fire had passed through destroying and consuming everything in its path. . . . Edifices of the Incas and the storehouses were, like the rest, destroyed and ruined."

When the destruction of the *tampu* system—that is, of the communication system—in Peru began as soon as the conquest was over, Francisco Pizarro gave in *encomienda* to each of his men a *tampu* and the surrounding land, together with its population. It was, in effect, an "allotment", yet the real meaning of *encomienda* is "a giving in trust", an ancient formula that, far from implying that the holder of the land had absolute ownership of the land and of the people living there, meant that such people simply owed him services. However, in Peru, far from Spain's control, each holder of an *encomienda* regarded it as his own property, and often maladministered it in such a way that the Indians were taken away from their normal, necessary duties and assigned to other tasks, the foodstocks of the storehouses and halting stations could no longer be replenished, and long sections of the road were destroyed or fell into disrepair.

The soldiers seemed at first blind to the fact that the people of each *tampu* had to tend to their crops and llama flocks and keep up by *corvée* all that fell within their jurisdiction. When the Indians were moved out of their normal orbit, out of their own *ayllu*, the functions of road upkeep failed. "I would not condemn the use of Indians", observed Cieza, "if it were done in moderation . . . but if a man had need of four Indians, he took twenty. . . .

Were one to enumerate the great evils, injuries, robberies, oppression and ill-treatment inflicted on the natives during these operations . . . there never would be an end to it."

In 1540 an official, Cristóbal Vaca de Castro, a lawyer sent out from Spain by Charles V to promote peace between the factions of Pizarro and Almagro (a war that did more than the conquest itself to destroy Inca culture) and named Governor of Peru, said, "I have seen with my own eyes riding all the way from Quito to Cuzco that most of the towns and settlements of the Indians are deserted, burned, destroyed. . . ." Thus one of his first acts after bringing a temporary peace to Peru was to prepare a detailed "Ordering of the Tampus" (the original of which is now in the archives of Seville).

The decree ordered that those *tampus* that had been there "from the time of Huayna Capac be restored", and went on to specify the weight of cargo an Indian would be obliged to carry (thirty pounds), the number of days of his service each year, and the care that each Spaniard must give to his *tampu* (disregard of which was subject to a fine of 300 pesos). Bridges were to be rebuilt, roads repaired, and the system of *chasqui*-posts made functional again in the form it had taken "in the time of the Lord-Incas". All this was to be effected within forty days of the signing of the decree, which was dated 1st June 1543. It was the first manual of its kind in the New World, and is of the greatest significance in the study of the Inca roads, for it lists in order all the *tampus* in Peru and Bolivia, together with the distances between them, and, for each *tampu*, the name of the *encomendero*, or holder of the territory in which it was situated. It is an invaluable document.

That this reform was carried out is evident from the curious holograph chronicle, *Nueva Cronica Buen Gobierno*, made by Felipe Huamán Poma de Ayalá. His list of *tampus* covers ten pages, and surveys the lands from Quito all the way south, through Ecuador and Peru, to Bolivia, The various types of *tampu* are indicated by symbols : a house represents a royal *tampu* reserved for the Inca and his entourage, while lesser ones are represented by a cross or a circle, which signifies the smallest *tampus*, called in the diminutive *tambillos*.

In addition, the chronicle lists the larger and important bridges, the chronicler differentiating between Inca bridges (*crisjejas*—"hanging") and Spanish-made bridges, constructed of cemented stone (*cal y canto*) and built after the conquest. This part of the chronicle is, in fact, a sixteenth-century Baedeker for 6,000 miles of Inca highway.

Felipe Huamán Poma de Ayalá was, as his name suggests, of mixed Inca and Spanish blood. He was born in 1535 in the province of Lucanas, which lay west of Cuzco in the Conti-suyu quarter of the empire. He traced his birth on his mother's side to a privileged member of the Inca caste, his grandfather being Auqui Topo Inca, who went with the Inca Pachacutic on his conquests of Quito, and held a position equivalent to that of viceroy over the vast Chincha-suyu quarter of the empire. Francisco Pizarro had him

23. A terracotta vase made by the Cañari of southern Ecuador. Vases of this type were filled with *chicha* (corn beer) and placed in graves to appease the dead.

24–27. Inca bridges: (*top left*) a bridge near Huanuco constructed of parallel tree trunks resting on permanent stone abutments; (*top right*) a suspension bridge (or *chaca*) across the upper Apurimac, made of steel cables in the Inca fashion; (*centre*) E. George Squire's drawing of an Inca bridge made of agave fibre (the agave plant is shown in the lower left-hand corner) spanning the Rio Pampas; (*bottom right*) an unusual stone cantilever bridge in the Carabaya country east of Lake Titicaca.

28–33. Pre-Inca stone carvings, all from Callejon de Huaylas on the Santa River off the main Chincha-suyu road: (*centre right*) a stylized human head carved in a wall of the little known Sechin culture on the Pacific coast beside the Conti-suyu road.

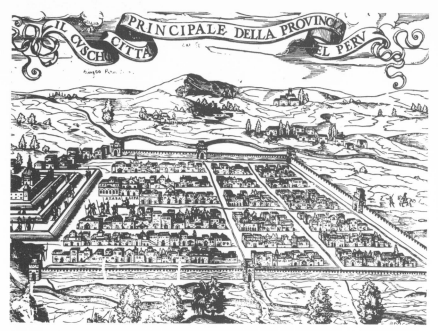

34–38. Cuzco: (*top left and centre*) two of de Bry's imaginary views of
Cuzco of 1596 based on reports from Spanish explorers – note camels in
foreground; (*bottom left*) a general view of modern Cuzco – the fortress of
Sacsahuamán on the left dominates the hilltop overlooking the city; (*top
right*) llamas descending the stepped northern road, known as "the road that tired the fox"; (*centre*)
a Renaissance doorway set into an Inca structure in central Cuzco; (*bottom right*) a narrow steproad
leading to Cusi-pata (Joy Square), the beginning of the Anti-suyu road.

39–43. Inca engineering at its most spectacular: (*top left*) the circular agricultural terracing at Moray, 15 miles northwest of Cuzco, originally thought to be amphitheatres but proven to have been dug deep into the earth to protect crops from frost (*Shippee-Johnson aerial photograph*); (*top right*) the fortress of Ollantaytambo controlling the entrance to the eastern jungles; (*centre*) Machu Picchu seen from the guard tower that leads southwest through Choquesuyoy to Cuzco; (*bottom left*) the course of the Anti-suyu road in the terraced Ollantaytambo valley; (*bottom right*) the Yucay valley north of Pisac.

44–45. Sacsahuamán, one of the greatest buildings ever erected by man, almost a mile long, composed of thousands of gigantic worked stones, employed 30,000 Indians for the 70 years of its construction: (*above*) Indians in replica Inca battle dress defending the fortress walls; (*below*) llamas grazing beside the immense stones of the fortress walls.

burned alive in Cuzco in 1534, for his failure to disclose, whether or not he knew it, the whereabouts of the missing treasures.

During this period, Martín de Ayalá married Juana Curi Ocllo, and from this union was born, in 1535, the chronicler Huamán Poma. He was one of the "new race", a mixing of Spaniard and high-caste Inca that was at first encouraged by the Spanish Crown as a symbol of the successful colonisation and of peaceful integration of conqueror and conquered. In following out this principle, Martín de Loyola, the nephew of the founder of the Jesuits, married Beatris Clara Coya del Inga. The ceremony is immortalised by an outsized mural in the Jesuit Church in Cuzco.

Further down the social ladder, such integration did not work. The low-placed Indian felt only too strongly the heinous pressure of Spanish occupation, and it was thus of this situation in particular that Huamán Poma wrote. His manuscript chronicle, written in 1615 and illustrated with naïvely constructed, yet historically instructive, drawings, consists of 1,179 pages of Quechua and Spanish. It was unknown either in Spain or Peru, and until 1908 lay unremarked, designated simply as Codex 2232, in the Royal Library at Copenhagen, where it was discovered by a German scholar. It was presumably brought to Denmark by a Danish Ambassador resident in Spain in 1650–3.

Its illustrated list of agricultural practices, its classification of human beings under the Inca system, its tabulation of their progress from womb to tomb, its description of Inca justice and illustrated list of ruling Incas, and, for the present purpose, its lists of Inca roads, of the locations and types of *tampu,* and of the names of the administrators of roads and bridges, are all of inestimable value. Moreover, the manuscript is unique of its kind. For, unlike Mexico, Peru did not have rebus or glyph writing. There were no artists who furnished illustrative ethnographic material such as has come down to us from pre-conquest Mexico. Only Huamán Poma's work supplies the deficiency—hence its great value.

In the valley of Jauja, wrote Pedro de Cieza, there were "many store-houses filled with everything to be found. And so many *colcas,* that, from a distance, they seemed to be like the towers of Spain." These *colcas* were ordered by La Gasca, in 1547, to be filled with the produce of the country, so that the immense number of soldiers coming into Jauja could be fed. Thus it came about that Cieza had ample time to note the types of food that were stored.

The most important were maize and potato (*acsu*), "which is like a truffle when cooked and is soft inside." The prehistoric Andean agriculturalists had, by selection, changed the wild tuber, the size of a walnut, into large potatoes of infinite variety. These, when stored in sacks made from woven llama wool and placed in the cold storage of the *colca,* could be kept for over a year. *Chuño* was dehydrated potato. This was made from a frost-resistant variety of potato that, when prepared in the normal way, was insipid and tasteless, but good when prepared as *chuño*. First left out to freeze, and then thawed in the day's fierce heat, the tubers were trodden upon until all the water had been squeezed from them. From this, a white potato flour was made; this was the basis of their bread. Then, as now, no *chupa*, or stew, was made without it, no journey taken without a supply of it. *Chuño*, "highly esteemed and valued", said Cieza, "could be stored for an indefinite period".

Maize (*sara*), cultivated at altitudes of up to 12,700 feet, was *the* Inca staple. When dried, it could be stored for years. It could be eaten parched, or could be boiled in slaked lime or ashes, which made it swell to twice its original size and gave it a bland taste. When the husks were removed, it became edible as *mote*, a form of hominy (maize porridge).

From maize was also produced the alcoholic drink called *accha*. "which is the *chicha* they drink, of which they always have great vessels". The women were the brewers, as was the case in all early Neolithic societies. Maize was allowed to germinate, for, when farinaceous grains germinate, an enzymatic diastase converts part of the starch into maltose. Mastication of a portion of the germinated corn helped in the process of preparing a diastase. This mash was then boiled, set aside to ferment for four days, strained, and served as *accha*, which had an alcoholic content of six to eight per cent. It was taken to excess on all occasions of ritual drunkenness. "It is amazing," Cieza observed, "how much of this beverage or *chicha* these Indians can drink, for the glass is never out of their hands." It was this beverage that Prescott referred to when he spoke of their "sparkling wine".

Quinoa, which is used in the Andes as oatmeal is used in the Scottish highlands, is a member of the goosefoot family (*Chenopodium*) and grows as tall as a man when cultivated at high altitudes. Its red pods yield a cereal resembling rice. "A very good food," confirmed Cieza, who went on to describe it as having "a reddish leaf like Moorish chard". Rich in minerals and proteins, it can, like maize, be stored for long periods.

Then there were beans: an infinite variety of them—red, black, yellow and white—all highly nutritious. Dried chilli peppers were also storable; these gave extra bite and flavour to food. From the sea coast came dried seaweed, rich in minerals, and appreciated for its taste and its iodine content, which kept down the incidence of goitre. The same source provided dried fish and shellfish. Proteins were supplied by dried llama and *cui* flesh. Llama meat cut thinly and sun-dried until it was as hard as leather was called *charqui*, a word that is sometimes rendered in English as "jerky". Whole *cuis* (guinea pigs, which were often raised in Indian houses) were smoked and dried and could then be stored for months on end.

Thus, when Cieza speaks of "storehouses filled with everything to be found" he is alluding to the basic storage foods described above. From these ingredients a cook could prepare a rich *chupa*, a stew of meat, corn and potatoes, thickened with *chuño* and given that extra bite with chilli peppers. All foods were, in essence, durable.

The *quipu-camayocs*, or knot-record readers (they would be secretary-accountants in our society), knew just how much was stored in each area at a given time, and, "wherever the Inca's armies went, they drew upon the contents of these storehouses without ever touching the supplies of the people of the lands through which they passed." If there was a lean year or, as sometimes happened, a year of drought, "the storehouses were opened for the people . . . and in a year of abundance, they paid back all they had received" from the *colcas*.

It can readily be seen that such a system dispensed with the necessity for a huge quartermaster section to look after the needs of troops on the move along the highways. All essential supplies were readily to hand.

*Colcas* in the highlands were constructed of dry-laid stone, the interstices plugged with *adobe* mud-cement. Roofs were made of slate or, where this was unavailable, of grass thatch (but this was avoided wherever possible, since it furnished nesting places for field-mice or rats). On the coast, storehouses were constructed of *adobe*, sun-dried brick, if stone were unavailable. Corn, beans and potatoes were stored in the greyish-brown sacks made from spun llama-wool, which was too coarse to be used for clothing. *Chuño* was stored in large pottery jars, as was salted fish, seaweed and chilli. Dried llama meat, *charqui*, was packed, or else hung from the rafters.


ON 8th January 1548, the royal forces under La Gasca began to move south towards Cuzco, following the long, narrow valley bordered to the west by the Mantaro river. They passed through Huancayo, even then a large market centre, then on to Marcavilcas.

The canyon created by the Mantaro river (anciently, "Angoyacomayu") determined the route of the highway for the next 100 miles, as it crossed the rugged land between Jauja and Vilcas-huamán, the geographical centre of the empire.

Unlike other rivers, which develop gradually as rills and brooks flow into them, the Mantaro leaps full-born, as a rushing brawling river, from the ice-fringed lake of Junín, on the borders of which lies the city of Pumpu (Bonbón), visited alike by Hernando Pizarro and Pedro de Cieza. By the time the Mantaro reaches Jauja, it has gorged out a chasm so terrifyingly deep and narrow that Pedro Sancho, the royal scrivener, said that there was a point at which one could throw a stone across it. Faced with this geographical fact, the Inca engineers constructed roads high up on either side of the canyon.

A few miles south of Jauja, and where the valley flattens out, was Marca-vilas, where "its chieftains built fine lodgings for the Inca with thick wooden beams which held a thatch-covered roof." Here the royal road divided. One branch, which was less used, proceeded directly southward over the high east bank of the river; the other crossed the Mantaro by a suspension bridge and proceeded in the same direction, traversing the high mountains on the western side, and overlooking the canyon in places.

The royal road crossed over a "net bridge" at Ancosyaco (which is mentioned by Huamán Poma as the "*puente de Ancoyaca*"), "where", said Pedro de Cieza, "there are white cliffs from which flows a spring of salt water." This geographical feature is still there. From this point the arterial step-road climbed to the *tampu* of Acos "settled in and among the craggy sierras". Just before Acos, a lateral turned west, and, climing the hills of Chongo Alto and passing through what is now the hacienda of Incahuasi (where there are natural hot baths), proceeded to Santa Rosa. Continuing west towards the desert coast, it descended by a series of impressive step-roads through Yuayos, Juniga, Cruz Blanca and Machurango, and then continued by way of the upper reaches of the Cañete valley, where the road was skilfully set into the canyon walls, to join up with the main coastal highway.

After Acos, the main route through the Andes went on to Picoy and led to the royal Inca lodgings, the road "being laid entirely with stone steps of small tread". The *tampu* of Paucara came next, and the way thither was "so well laid out and broad that it is almost like walking on level ground rather than in the mountains". Paucara was built on the crest of the sierra, and its "Indians lived among the hollows of the craggy hills". The Incas had built into the rock "a *pucará* [fortress], which looked like a turreted castle in its thickness." "I slept in it one night," said one itinerant Spaniard, ". . . it was 400 feet high, with so many natural hollows that more than a hundred men and horses can take shelter in it." This description was confirmed in the next century, in 1616. In the course of carrying out his clerical duty of visiting his flock of new Christians, the Carmelite friar Antonio Vásquez de Espinosa came riding through here on his mule, on his way over the Inca highway. His *Compendio y Descripcion de los Indianos Occidentales*, which was lost for a long time and published only recently (ed. C. U. Clark, The Smithsonian Institution, Washington), contains much detail regarding the road. He described the *pucará* as "looking like a battlement of towers, so that from a distance it looks like a city with fine buildings. There are very large caves and caverns that people can live in near the [royal] road, besides which there is a small watercourse."

On 27th October 1533, Francisco Pizarro, after a stay of two weeks in Jauja, took this same road on the final stage of the journey to Cuzco. Without these superbly engineered roads, it would have been impossible for mounted men to have reached it ("After God, it was the Inca's roads that gave us victory"). The Mantaro canyon is only sixty miles in length, but to negotiate the road was, for the mounted Spaniard, "like a little journey in hell".

The next *tampu* after Paucara lay some five leagues or fifteen miles away, at Parcos. To reach there it was necessary to climb still further. Pedro Sancho, the young secretary who wrote the record of the distribution of

Atahuallpa's ransom, and who also left an account of his part in all these affairs, described the terrifying ascent to Parcos: "We had to climb another stupendous mountain [the Jauja–Mantaro strip]. Looking up at it from below it seemed impossible for birds to scale it by flying through the air, let alone men on horseback. . . . But the road was made less exhausting by climbing in zigzags rather than a straight line. Most of the way consisted of large stone steps that greatly wearied the horses. . . ."

After the *tampu* at Parcos, "which is built on the crest and absolute edge of the sierra", the road began to descend, and Sancho and all the rest had to negotiate another steep road, this time going down, towards the Mantaro. Cieza remembered that, from above, the river looked much like a writhing serpent. The road accomplished its 2,000-foot descent to Marcas—close by, but out of reach of, the river—by means of a long series of stone-laid steps: and crossed a suspension bridge "hung from large stone towers". These towers are still visible today. The royal road then proceeded to the Tambo de Yangar, where the town of Azángaro, with its impressive ruins, now stands.

The original route of the highway then went near Viñaque (now Hauri), "where", Cieza found, "there are some large and very important old buildings which, judging by the state of ruin and decay, . . . must have been there for many ages." Cieza rightly judged that the ruins bore resemblance to those on the famous site of Tiahuancu in Bolivia.

Beyond Hauri, and at an altitude of just under 8,000 feet, the road entered a warm, cactus-dominated valley: this led to Quinoa. The present-day folk art of Quinoa is widely known, for it retains, albeit distantly, some of the old techniques of pottery making.

Continuing through Chupas, the road bore to the south-east, its level rising with the land to over 10,000 feet above sea level. Here it began to cross the lofty *puna* of Sachabamba, a vast pampa of golden-coloured grass, where even now the highway, twenty-four feet wide and bounded by low walls, can be clearly seen, on its way across the plains. From here, the highway then began a 2,000-foot descent to the small lake of Pomacocha, which lies in a hollow and is like an oasis in this sterile, arid region.

The lake, which a *conquistador* described as less than four crossbow shots (400 feet) across at its broadest, was, and still is, terraced with precisely laid retaining walls. At its narrowest end, it was dammed. The controlled overflow then emptied into the Vischongo river.

The ruins of Pomacocha give much evidence of the extreme technical precision of Inca construction methods, since all the stone ashlars are, as in all Inca architecture, uncemented and held in place only by their own weight. On firm ground by the lake there is a twenty-foot-high free-standing rock. Its sides have been rounded and ashlars chambered into the rock mass so carefully and skilfully that one can only with difficulty distinguish between what is man-made and what is the living rock. On the top and in the centre of this huge rounded and flattened rock surface is a stone gnomon a yard high, said, by "the Inca" Garcilaso de la Vega, to have been used by the priests to determine "which days were long and which were short and when the sun departed and when it returned." This site has had only a slight brush with history, having been mentioned during the civil wars as "a place of strong position".

After an hour's ride from here, Vilcas-huamán is reached.

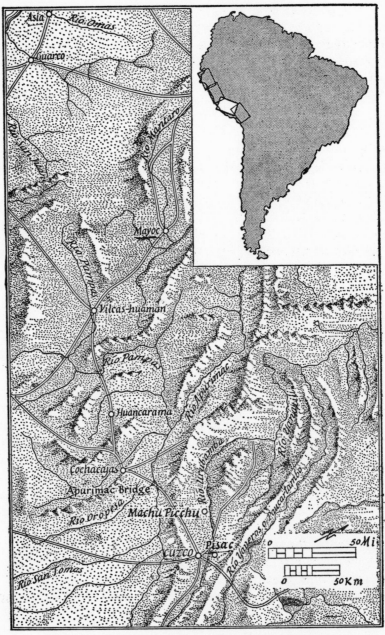

The Chincha-suyu road from Vilcas-huaman to Cuzco.

was to send a company of his men in December 1537 to hold Huaytara, and in particular the strong Inca *pucará*, which defended the pass. Later Francisco Pizarro pursued Almagro's troops along this route, and, on reaching the "snowy heights" at the *tampu* of Incahuasi, his soldiers "were attacked by giddiness, and suffered so much anguish that they vomited, staggered and threw down their arms". This was a route over which the armies of the Incas constantly passed, and was one of the routes they used in carrying out their own conquest of the coast.

At Huaytara began the descent, which followed a zigzagging step-road for over two leagues and was described by Pedro de Cieza as "rugged". Below Huaytara the road divided, one branch going down the Pisco valley, and the other over difficult terrain to Ica, also on the coast. Another coastal-bound route beginning at Vilcas-huamán crossed the suspension bridge over the Pampas river, traversed the forbidding heights inhabited by the Sora and Rucanas tribes, then followed a river valley to the junction with the road coming down from the sierra. The road then continued to the Nascas, a series of large valleys along the hot desert coast, and so linked up with the Inca's coastal highway.

The army of Pizarro, proceeding on its way to Cuzco with all of its famed *capitanes*—Hernando de Soto, Almagro, Juan Pizarro (the youngest brother of Francisco), and others—rode into Vilcas-huamán at dawn on 29th October 1533. The speed with which the army travelled had taken the Inca troops by surprise. "They left their tents, their women and some men in Vilcas . . . we captured these and took possession of everything. . . . The next day the Indians attacked us, killing a white horse that belonged to Alonso Tabuyo. We were forced to retreat to the square of Vilcas-huamán."

Neither the great square nor the town itself had changed noticeably fifteen years later, when, on 15th January 1547, a new army arrived, that of President La Gasca, now doing battle in the name of the King against many of those who had made that first entry into Vilcas. The approach to the town had been made with great caution, for La Gasca had been informed that Francisco de Carbajal was moving with massed men to prevent the loyalist forces from passing over the great suspension bridge ahead of them at the Pampas river. He was already threatening them at the next main stop, Andahuaylas, so that La Gasca—as he explained in his long report to Spain, dated 7th March 1548—ordered that his "*capitanes* take and hold the bridge at Vilcas".

The Capac Ñan, the royal road to Cuzco, left from the south-east part of the plaza. "From here,' Cieza said, "the highway proceeds to the next *tampu* at Uranmarca."

To reach "the bridge of Vilcas" the traveller has to descend 5,000 feet in less than three miles, zigzagging back and forth over a stone step-road. Even in 1533, when the road was in pristine condition, Pedro Sancho complained that, "although the journey [between Vilcas and Uranmarca] was short, . . . it was laborious, since one had to descend a mountain all the way, the road consisting almost entirely of stone steps." Beyond Vilcas-huamán stood Pillau-ccasi, a toll station, now in ruins. From that point the von Hagen expedition counted more than 3,000 steps, the road being six feet wide. Most of the steps are still in their original position.

After the highlands 5,000 feet above, the valley seems like an oven. It is verdured with enormous cacti holding spiny arms aloft, and an immense variety of spined xerophytic plants. It was called the *yungas* (a word applied to hot regions), since it was hot, and it was here, "on this same river of Vilcas", said Cieza, that Diego de Almagro, retreating from the heights of Huaytara, "was so ill that he spent four days in the heat, where he might be cured".

At the property of de Pariabamba, where two other rivers join the Pampas, the Pampas valley flattens out into a large canyon. Here, in the absence of a rock overhang, the Inca engineers constructed two massive stone towers on which to hang the suspension cables of the second largest bridge in the Inca realm. Pedro Sancho admits he was terrified to cross the bridge: "to someone unaccustomed to it, the crossing appears dangerous, because the suspension bridge sags with its long span . . . so that one is continually going down until the middle is reached and from there one climbs until the far bank. In addition, when the bridge is being crossed it trembles and sways very much, all of which goes to one's head when unaccustomed to it."

The reliable Pedro de Cieza states that, "When I crossed it there were two immense stone towers with deep foundations [parts of them can still be seen] on which to hang the suspension bridge. It was seventy-six paces long . . . and so strong that horses can gallop over it as though they were crossing the bridge of Alcántara [built by the Emperor Trajan across the upper river Tagus] or that of Córdova." Pedro Sancho de la Hoz, who crossed it with Francisco Pizarro's cavalry in 1533, thought it to be "361 Spanish feet long, and wide enough for two horses to pass abreast on it." However, in 1547 when La Gasca moved horses and artillery across it all day long, he found that "the bridge was not very strong, and, periodically during the night it had to be repaired with new rope-cables."

The bridge, with its thick rope-cables made of cabuya fibre, had to be renewed constantly—at least once every two years. It was still in use in the seventeenth century, since Huamán Poma, the historian of things Inca, recorded where the people who guarded the bridge lived.

On the other side of the Pampas river, there was another stone step-road. This climbed to almost the same height as the road had descended from previously. Halfway up was the village of Uranmarca, "where", said Cieza, "are the lodgings of Uranmarca, which is a settlement of *mitimaes*." This colony of loyal Quechua-speaking people had been purposefully transferred to, and given aid to settle in, an area where there had been no settlement before, their task being to provide lodgings for those using the road and to keep the Vilcas bridge in repair.

Andahuaylas, situated further along the road on a broad, fertile plateau at an altitude of 10,500 feet, was, as Huamán Poma recorded, "a city and royal *tampu*". "When I first came here in 1548," said Pedro de Cieza, after making the long, difficult ascent from the Pampas canyon, "its lord was a *curaca* called Huasco. The original people were Chancas. They went clothed in blankets. . . . In former times, the Chancas were most valorous. They fought and won lands and large domains, and were so strong that they besieged Cuzco itself. . . . Hanco Huallu, the Chanca chief who surrendered to the Incas was renowned in this Andahuaylas province as being unable to endure Inca rule, with the result that he fled with his followers into the most remote mountains and settled on the shore of a lake below the Moyabamba river." Moyabamba is in the *montaña* of the Upper Amazon, over 1,000 miles from Andahuaylas. It shows the determination of the Chancas to escape Inca rule, that they should have crossed such a vast tract of Inca-controlled territory and still brought out so much of the tribe intact; and it shows the extent of the Incas' fear of the Chancas, that, in order to reach and subdue them again, they were prepared to build one of the most spectacular roads in history, from Jauja to Chachapoyas along the upper reaches of the Marañon river, in order to find them.

The Chancas were only one of many Andean tribal units, yet, like the Incas, they were turbulent and indomitable. They claimed totemic descent from the puma, and on their great festive days the *curacas* dressed and danced in puma skins. Andahuaylas had long been a buffer state between the Chancas and the Incas, but in 1400 the Chancas moved further southward to take control of the strategic areas of Abancay and Curahuasi, each of which controlled two vital bridges. The Chancas delayed their attack on Cuzco until the eighth Inca, Viracocha, was an old man. In 1437, they crossed the Apurimac river, took control of all the surrounding area, and put Cuzco under siege. The old Inca fled, but his son Pachacutic rallied his troops, defeated the Chancas, and visited upon them the ritual reprisal, so that the Chancas passed into obscurity until the time that Hanco Huallu made his escape with 8,000 members of his tribe.

Tribal memories being long, the Chancas did not aid the Inca's forces when they were pursued by the Spaniards. Thus they were easily subdued, and Andahuaylas was given in *encomienda* to Diego Maldonado, nicknamed "the Rich". Hailing from Salamanca, he had taken part in the capture of Atahuallpa and had been rewarded with 362 marcos of silver and 7,760 pesos of gold. In 1548, he was with Gonzalo Pizarro, but waiting to escape into the forces of La Gasca.

Pedro de Cieza found Andahuaylas "well supplied with food. We spent many days there with President La Gasca, while he was preparing the army to put down the rebellion of Gonzalo Pizarro".

La Gasca said that he arrived there at the end of January and "was consulting those people who know how the land lies, and making a plan of campaign", for there were many places where a determined abmush could rout his whole army. "On 2nd February," continued his official report, "Sebastián Benalcázar arrived at Andahuaylas with twenty horseman, his presence giving great pleasure, as he is held in great esteem." Pedro de Cieza was among those horsemen.

The army now moved again over the royal road, shaping their way southward to Cuzco. The highway passed the *abra* of Cumu Huillca, then descended into the valley of Pincos, where a Spaniard, despite the civil war, had set up a *trapiche*, or sugar mill, to grind the sugar cane grown in the valley. A short climb out of Pincos, and the road, paved here because of the rain, was within five miles of the fortress of Curambá.

The site of Curambá, situated beside the Inca highway, on a plateau 12,500 feet above sea level, has been noticed since 1534. It is remembered with reason, for here the Spaniards found two twenty-foot-long silver ingots. The road enters the rectangular plaza from the north, after negotiating a pass. The plaza was built on four stone-laid *andenes*, on which there were three crescent-shaped lines of buildings; these might—according to Pedro Pizarro, the young page of his uncle, the conquistador—have housed "a village of sun virgins." In the centre of the plaza was a truncated pyramid, reached, like the one in Vilcas-huamán, by flights of stone steps.

Besides being a *tampu*, a temple city and a *pucará* midway between Andahuaylas and the next bridge, Curambá was important as a centre for the smelting of gold, copper and silver. The smelting ovens, of which many can still be seen, faced the north-east, from where strong winds, blowing from the heights of the wilderness of Vilcabamba came. The ovens, called *huayra*, were dotted about Huayra-pampa—the "plain of the wind ovens". Hand-operated bellows were not always able to produce sufficient heat to melt the ores, so the Incas relied on the consistent winds blowing from the Vilcabamba mountain range to produce the desired high temperatures. As there were many Inca-worked placer mines throughout the Vilcabamba area, a road had been built linking them with Curambá.

The eastward road led to Wiñaysunu and was connected with the remarkable fortress city of Choqquequirau, built above the Apurimac river, on its north-eastern side.

Curambá was therefore a place of great strategic importance, since it could effectively block passage along the royal road and prevent access to the bridge. It was also one of the sallyports of Manco Inca II, who after 1536 established his neo-Inca state in the inaccessible Vilcabamba, a hundred miles from Curambá as the crow flies.

After Curambá the road descended. It went through the pass of Bajada de Huancarama to the village of the same name, where the paved road can still be seen. Further down, the road came to a small freshwater lake (*cochas*) and to the village and *tampu* of Cochacajas. This place, like all such strategically placed sites, was there to protect, repair and guard a bridge—in this case, the bridge over the Pachachaca river. Cochacajas was also an important road junction.

Before reaching the bridge, the main highway met a lateral road, which led west, towards the Pacific coast. The Inca engineers planned this road so it would run along the north (or left) bank of the river and so dispense with the need to build another bridge over this truculent, Amazon-bound river. The lateral ran nearby, its route lying more or less parallel with that of the modern road through the area, and proceeded through Pichichua, Tintay and Toraya, across the high *puna*, occupied for the most part by huge flocks of wild vicuñas and viscachas (related to the chinchilla), to reach the freezing lake of Parco. This lies within the Pacific watershed. From this point the road ran downhill all the way to the desert valleys of the Nascas, where it connected with the coastal road.

An hour's walk away from Cochacajas, proceeding by way of the main royal road, were the river and bridge of Pachachaca (*chaca* being Quechua for "bridge"). The Pachachaca is a narrow, swift-flowing stream that rises in the Aimaraes Mountains in the western Andes. At the point where the road crossed it, it flowed through a sheer-sided canyon and was unfordable. Thus the Incas had bridged it using suspension cables mounted "on strong stone pillars".

During the conquest and the civil wars, the bridge was repeatedly burned. On 12 July 1537, two opposing forces faced each other across it, and bombarded each other in order to obtain possession of the bridge. Afterwards it became a place for the two sides to parley. "I myself was selected", wrote Alonso Enriquez de Guzmán, who described the incident in his autobiography.

Bordered by white lilies of a type known as *abancay* ("like ours in Spain but without their fragrance") the Inca road then climbed out of the valley, and, after passing the *tampu* of Abancay, came to the high, treeless *puna*, fiercely hot at noon and bitterly cold at night. Here, where it was unrestricted, the road broadened, gaining its official standard width of twenty-four feet. It kept to this width as it went through the *abra* of Abancay, the "opening" at the highest point of the *puna*.

Here, thanks to an unusual chain of circumstances, there is a well-preserved section of the road, with the remains of a small rest-house close by, and, at the top an *apacheta*.

The *apacheta* was a propitiatory cairn, a pyramid of small stones usually found at the highest part of the road. A translation of the word *apacheta* defines its function: *apa*—"burden"; *cheta*—"depositor". Each passer-by added a stone to the cairn, the stone being a symbol of the burden he was carrying. "The Indians," said that observant Jesuit José de Acosta, "carry a small stone picked up on the trail a little before arriving at the *apacheta*. They believe that by adding it to the *apacheta* they leave their tiredness behind and the gods will give them new strength."

Having reached the top of the pass, the road descended and entered a long valley. At this point are located the Stones of Conchaca or Sayhuite— several free-standing limestone boulders, one of which, oval-shaped and twenty feet long, fourteen broad and twelve high, is carved with the most fantastic shapes and forms. The sculptors, working mostly with stone celts, handled this immense rock as easily as an Oriental craftsman would a piece of ivory, carving lizards, pumas, viscachas, snakes, guinea pigs, and steps— an intricate maze of symbols, the precise significance of which it is impossible to determine.

Our earliest record of the stones dates from 1847, when the inquisitive French Consul, Léonce Angrand, visited them, leaving us a series of drawings of the large oval stone. These drawings have been preserved in the Bibliothèque Nationale in Paris. E. G. Squier made a photograph-drawing of another of the stones. He thought that this one, reached by a flight of steps cut into the rock, and with a reservoir for about a gallon of liquid which flowed into the conduits cut on all sides, was for libations of chica-beet, which priests (*amantua*) drank, believing that they were partaking of the god of the oracle that lived in the rock. On the other side, a door, and a hollow large enough to receive a man had been carved from the rock. But the exact purpose of the stones remains a mystery.

From here it takes about an hour to reach the next *tampu*, at Curahuasi, which is listed by Huamán Poma as "royal *tampu*, village, bridge of the Apurimac". The function served by the people of Curahuasi is thus not in doubt: they were to repair and maintain the road leading to the bridge, and to replace every two years the immense rope-cable from which the bridge was suspended. There are still extensive remains of the settlement of Curahuasi, including some buildings three storeys high—for Inca constructions, an unusual architectural feature. It is still possible to see where the royal road entered and left the plaza.

It takes three hours to walk the distance—"about three leagues", or nine miles—from the village of Curahuasi to the tunnels leading to the bridge over the Apurimac, the great bridge of Peru.

## CHAPTER SEVEN

# Apurimac: The Holy Bridge

The river Apurimac emerges from the edge of the western Andes as a mere rill, fed by the run-off from the glaciers of the lofty Cerro Huachahui (17,887 feet high). Flowing in a north-easterly direction, it receives a number of tributary rivers and streams, and gouges out an impressive canyon on its way to join the Amazon. By the time it reaches the site of the bridge, it has descended from a height of 10,000 feet to one of 5,000 feet. Heard from above the high canyon walls, its cascading waters have a dull echoing roar, and it is this that gives it its name of Apurimac—the "Great Speaker".

It had been the Rubicon of the Incas, since for a century it had held them in check, and prevented them from extending their empire northwards. It remained a considerable obstacle until 1350, when the engineers serving the sixth Inca, Roca, made the first attempt to bridge it.

That bridge, the Huaca-chaca, or "Holy Bridge", was *huaca* ("holy") to the Incas because it was thought to possess soul. On its Cuzco side, a very important oracle was erected; this spoke through the deafening roar of the river to those who implored it. Pedro Pizarro, writing in his old age, said that it was known as "the Lord that Speaks or the Apurimac, the 'Great Speaker'. It was in a richly painted hut, which contained an idol, a thick log spattered with blood."

The first Spaniards thought of the bridge *as* Peru. Hiram Bingham, the discoverer of Machu Picchu, said that the illustration of it in E. G. Squier's book "was one of the reasons that I wanted to go to Peru". Thornton Wilder used it as a literary device in *The Bridge of San Luis Rey*, in which the cables of the "great bridge between Lima and Cuzco" break before the eyes of Fra Juniper.

The first Spaniards to cross it were chilled with terror. Journals and reports are filled with their plaints about the way the bridge swung in the wind; about how deep the canyon was, and how terrifying the roaring of the river was as it reverberated against the vertical rock walls; about how their pulses raced, their eyes grew dim and their hearts faint as they clung to the slender rope-cables. Wrote one conquistador, "It is no small terror that is caused by what men must pass through in these Indies."

When Pedro de Cieza came to the river Apurimac in March 1548, he thought it "the largest to be crossed between here and Cajamarca. The road to the bridge is well laid out along the slopes and mountains. Those who built it must have had a terrible time breaking the rock mass and making the road level, especially when the road descends. . . ." He also said that, "the road is so rugged and dangerous, that some horses laden with gold and silver have fallen in and been lost. . . ."

From the *tampu* and village of Curahuasi, the road made its descent by the now familiar zigzag stairway road. After two hours' walking distance, the road comes to the vertical walls of the canyon. There being no rock ledge on which the road could be rested, the Inca engineers tunnelled into the sheer rock walls. The approach tunnel leading to the bridge platform is cut through 1,000 feet of friable rock; it is twelve feet high and less than six feet wide. Air vents appear about every thirty feet.

The Incas' methods for handling rock differed little from the Romans'. Holes were drilled in natural fissures, and wooden pegs inserted and wetted; in expanding they split the rock, which was pried out with the help of huge bronze crowbars. Another method was to build fierce fires against the rock surface (the blackened interior of the tunnels gives evidence of this); when the rock was white-hot, cold water was thrown upon it, causing the rock mass to crack.

Where the tunnel ended, a spiral, stone-laid stairway was cut into the rock and wound its way downward to a huge platform cut away from the canyon wall. Two stone towers were built on the platform, and the huge rope-cables were hung over these towers and then buried deep in the platform. The two cables from which the bridge was suspended, and the three cables that held the floor of the bridge were, as Garcilaso de la Vega, who had often seen it, explained, wrapped around five joists, each as thick as an ox, and buried in the platform under a great mass of rock.

The rope-cables were hand-spun from the fibres of the cabuya, an amaryllid belonging to the *Agave* genus of tropical America, and one of the most characteristic floral elements of the Peruvian and Mexican landscape. It had fleshy, sharply pointed, spine-edged, beautifully curved, blue-grey pads, which are both long and broad. These succulent pads, which grow as long as six feet, are veined with strong fibres—the sisal of commerce—which, when dried, washed and combed can be used to make sandals, saddle-bags, halters, and, in this case, rope-cables.

"Let me tell you the way they were spun," said "the Inca" Garcilaso de la Vega. "Three strands of three fibres apiece are braided together, producing a cable of nine fibres; then three of these are braided together, producing a cable of twenty-seven fibres; and so, by repeating the operation several times, they finally obtain a rope-cable as thick as a man's thigh." The braiding of the rope-cables was done *in situ* (just as Johann Augustus Roebling, the German-born engineer, had the steel cables for Brooklyn Bridge spun on the spot), for they would otherwise have been too unwieldy, and impossible to transport. Cables were stretched across to the opposite side of the canyon in the following manner: first an Indian crossed the river on a raft, holding a small rope that was in turn attached to a larger one, and so on, with one of the main cables at the end of the chain; then with the help of legions of workers, the cable was pulled and lifted to the stone tower. The two principal suspension cables were buried on either side of the canyon, by wrapping them around five wooden beams placed like steps, which, once buried, held the cables taut, to prevent them from slackening too much.

Although we know that the cables were enormous—"as thick as a man's thigh"—no one has left an estimate of the size, length and weight of the cables. However, an idea can be gained by deduction. The length of the bridge from end to end was accurately recorded (by E. G. Squier) as 148 feet, the cables naturally being much longer due to the fact that they of necessity sagged a good deal, while, for each cable, a length of fifty feet was buried at either end of the bridge. After being wrapped around enormous beams, they were buried deeply and covered with huge stones, thus converting the inward and downward thrust in the towers and upward angular tension in the stays. The observation that the cables were "as thick as a man's thigh" suggests that they had a circumference of twenty-five inches; the weight of each cable would thus have been about 5,000 pounds, able to withstand up to fifty tons of pressure. The bridge floor was made up of woven wickerwork or boards, inserted through the cables. The suspension and bridge cables were joined by a skein of ropes that acted as a guard rail. As the bridge swayed in the wind, it was held in check by guy ropes lashed to the vertical walls.

On the Cuzco side of the river the road had been cut out of the rock and walled, these walls having since been destroyed. It ascended by a series of abrupt zigzags to the high point now called "La Banca", and varied in width from four to seven feet. "There was no additional room," someone remarked, "even for an echo."

When Ephraim George Squier, the American diplomat-archaeologist, crossed the bridge in 1869 (it is to him that we owe the only authentic illustration of it), he noted that it was still being maintained, its Indian custodians living nearby in "hovels, like goats". From this point, on the south or Cuzco side, "the bridge could be seen swinging high in a graceful curve between the two precipices on either side, looking wonderfully fragile and gossamer-like".

Under the Inca empire, all bridges, their construction and maintenance and the collection of tolls, were managed by Inca officials of the Acos lineage, the title of the governor of bridges being in Quechua, *Chaca-suioioc-acos-Inga-guamnochaca*, as Huamán Poma tells us. When one considers that the highways spanned the length of the South American continent, from Colombia to Chile, and that no less than 892 streams and canyons, large and small, had to be crossed, in a land where rivers change their course with infuriating ease, it becomes clear that the Incas' technical achievement in building and maintaining close on 1,000 bridges over a distance of 4,000 miles was indeed formidable.

Until the advances of nineteenth-century technology, when iron chains began to be used for suspension cables, these Inca-constructed suspension bridges were the largest known. The Incas had no knowledge of the arch; nor for that matter did any other preliterate people of the Americas. The arch, a matter of weight, gravity and pressure, is relatively passive and earthbound, but the suspended cable reverses the arch curve and, in the process, achieves strength without apparent mass or weight.

The men who conceived and carried out these and other immense structural undertakings are properly called "engineers". As Neolithic man gained mastery over nature and its materials, so he learned the art of pottery, weaving, agriculture, metallurgy and the domestication of animals, and thus became more civilised. "No one today," writes Claude Lévi-Strauss in *The Savage Mind*, "would any longer think of attributing these enormous advances to fortuitous accumulation of chance discoveries. . . . Each of these techniques assumes centuries of active and methodical observation of bold hypotheses tested by means of endlessly repeated experiments. . . ."

The Incas were heirs to a long technological history. Although it was their policy to denigrate the contributions of other tribes to their material culture, making it appear that before their advent all was void and barren (in reality, Inca civilisation was only an intensified form of the typical Andean culture), yet it is true that under the Inca system man did achieve the systematic benefits of the exploitation of nature. The symbol of that technological achievement was the great bridge across the Apurimac.

When the armies of President La Gasca reached the Apurimac canyon in the first week of March 1548, all the *three* bridges across the gorge, the Huaca-chaca, Cotabamba and Accha, had been destroyed on the orders of Gonzalo Pizarro. La Gasca said in his report that he was careful not to allow Gonzalo to find out where he and his troops would cross or where he would "most likely put a bridge across the Apurimac". Indians, appearing in the distance like so many leaf-cutting ants, arrived daily, carrying cabuya pads, and La Gasca determined that the "natural conditions of the Cotabamba" site made it the best place to replace the suspension cables. The Cotabamba bridge was used to cross the Apurimac gorge on the Conti-suyu road to the coast. "I gave," wrote La Gasca in his report to Spain, "instructions for

Lopé Martín to hurry up the flow of materials for the bridge [the cabuya with which to spin the cables]." Within two weeks, which gives some idea of the speed with which cables could be braided, the two great cables were in place, but troops of Gonzalo Pizarro suddenly appeared and "burned two of the cables of our bridge". However on 7th April, by which time the bridge heads had been secured and suspension cables and the bridge laid, the army of La Gasca passed over it. From here they regained the royal road without opposition, and, at Xaquijahuana, prepared for battle.

It was less a battle than an *affaire*, as La Gasca describes it, without any great hurt to either side. Gonzalo Pizarro's army just melted away, men leaving singly, then in groups, until the surrender was general. It would have been very different had Francisco de Carbajal directed it. Having yielded command to Gonzalo, he sat on a hillside astride his reddish mule laughing at the *contretemps* and singing an old Spanish ditty about the wind and the loss of an old man's hair: "O mother my hairs, my hairs,/one by one they fly away in the air./O poor mother,/my hairs." But before he could take flight he was captured.

"I decided to deal with Gonzalo Pizarro and Carbajal at once," said La Gasca, "for so long as they lived there could be no assurance." They were duly beheaded, and Gonzalo's head was put in a frame of iron mesh and hung on the royal pillory in Lima.

Pedro de Cieza recorded it all for his "histories", but unfortunately he lost in the *melée* some of his notebooks and parts of a manuscript, "which I much regretted". A search for the lost papers brought him to the attention of La Gasca, who, upon learning that there was a historian present, asked to see, and was shown, parts of the "histories". Pleased with what he had read, La Gasca created Pedro de Cieza El Primer Cronista de las Indias; and so, armed with letters signed with the rubric of the triumphant La Gasca, Cieza figuratively changed his soldier's jerkin for the long cloak of a historian and once more continued his travels along the royal road towards Cuzco. "From the Apurimac," Cieza stated, "one continues until arriving at the lodgings of Limatambo." This massively conceived building, the polygonal stonework of which is still in evidence, is twenty feet high and 800 feet long and set on terraces cut out of the rock. It was the residence of the governor, and was in all probability the administrative centre of Chincha-suyu.

After this, the road crosses the Sierra de Vilcaconga, then descends "to the valley of Xaquijahuana, which is low-level, lying between the mountains. There were in this valley sumptuous, rich palaces. . . ."

It was here that the Chancas tribe were finally defeated in their preventive war against Cuzco. When two old conquistadors, Peralonso Carrasco (one of whose holdings was the *tampu* of Abancay) and Juan Pancorvo (one of the founders of Spanish Cuzco), entered that land with Francisco Pizarro, the tombs that the Incas had built for the dead Chancas were still to be seen.

They had been set up as a warning. The dead had been skinned, their skins being stuffed with ashes and straw to resemble human beings; these figures had been positioned in a hundred different ways. Cieza was told that some had their skin stretched at the stomach like a drum, while others seemed to be playing a flute. They remained in place until the Spanish conquest.

The Spaniards, familiar as they were with rapine and death in all its forms, were aghast when in 1533, on their way along the last stretch of road before Cuzco, they came across the bodies of the defeated Huascar's family, spitted on posts spaced along the royal road. Men, women, children and even foetuses were hung there, and in this position would have greeted Atahuallpa on his triumphal march to Cuzco.

Xaquijahuana was the last stop before the swamps of Anta. This place was well known as being the *ayllu* of the Anta lineage of Incas. Those from Anta held the hereditary right to provide the whole empire with overseers for the maintenance of its roads.

Anta lies fifteen miles south of Cuzco in a low-lying plain; water from the surrounding hills collects there, causing the quagmire. In order that the road should be above the flood plain as it crossed the area, the Inca engineers raised a causeway about six miles long, with walls on either side. Further protection was provided by thirty-six well-engineered culverts, which regulated excessive flooding. When Cieza travelled this way he observed, "It would have been very difficult to cross this bog without the broad and solid causeway that the Incas ordered to be built."

The causeway ends at Izcucacha, where the road crosses a stone-laid bridge. After mounting a hill, it arrives at Carmenca.

From here, the traveller on the royal road looks down upon Cuzco.

E. George Squier's drawing (1864) of the famous suspension bridge across the Apurimac ("the talking river"), The Bridge of San Luis Rey. It was 148 feet long and one reached its left or northern end through tunnels 250 feet long.

# PART II

# CUZCO

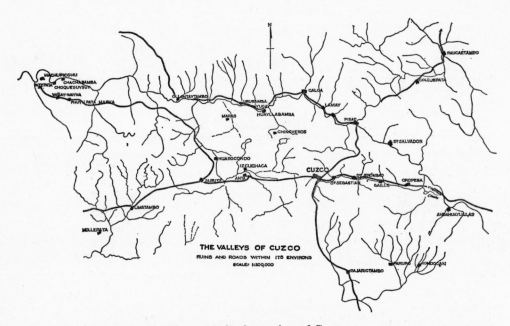

The roads in the region of Cuzco.

## CHAPTER EIGHT

## Cuzco, Capital of the Four Quarters

Carmenca, now the parish of Santa Ana, was the final checkpoint. It was a toll station, a *tampu*, and at a distance of 1,250 miles from Quito, the terminus of the Capac Ñan, the royal road. From Carmenca the traveller had his first unrestricted view of Cuzco. If he were just beginning his journey along the road, however, he would stop in Carmenca at the Huaca-puncu or Holy Gateway, and there make a *mocha* (a bow) to assure himself of a safe journey, with a prayer that the highway would not collapse.

When Pedro de Cieza arrived there in April 1548, the Cañaris, whom he recognised from their headgear—"a knotted crown as fine as sieve wire"—were the guardians of Carmenca. They were a colony of *incap-michuscan-runa*, of people transferred from their homeland 800 miles to the north, and formed an élite guard, with responsibility for the northern entrance to Cuzco.

Pedro Sancho de la Hoz, the young scrivener in the service of Francisco Pizarro, was the first Spaniard to describe Cuzco, his account dating from 1533. At that time the temples had not yet lost all the gold plate that decorated their walls, and the city still functioned as it had done under the Inca empire. Pedro Sancho thought it so big "that one could not see it all in a week. It is grand and stately and must have been built by a people of great intelligence. It has fine streets except that they are narrow . . . and the majority of the buildings are in stone, although there are many houses built with adobe. Cuzco is the richest city of which we have knowledge in all the Indies, for often great stores of treasure were brought there to increase the grandeur of the Incas. . . ."

Cuzco was founded sometime in the eleventh century A.D. by the first Inca, Manco Capac. It lies in a hollow—people called it a "navel" of a valley—at 11,000 feet above sea level. On three sides the mountains rise precipitously, while to the south-west stretches the valley, which forms a broad corridor between the mountains, and consists of fertile plains alternating with bogs. It was in Cuzco that Manco Capac ended his search for a home for

his people. According to legend, he thrust into the earth at Cuzco a golden
staff given to him by his father, the Sun God, and when the staff disappeared
he became aware that the soil was unimpeded by rock and that the land was
fertile. Whoever was then occupying the area was displaced. Archaeology is
here in agreement with Inca myth: the Incas' culture and history developed
in this valley, in the immediate neighbourhood of Cuzco.

The residences of the Incas in Cuzco were grouped about the principal
plaza, Huaycapata ("Leisure Square"), where festivals were held; just outside it were the main public buildings of the empire—the Temple of the Sun,
the House of the Sun Virgins, and Curicancha (the "Golden Enclosure").
From this square issued the narrow streets of the city, which was divided
into twelve administrative units. The King of Spain's inspector thought that
there were 100,000 houses—obviously a gross exaggeration, though there
may have been that number of people living there. However, he affirmed,
"In the eight days that I was there I was not able to see everything." No
plan of Cuzco as it was at the time of the conquest is known to be in existence. The earliest known plan—which anyway shows only the centre of the
city—was drawn by Huamán Poma, seventy-five years after the conquest, by
which time the city had been rebuilt on Spanish lines.

When Francisco Pizarro arrived there on 15th November 1533, with his
full war party of 175 Spaniards and 1,000 or more Cañari auxiliaries, the city
seemed to be ablaze with gold, for the façades of some of the more important
buildings were still covered with hammered gold plates. "I saw," reported
one of the Spaniards, "a quadrangular building measuring 300 paces by
fifty, plated entirely with gold. Of these plates we took down 700, which
together weighed 500 pesos [a peso is approximately 0.147 ounces]."

Manco Capac II came with the Spaniards, but, even while he was being
crowned (the Inca "crown" being the tasselled, wool-fringed *llautu*),
Francisco Pizarro was dismembering Cuzco and parcelling out palaces and
houses to his conquistadors.

Pedro de Cieza entered Cuzco on 11th April 1548, thus ending the first
stage of his journey over the royal road. However, the Cuzco he looked upon
was not the city of 1533, for in 1536 the seemingly docile young Inca,
Manco Capac, had escaped his captors, revolted, raised a great host of
followers, and held Cuzco under siege for eighteen months. In the process of
siege and counter-siege, the straw-thatch of the majority of buildings had
been burned and a great number of adobe structures had been torn down by
the Spaniards to give themselves more room for manoeuvre. The city had
thus been greatly transformed. One of the Spaniards who settled in Cuzco
averred, "I believe that it can be said of us Spaniards that we did more
damage in four years alone than the Inca ruler achieved in four hundred."
Thus, the city that Pedro de Cieza saw was a rebuilt Cuzco founded by
Francisco Pizarro.

All the same, enough of the sub-structures of the original buildings re-mained to show that Cuzco had been and still was the microcosm of empire. For within it lived people drawn from all parts of the Inca realm. "Each tribe is distinguished by differences in headdress . . . so clear and distinct that when 1,500,000 men were assembled, one tribe could easily be distin-guished from the others." Different groups inhabited different areas of the city, but all lived in one-storied steep-gabled houses made of adobe baked-mud bricks, painted red, yellow or black, and thatched with thick straw.

Pedro de Cieza learned that there had once been royal storehouses throughout the city. These had been filled with the goods paid as tax by people all over the empire: from the desert coast came cotton, shells, dried seaweed, salted and smoked fish; from the direction of the Anti-suyu jungles came bird feathers, coca leaves, chonta wood, skins, tropical foodstuffs, and gold from placer mines. Cuzco also being an arsenal, the raw materials for making slings, cotton armour, swords, battleaxes (these were star-shaped) and javelins were stockpiled there.

Sections of the city were reserved for the royal artisans, professional gold-smiths who were relieved of paying tax, and gave themselves wholly to turning out castings in gold and silver. "There were", said Cieza, "a great many gilders and workers in silver and gold, who understood how to work things ordered by the Inca."

All this specialisation presupposed organisation; indeed, for the prag-matic Inca, truth was orderliness. Of course, order is not necessarily always good, and can be worse than lack of order when it is a forced and inappro-priate arrangement without regard for circumstances or the natural course of things. However, it was a necessity for the Incas, who were plenary rulers, their absolutism held in check only by custom and the fear of revolt. "The myth of the great Inca socialist State", to quote the late Alfred Métraux, "springs from a cursory acquaintance with its institutions." Laws of property and the Indians' duties to the empire have been interpreted in terms of European ideals. Garcilaso de la Vega ("the Inca"), born in Cuzco in 1535, explained the Inca system with an idyllic and admirable simplicity: "They divided the land into three parts, the first for the sun [religion], the second for the Inca, and the third part for the people." All three divisions were cultivated by the people, the produce being divided into three parts; personal possessions were limited to house, animals and household goods, everything else belonging to the State—that is, the Inca. "If such were the economic framework of the State," wrote Dr. Métraux, "one could truly speak of State socialism grafted onto agrarian collectivism. But was it really like this?"

The Inca caste, including both those who were Incas by blood and those who were Incas by privilege (great war captains, for instance), were the rulers, governors, war leaders and priests. Apart from them, no individual owned land in his own right, since all land belonged to the communally-held *ayllus*, each of which was responsible for, among other things, constructing and maintaining the irrigation systems within its area and managing the community's flocks of llamas and alpacas. Each *ayllu* was ruled by a selected leader and guided by a council of old men. A group of several *ayllus* came under the jurisdiction of a district leader, a ruler of 10,000 tax-paying workers. These districts or provinces were in turn divisions of the four quarters (*suyus*) of the Inca empire. Each quarter was ruled by an *apu*, who was answerable to the Sapa Inca himself. The imperial capital was Cuzco.

The Incas, unlike the Mayas or Aztecs, did not have slaves, so onerous work, such as that involved in road building, mining and irrigation, could not simply be foisted on to slaves. There was no money. Tribute was paid in produce and the *mita* as services rendered. It is assumed that only professional architects, artisans, and a small body of professional soldiers escaped the *mita*.

In order to unify this vast area of coast, cordillera and *montaña*, the Inca developed communications. In many instances, previously developed local roads were incorporated into the road system, which was rendered more effective by the systematic construction of *tampus* and extension of the *chasqui* service. However, only with a highly disciplined people living in a land where there was a high degree of political cohesion was such a road system possible.

Pedro de Cieza, after having observed all these factors, thoughtfully put down his conclusions in a chapter entitled, "Of how the Lord Incas constructed the highways to travel throughout the empire".

"One of the many things that captured my attention . . . was how the immensely splendid highways we see throughout the empire could have been built, and, moreover, how may workmen it must have taken to build them, and, finally, what types of tools and instruments it took to level mountains and tunnel the rock to make the roads so broad and excellent as we see them. For if our Emperor Charles desired to build another highway from Quito to Cuzco and another which goes from Cuzco to Chile, *truly* I do not believe that with all the power and people at his disposal he could do so *unless* he were to employ the methods and techniques of the Incas.

"For this was a long road, over 1,100 leagues [3,300 miles], which went over rugged mountains and along precipices so sheer in many places that one could not see the bottom of the chasm, some of the sides of which were so sharp that the road-builders had to cut through the living rock to keep the level and maintain its proper width. In other places the road's incline was so steep that they had to build steps to ascend to the top, with platforms every so often so that the travellers could rest. In other places the road had to be forced through snow drifts and glaciers, which was the most dangerous. Yet through these drifts or through forests they built the roads level and, when necessary, well-paved with stone.

"Let those who read this and have been in Peru recall the road that goes from Pachacamac on the coast to Jauja, over the craggy mountains of Huarochiri and across the snow-bound peaks of Pariacá. . . . Let them also recall the tunnels and the twisting step-road that runs down to the bridge at the Apurimac or how the road crosses the sierras of Paltas, Cajas and Ayabacas and other regions of this realm where the road is some fifteen feet wide . . . and in the time of the Incas clean of grass or any refuse (for they were always caring for it).

"How were these roads built without inflicting undue hardship upon [the Inca's] subjects? Now, when an Inca decided to build one of these famous highways, no great provisions or levies were needed. An inspector went out ahead through the lands, laying out the route and assigning Indians [by *corvée*] each to their own section, for the building of the road. . . . In this way, with each province responsible within its own boundaries for the building of the road, which it undertook at its own expense and with its own Indians, the road was built and laid out in a relatively short time. When the road came to a barren or unpopulated place, the Indians that lived nearest came with the necessary tools and victuals, and so all was done with sustained effort and, in a sense, joyfully, for they were not oppressed in any way."

This method of road building was confirmed by Huamán Poma fifty years later. He also wrote that in Inca times "there were six royal roads, which were administered by an Inca governor of the Anta lineage. . . ." He has also left us an illustration of such an inspector. "The roads were measured and delimited and each built eleven feet wide, and on both sides stood a stone wall. [The standard road, based on many measurements, was twenty-four feet.] The road went straight and wide. And on its sides they built way-stations [*tampus*] where one could rest, also places for the *chasqui* messengers. The roads were clean and, when going through swamps, paved."

Huayna Capac, who in 1485 ordered the royal highway from Quito to Cuzco to be built, had it joined to the road from Cuzco to Chile that Topa Inca had had constructed. "It is", rhapsodised Pedro de Cieza, "the finest road in the world and the longest [3,250 miles]. . . . In the memories of any other peoples I doubt that there is a record of another highway comparable to this."

E. George Squier's drawing of the magnificent gateway that led into the valley of Ollantaytambo.

# PART III

# ANTI-SUYU:
# THE SECOND QUARTER

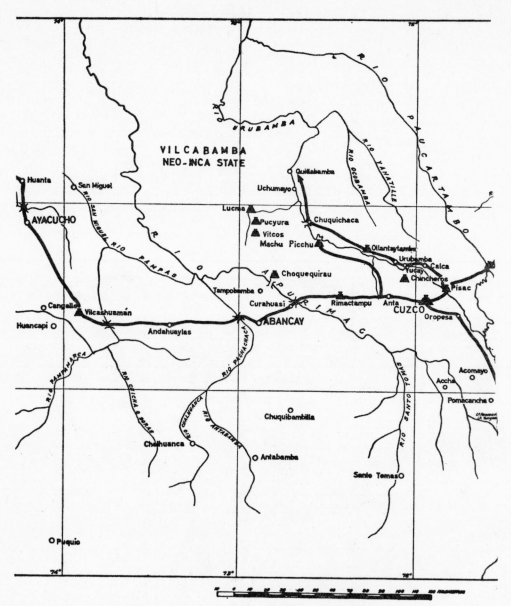

The Anti-suyu roads and the megalithic cities.

## CHAPTER NINE

## Megalithic Cities of the Anti-suyu

Anti-suyu, or Antis, from which the word "Andes" is derived, was the second quarter of the Inca world. Its vague boundary lay in the forests of the eastern slopes of the Andes, an area that stretched far to the north-west and south-east and embraced the Amazon and its tributaries in Peru and Ecuador. Anti-suyu thus included Pisac, Ollantaytambo, Machu Picchu and was connected with satellite cities, as well as the vast Vilcabamba complex, the last area to be conquered by the Spaniards.

Although Cuzco is located in the heartland of the towering Andes, it is nonetheless only a day's walk away from the lower Vilcanota river which runs to the east of the city, and two day's walk from the heavily forested area—the *ceja de la montaña*, the "eyebrows" of the forest. For the inhabitants of these hot lands, the Incas had one word, *yungas*. It is significant that the walls of the greatest fortress, or *pucará*, ever built by the Incas faced the eastern quarter—Anti-suyu.

The road to Anti-suyu began at Aucapata, "Joy Square". From here it went south-easterly direction through Hatun Rumiyoc, the high stone walls of which are composed of closely fitted ashlars, to Tococachi, where it crossed the Tullumayo river by means of a stone (*ullus*) bridge. At this point began its ascent of the hills.

Once the Incas had completed their conquest of the Andean tribes, they found that they were still vulnerable from the east, Cuzco being only two or three days' march away from the eastern jungles. As the Incas conquered the tribes living on the periphery of their realms, so they upset tribal space patterns and forced the defeated to fall back on other territory, thereby causing secondary wars. The shock waves resulting from this invasion by a mountain people who used llamas for transport, cast bronze axe-heads and had metal weapons were felt hundreds of miles away, the alarm being passed from tribe to tribe until it even reached the Guarani, an aggressive Paraguayan tribe who lived a thousand miles east of Peru. By means of indirect trade, they obtained copper axes and silver ornaments from the Incas. This led them to attack Inca outposts in the Bolivian *chaco*. Such raids were repeated all through the hot, forested section of Anti-suyu.

Direct trade relations were established between the Incas and forest tribes, the latter bartering forest products in return for copper axes, bronze axe-heads, and silver and gold ornaments from the Incas. When these articles were not obtained by trade, Inca outposts were attacked, particularly in the region of the Amazon. Indeed, the first white man to set foot in the Inca empire did so by joining one such attack, on an outpost near the Bolivian *chaco*.

When the Spanish navigator Juan Díaz de Solis was named Pilot Major following the death of Amerigo Vespucci, he sought to find a route to the newly discovered Pacific by way of the great river that at first bore his name and is now known as the Río de la Plata. In 1515, upon hearing from the Carío Indians that they raided a people who lived where the sun set, and that these people lived on a mountain of silver, in houses built of stone, domesticated "long-haired deer" (that is, llamas), and possessed an unlimited quantity of gold and silver, some pieces of which were displayed to him, he "decided that it must be seen". As a result of this, García Alejo, a Portuguese, joined the Guarani and raided several Inca jungle outposts. The dark-bearded white man was recognised as a "new being", and in 1515 (twelve years before Pizarro) became the first of his species to set foot within the Inca empire.

As a rule, the inhabitants of the upper Amazon lived on a relatively high cultural plane, and they made many significant contributions to the development of agriculture. As early as 2000 B.C., they were cultivating manioc, from which tapioca is derived; and, in addition, they grew sweet potato, arrowroot (widely used for starch), ingas, cashew nuts, avocado, zapote, papaya and pineapple. Cultivation of all these foodstuffs spread to the warmer valleys of Peru and Ecuador. These people, who belonged to varying cultures and were widely dispersed geographically, terraced the eastern slopes of the Andes, since this was a region of high rainfall, providing soils of high agricultural potential. Cities, constructed of dry-laid stone and built just above the *ceja* were scattered over a wide area. The one called Kotosh is still in good condition, and is perhaps a thousand years older than the first Inca cities: it dates from 1000 B.C.

The peoples living in the region of the upper Amazon were cultivators of narcotics and hallucinogenic drugs. One such drug, used for divination, was produced from the Banesteria vine, known to the Incas as *aya-huasca*, the "vine of the soul". There were numerous types of hypnotic snuff. Datura is a *yunga* product, and most important in Inca and in modern history; the cocabush, which grows on the moist eastern slopes of the Andes, is the source of cocaine. Thus, when the Incas began their systematic invasion of the

I. D'Orbigny's drawing (1830) of Chuquisaca Indians in beautifully colourful
handwoven native costumes.

II–V. The terrain of the Great Royal Road through the mountains, the highest mountain road in the world: (*top left*) the Royal Road skirting Lake Titicaca; (*left*) the man-made terraces of Pisac joined to an Inca Road; (*top centre*) the Royal Road in the *altiplano* of Bolivia *enroute* to Chile and "the Ends of the Earth"; (*right*) Machu Picchu joined by the Cuzco road.

VI. The Royal Road in the *altiplano* near Vilcas-huamán north of Tihuanti-suyu, Cuzco, the heart of the Empire. On it is a modern descendent of the Incas wearing the traditional poncho.

VII. Detail of a large eighteenth-century Indian colonial altar hanging of the Passion painted on woven cotton cloth in the Ancient Inca manner – Indian influence is apparent in the stylized figure and the mannered hands.

VIII-IX. Two examples of Indian textiles: (*above*) A modern Quechua woman wearing the typically brightly coloured hand-woden alpaca wool cloth. (*right*) a pre-Inca tapestry from Chancay, eleventh century.

X. The author with the polychromatic wall decoration on a Mochica building near Casa Grande on the Pacific coast (Conti-suyu) road.

region, they were hardly entering a land that was agriculturally backward.

"In 1400," Pedro de Cieza was told, the eighth Inca, "after he had taken the name Viracocha, one of their principal gods, and married . . . decided to set out and conquer the various peoples who lived a short distance to the east of Cuzco". Thus began the conquest of the Vilcanota valley, the most beautiful, benign valley of all Peru. The conquest was hastened by Viracocha's son Pachacutic ("Earth-shaker", so called because of his victories and his re-organisation of Inca institutions, his stern application of Inca justice, and his remoulding of history through a selective manipulation of the facts).

As he penetrated the area east of Cuzco, so Pachacutic became aware just how vulnerable to attack the city was from this quarter. He therefore ordered his architects to build the gigantic *pucará* that frowns down upon Cuzco from the rocky heights above.

The *pucará* of Sacsahuamán is not only one of the greatest single structures ever built in preliterate America, but is also unlike its counterparts in that we know the identity of its architects, who gave their names to the three gateways to the fortress. This is all the more unusual as, among the Incas, building was generally a communal activity, with no particular individual singled out above the rest. Speaking of the *pucará*, Garcilaso de la Vega, who was born in Cuzco in 1535 of an Indian *coya* and a Spanish father, wrote, "Four master architects contributed to [its] construction. . . . The first and principal one was Huallpu Rimanchi Inca, who designed the general plan. . . ."

The fortress was built into a limestone outcrop 1,800 feet long, and formed of three tiers of walls rising to fifty feet high. Access could be had at only three points, through massive trapezoidal doorways. The whole is composed of immense polygonal stones (some weighing over twenty tons) bonded and joined together, and represents a supreme example of stone construction. The stone was quarried—with heavy haematite hammers, copper or bronze chisels, and crowbars—from limestone outcrops two to fifteen miles away, and was dragged to the site with the assistance of rope-cables, wooden sledges, and rollers over which the sledges were pulled. It was put in place by means of earth ramps. The precise Inca records, as revealed in their *quipus*, state that "20,000 labourers, in continuous relays", worked for sixty-eight years to build Sacsahuamán.

Pedro Sancho de la Hoz, who saw it in 1533, when he was twenty-one years of age, said: "It is the most beautiful thing to be seen in this land. The ramparts are made of such huge stones . . . they are as big as pieces of mountain; there is not a single one small enough for even three carts to be able to transport it. . . ."

There were two rounded fighting towers; a reservoir for water, which was distributed by culverts to the whole *pucará*; apartments for the Inca; underground storage for arms; and many *colcas* to preserve food. The fortress was large enough for most of the population to be able to take refuge there in the event of a siege. However, it was not put to the test until 1536, when the Spaniards besieged and captured it from the forces of Manco Capac. As a result of that siege, much of the upper structure of Sacsahuamán was destroyed, but Pedro de Cieza, who visited it in 1548, found that it was still "a great thing to see".

On its way out of Cuzco the Anti-suyu road ran alongside the well-laid walls of the Suntu-Hausi palaces, then with Sacsahuamán on its left, ascended as a step road to the grassy pampa above the city, passing the square of Tocacachi ("Salt Window") on its way. After passing the eastern sun pillars (used, it is said, as a clock), it reached the first checkpoint, the station and *tampu* of Puca-Pucará, which was squarely built with carefully and symmetrically aligned stonework. It was designed to guard the road, all traffic into Cuzco being examined there and tolls collected. These were paid in kind from whatever goods were being taken into the city.

Crossing the *chitapampa*, fiercely hot at noon and icily cold at night, the road proceeded to the *tampu* of Huancaye. Then, just fifteen miles east of Cuzco, it descended a full 2,400 feet to the upper Vilcanota valley. Here it crossed the river by means of a suspension bridge, the original rope-cable bridge having now been replaced by a modern steel construction.

Just on the other side of the bridge lay Pisac, which commanded the route to Paucartambo and controlled the rivers of part of the upper Amazon watershed. Though only fifteen miles from Cuzco, none of the principal chroniclers mention it. Pisac is, in fact, a massive mountain rising from the floor of the Vilcanota valley; in shape an irregular oval three miles long, it rises to 4,500 feet above the valley, and was substantially reconstructed by the Inca engineers. Agricultural terraces, beginning at the riverine plains at the bottom of the mountain, majestically range up its sides for over 1,000 feet, following the natural contours of the rock. Aqueducts link the terraces, conveying water from the higher to the lower levels, and through these terraces marches the Anti-suyu road, on its way to Paucartambo and the *montaña*. Agriculturally, the terraces served the dual purpose of extending the planting area and conserving the soil, which the heavy rains would otherwise have washed away, but they also had a defensive function, for above, below and around them were grouped houses, storage places, fortresses, tunnels, gateways and checkpoints. The defences were so extensive that the entire population of the Vilcanota valley could have taken refuge at Pisac in the event of an attack.

The citadel of Pisac is filled with narrow, paved roads, tunnelled through the rock. The number of dwellings found indicates a fairly large population, scattered over the mountain.

Passing through the Amaru-puncu (the "Serpent Gate", reflecting the Incas' fascination with the giant anaconda, which lived in the jungle rivers), the road proceeded towards Paucartambo, twenty miles to the north-east. On the way there, several of the roads to Anti-suyu converged, forming one principal route.

Eight miles further on, the road reached the *tampu* of Colquepata, then climbed to Paucartambo, from which vantage point can be seen a seemingly endless wilderness of jungle, stretching far into the distance, and a number of rivers on their way to join the mighty tributaries of the Amazon. Garcilaso de la Vega was told that in the time of the Inca empire his mother's relatives, who ranked high in the social hierarchy, had entered the *montaña* at Challa-pampa, which had few inhabitants; from there they went on to a place called Pillcupata, where they settled "four populations"—that is, *ayllus* of *mitimaes* who were inured to the hot climate of the region. At Tunu they laid out the first Inca-controlled cocabush plantations.

Coca (*Erythoxylon coca*), from which cocaine is derived, is a tall shrub native to the lush plains of the *montaña*. Its leaves, which in shape, colour and smell resemble those of the tea-plant, yield cocaine, which is obtained by careful curing. The cultivation and use of coca antedates the Inca civilisation by thousands of years, for in coastal graves dating from A.D. 500 pouches of coca leaves have been found together with ceramics modelled on the form of the human face and accurately depicting people chewing coca leaves, the coca cud extending the cheek, which thus resembles the buccal pouch of a hamster. The usual practice is for a quid of coca leaves, to which is added an alkali—lime or ashes—which hastens the breakdown of the leaf and so releases the cocaine, to be placed between the teeth and the side of the mouth. The amount of cocaine consumed with each quid is minute—just 300–400 milligrams—yet this seems sufficient to anaesthetise the senses of the chewer and render him less hungry and quite impervious to cold and thirst. Cocaine was present in all ancient Indian cultures from Argentina to Colombia, and still claims millions of addicts; the Incas were the ones who systematised its production. An examination of their own histories suggests that the use of coca was limited to priests (for the purposes of divination), the Inca caste, *chasquis*, and old people, who used it to dull their senses as they waited for death. However, the Spanish conquest broke down the restraint, and coca-chewing spread to all classes. "All through Peru," Pedro de Cieza observed, "it was and is the custom to have this coca in the mouth; they keep it in their mouths from morning until they go to sleep. This coca is so valuable that it brought certain people an income of 80,000 pesos annually. There are many now living in Spain who have become rich from buying and selling coca at the *catu*-markets." Now all labour in the sierra is geared to it; if it did not exist, Peru would be very different.

While coca was one of the reasons for the Inca takeover of the *montaña*, the main reason was their anxiety to protect their eastern flank by forming an alliance with the tribes in the region, thereby using them as a buffer against any possible invasion. So firm did this alliance become that, in 1536, Manco Capac had numerous Anti tribesmen in his neo-Inca realm.

At Pisac, the Anti-suyu road divided. The north-eastern branch went to Paucartambo, as described above, while the other branch ran in a more westerly direction, along the Yucay valley towards Machu Picchu and, to the north of this famous city, the jungles of Urubamba. The Incas were fully aware that this valley was not only another gateway to the upper Amazon, but also another potential invasion route. Under the régime of Pachacutic, the Incas gained control of the whole area. On the east or left bank of the Yucay, there was a string of cities: Calca, its agricultural terraces nurtured by canalised streams, formed from the run-off of the glaciers high above and consequently very cold; Colla, and then Yucay, the most Arcadian spot in the whole valley, and once a favourite refuge of the Inca court during the winter, when an arctic-like cold settled on Cuzco. Both sides of the narrow river valley are terraced.

Beyond the terraces, where the valley widens and its sides become less sheer, stands a fortress, which guarded the right or north bank of the Urubamba river, and could effectively check the progress of any army using this side of the road. Below it is a bridge. The original suspension bridge hung from three massive towers, an unusual feature in Inca bridge-building. In 1880 the rope-cables were exchanged for steel, but the renovated bridge continued to (and still does) use the original Inca support towers. At this point the two Anti-suyu roads joined and, as a paved road—for there is considerable rain here—proceeded to the administrative centre of Ollantay-tambo.

The only way into and out of Ollantaytambo was through a magnificent gateway. This was still reasonably intact in 1865, and much of it is extant even now. It so impressed E. G. Squier that an illustration of it was used as the frontispiece of his book on Peru, published in 1877. All traffic into the Anti-suyu was funnelled through this portal. To the right was the escarp-ment of the valley—high, sheer, and impassable; to the left, the cataracts of the Urubamba.

The road entered Ollantaytambo by way of a narrow street bounded by walls of superbly laid polygonal masonry; crossing a small rivulet it entered Maynaraqui, the "place of petition", around which were houses built of adobe and with steeply gabled, grass-thatched roofs. From the top of the fortress it is still possible to discern a number of *canchas*, or groups of houses built in a square and with a common backyard. This typically Inca structural pattern has remained unchanged since 1500. Even the most imposing Inca buildings were planned on this principle, and were never more than a group of such *canchas* regularly disposed within an enclosure wall.

A wide and handsomely laid stairway leads directly from the village to the fortress towering above it. On its way it passes through a series of

E. G. Squier appeared at Ollantaytambo, and it is through his careful and thorough work that the site became known to the world at large.

It was, however, a Frenchman, Charles Wiener, who, ten years later in 1877, brought the Anti-suyu route into focus. He also published two works that, when transformed from words into deeds, forty years later, had a tremendous impact on South American archaeology. At Ollantaytambo he wrote "*on parlait d'autres villes encore, de Hauina Picchu et de Matcho Picchu [sic]*". He did not pursue this hint, however; that was left to another, a young American called Hiram Bingham, whose discoveries are discussed later in this chapter. Wiener himself decided to continue to the east and follow the route to Anti-suyu.

East of Ollantaytambo, the river Urubamba drops in an unbroken line of cascades through precipitous granite gorges. The Incas never attempted to build a road there. The terrain and climate change rapidly: the land height drops and an area of thick vegetation begins; it becomes warm and humid, and coca plantations appear. This is the *ceja*, the eyebrow of the forest, and immediately beyond it lies the jungle.

The valley behind Ollantaytambo is extensively terraced on its eastern side, where the canyon walls are not too precipitous. Mount Veronica, the summit of which reaches the height of 19,627 feet, rises nearby. The Anti-suyu road, once much wider than it is now, kept to the east of the canyon, and was bounded by a high wall, which prevented wayfarers and llamas from trespassing on the terraces. Moving sharply east, it then ascended the side of the valley, cutting through the terraces. A five-hour climb brought the traveller to the *tampu* of Avaspampa, situated at an altitude of 8,656 feet. At this point the snow-capped Veronica seems near enough to touch; the temperate Yucay valley can be seen to the left, and the warmer tropical lands to the right. On nearing the Panticalla pass, it is still possible to see the road, its well-laid stones still in place. Indeed, when the von Hagen expedition passed this way in 1953, large sections of this part of the road were found to be still intact, still used, and, in places, in surprisingly good condition. Further on, the *tampu* of Panticalla, now amorphous, was clearly once large and spacious. To the west of it rises the peak of Cerro de Padre Eterno (17,421 feet), the original Inca name of which is now unknown.

Beyond the *tampu*, the road turns sharply left to go through "the Door". This was the strategic pass that guarded the road down to the bridge of Chuquichaca, which spanned the Urubamba and in turn guarded the way into the final Inca sanctuary of Vilcabamba. On its way there the ancient road followed the furiously descending Lucumayu, keeping to its left-hand (western) bank, since on the other side the river received many tributaries. To have built the road there would thus have necessitated building and maintaining many bridges, instead of the one that was actually necessary. This bridge was the Chillichaca, the abutments and towers of which can still be seen.

Continuing down the valley, the Anti-suyu road passed through Umasbamba, Huirto and Huayopata, eventually reaching the Urubamba river and the famous suspension bridge of Chuquichaca.

The Vilcabamba river, one of the larger affluents of the Urubamba, drains much of the low-lying *montaña* behind—that is, to the north-east of—the towering granite peak of Machu Picchu. Manco Capac, having crossed the Chuquichaca bridge with the remnants of his army and then cut the cables of the bridge, followed this river into the jungles of Vilcabamba province. The area of the neo-Inca state established there was roughly triangular in shape, lying between the rivers Apurimac, Urubamba and Vilcasmayu. Manco, closely pursued by the Spaniards, who had repaired the bridge, followed a well-laid paved road near the Vilcabamba river, and retired deeper into the jungle, into cities that had been built there specifically as safe retreats. Throughout this region there were good paved roads, together with bridges of various types, spanning the many rills and rivers that scar the jungle.

Although the nucleus of this new-Inca state, which was constantly being augmented by Indians fleeing the *Pax Hispanica*, was from the mountains, it also had loyal support from people of the *yungas*, the tribes of the Antis. The Chunchos, Piros and Campas had long since made their peace with the Incas, and they actively assisted Manco in his efforts to establish a new Cuzco in their hunting areas. Within this sanctuary Manco built up his defences. Roads were extended deep into the jungle. Fortified positions in the *montaña* allowed the Incas and their allies to keep the main Andean roads under constant attack. Horses were captured and Manco learned to ride. Supplies moving between Vilcas-huamán and the Apurimac bridges were seized, giving the Incas guns, swords, crossbows and armour. So strong did they become that during the civil war Manco and his forces took part in the battle of Chupas (near Vilcas-huamán) on the side of the army of Almagro. When the "Men of Chile" were defeated and the Incas again retreated to their stronghold, seven Spaniards whose lives were forfeit asked for and received sanctuary there. During the five years in which the seven lived in New Cuzco, as it became known, they set up forges, made horseshoes and swords, and repaired guns. Betweentimes they even taught the leading Incas to play bowls and draughts. All this gave Manco insight into Spanish strategy, and helped him develop his guerrilla tactics. Inca raids became a considerable threat to Spanish communications, and the raiders' successes attracted more Indians to their cause, making the continued Inca resistance to Spanish occupation a matter of immense concern to the Viceroy. Eventually, however, the resistance was suppressed, the last Inca-in-exile, Tupac Amaru, being beheaded in 1572. The final stage of Inca civilisation was stifled, the whereabouts of the villages and fortresses that made up New Cuzco—which very few white people have actually seen—forgotten. Only lately have its precise location and some of its history been revealed. Victos, one of the last Inca capitals, was however visited by two Spaniards, one of whom reported that "there was a large area paved with flagstones and covered with sumptuous buildings, skilfully and artistically constructed in stone".

Until 1909, when a young Yale professor, Hiram Bingham, set out to find the last capital of the Incas, there was no clear evidence about its location. Bingham's momentous discoveries cleared the way for later explorers and a subsequent widening of our knowledge of the subject.

In 1953, the von Hagen expedition, in its attempted survey of all Inca roads, pushed further into the *montaña* than Hiram Bingham had done. Inca structures, many exhibiting Spanish influence, were discovered at Puncuyoc, and a whole complex of paved roads eight feet wide revealed. The sheer scale of these discoveries made it impossible to survey all the roads in detail, and this project had to be abandoned in favour of an overall survey of the Inca road system; yet everything pointed to the fact that Vilcabamba was still "out there". In the summer of 1964, Gene Savoy, a young American archaeologist long active in Peru, made an extended and hazardous journey into Vilcabamba, and discovered sixteen distinct Inca communities within the area. He found dwellings built mostly of granite, fountains and terraced gardens, glazed pottery and horseshoes. A strong Spanish influence was evident in these finds.

In 1909, however, all this was unknown. The fact that it was intrigued Hiram Bingham and impelled him to begin the search for Manco Capac's "New Cuzco". First its outer bastion was found, and then, as Bingham continued his explorations, he learned of a mystery city built high on the granite precipices that overhang the Urubamba.

This city was Machu Picchu, situated forty miles west of Vilcabamba (the old), and perched 2,000 feet above the raging waters of the Urubamba. It bore no direct relationship to the centre of the last Inca resistance, and there was no direct route of communication leading to it. It was not a citadel and definitely not a fortress, although it had its defences. It had never been seen by the Spaniards and was never referred to by the Spanish chroniclers. That it was known to the local population was shown by maps that Charles Weiner made in 1875.

In 1911, Hiram Bingham and his able team of specialists made the 2,000-foot climb through thick undergrowth to Machu Picchu. As they felled the forest concealing the ruins, they saw slowly emerge a city with its dwellings, palaces, plazas, stairways and fountains; gradually these were retrieved from the green chaos of vegetation that had covered and preserved them for 500 years. It is the dream of almost every archaeologist that some day, in the hushed sanctity of a forest, he will find a ruin, a city, a site that no one knew existed, and such was Hiram Bingham's good fortune.

The city's position was daring enough. Below, the Urubamba made a horseshoe turn, isolating Machu Picchu on three sides. Wherever possible the precipitous slopes were terraced. In time, this impressive site appeared as those who lived there had left it, but the work of exploration continued for years and brought in its wake a stream of publications containing the most painstaking and thorough accounts of any yet produced in the field of Peruvian archaeology. However, Machu Picchu's discoverers soon learned that it was not unique, except for the finish of its stonework and its exceptionally impressive geographical setting, for beyond the city gate they found a well-laid stone road leading south and connecting Machu Picchu with a chain of other sites, spaced at intervals of five or ten miles all along this road. It is obvious that only a people in full control of the whole area, with undisputed command of the population, could have built and maintained such a complex.

Judging by the amount of usable soil yielded by the agricultural terraces, and, consequently, the amount of food that could be produced, it seems certain that Machu Picchu could have supported only a meagre population, something less than 500. Water was conveyed through an open aqueduct; the carefully prepared stone water fumes can still be seen from above the city. When the supply failed, as it occasionally must have done at the height of the dry season, water would have to have been drawn from the river—some 2,500 feet below.

So what was Machu Picchu? To Hiram Bingham it was the last refuge of the Incas, as well as the first—for he saw it as the "Origin *tampu*" from which the Incas appeared after the flood. However, the truth is that Machu Picchu was late Inca, as is shown by the fine pottery carefully unearthed from the site, which has yielded nothing older. Moreover, it was not unique, but simply one of a galaxy of small communities perched above the Urubamba canyon. One of the laterals of the Anti-suyu route connected them all together and linked them with Cuzco.

Between Cuzco and this area is a high, undulating *puna*, ranging from 8,500 to 13,800 feet above sea level, and to a large extent under cultivation. This continues as far as the Pampapaccahuana, a glacier-fed river that flows into the Urubamba just below the great fortress of Ollantaytambo. North of here lie Machu Picchu and its connected settlements, joined by a road about thirty miles long.

The route to Machu Picchu from Cuzco lay along the Chincha-suyu, the northern route, as far as the marshes of Anta. Beyond this point at Zurite, the road turned north, and continued to Huaracondo (fifteen miles north-east of Cuzco), where the remains of an Inca bridge and road are still visible. Turning west and running parallel to the main Anti-suyu route along the Urubamba, the road passed through Incasamana and Pauccarcancha, where it bridged the Pampapaccahuana. Beyond here, the road was engineered to follow the side of the Urubamba canyon, 2,500 feet above the river.

The first known village in the chain of settlements to which Machu Picchu belonged is Runca Raccay, a cluster of houses with a small plaza and some agricultural terraces; less than fifty people could have lived there. About ten miles further on, at an altitude of about 12,450 feet, is Sayac Marca, a group of five *canchas*, with two baths and a small plaza. The inhabitants were supported by the food grown on the terraces or obtained by such barter trade as was possible with other settlements in the region.

Passing through a dense forest, the road is supported by a dry-laid retaining wall built into the rockface, which has been cut away to make room for the base stones of the wall. Then, midway between Sayac Marca and the next "hanging city", six miles further on, the road passes through a tunnel. Here the road-builders found the way barred by an exposed outcrop of granite, smooth and sheer, and offering no natural base for the six-foot-wide road; they therefore had no option but to tunnel through the rock for nineteen yards. In the latter half of the tunnel they carved stone steps, so that the road would be level at either end of it. The most striking feature of the road along the top of Urubamba canyon is that, despite the inconstancies of the terrain, it is horizontal almost throughout; only occasionally is there a slight gradient.

From end to end the road is paved with granite, quarried *in situ* and dry-laid, as was all stonework. The bases of the retaining walls—which are often as high as fifteen feet—are placed in niches cut out of the granite. There is occasionally a small *tampu* between settlements, but such halting stations can seldom have been needed, since the distance between villages averages only ten miles. These villages form a chain along the Urubamba canyon: after Sayac Marca the road passes through Phuyo Pata Marka, Wiñay Wayna, Inti Pata and Choquessuysoy and then, with nowhere else to go, ends up at Machu Picchu.

Why should there have been such a vast expenditure of human energy to build this road? The hundreds—thousands—employed to construct the agricultural terraces and road system brought trifling and unneeded acreage into production. The total population of these dangerously perched settlements could not have exceeded a thousand. The area was of no strategic importance, since no enemy could have undertaken to move through that thick and difficult forest. Were these magnificent and daring roads really necessary? Could it be, as one Spanish chronicler suggested, that the Inca caste believed that sloth causes a people to decay and that, in order to keep the population disciplined and active, they devised gigantic work programmes, regardless of their final utility?

It is difficult to see any other explanation for the road, terraces, and villages on the way to Machu Picchu.

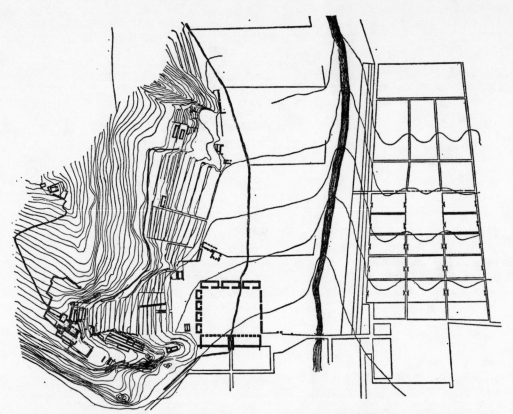

Ollantaytambo, 24 miles northwest of Cuzco on the upper Urubamba River. This typifies "ideal" Inca planning: the self-contained city formed of a series of *cancha* complexes with the *pucara* or fortress above.

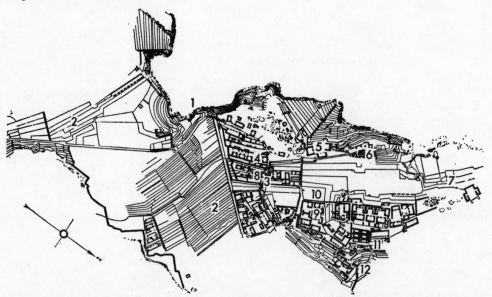

Machu Picchu in the saddle between two peaks, 2000 feet above the rapids of the Urubamba River. It is essentially a fortified city: 1) the gateway to the city; 2) agricultural terraces; 3) stairway of the fountains, which supplied the city with water brought by an aqueduct from a mile away; 4) one of the residential sections of the clans; 5) the sacred plaza and the Temple of Three Windows; 6) the Intiahautana, "hitching post of the sun"; 7) northern terraces and the road to Huayna Picchu; 8) the semicircular temple, the Palace of the Ñustas; 9) house of the clans; 10) a clan section of the "Three Doors"; 11) the royal mausoleum; 12) the place of the stairways and the cemeteries. (*Redrawn from Hiram Bingham's* Lost City of the Incas, *New York 1951*).

## CHAPTER TEN

## Vilcanota: The Royal Passage

In the summer of 1549, Pedro de Cieza prepared to leave Cuzco and travel south. First, however, he had to stop at Rimac-pampa—the "Speaking Place", so called because "it was here that proclamations were made". Rimac-pampa, the sixth ward of Cuzco, was the starting point of the great road south to Lake Titicaca and beyond, and also a guarded checkpoint through which all travelling in that direction had to pass. The road commencing there was begun in 1452 on the orders of Topa Inca and was extended 2,100 miles south, into Chile.

After the battles of 1548, which brought to an end the revolt of Gonzalo Pizarro, Pedro de Cieza was made El Primer Cronista de las Indias by Bishop–President La Gasca. Thereafter he bore letters instructing all officials that he was to be given the assistance he required in order to write his histories.

Now Cieza no longer had to walk while his horse carried his manuscripts, nor pay, as he once had to, "thirty pesos a sheet for paper". In addition to his own mount, he had a pack horse for his papers, and a servant attended him. However, other soldiers who had fought for La Gasca received titles, land grants, and *repartimentos* of Indians (mostly from those who forfeited their rights by being on the losing side); but, as Cieza himself states and the records confirm, he received little more than his title.

This immense third quarter of the Inca empire, the Colla-suyu, took its name from the Colla tribe, who lived around Lake Titicaca. It stretched far to the south, and included southern Peru, all Bolivia, the *montaña* down into the jungle, a fragment of the Paraguayan *chaco*, the Andean section of Argentina (where Tucumán, a large, completely modern city whose name is Quechua, stands), and the whole of Chile down to a latitude of thirty-five degrees, an area with an arid coast and the highest mountains in South America. South of this region the Incas encountered fierce resistance from the Araucanian tribes, and thus progressed no further.

Starting on his way south, Cieza took "this road by which one goes from Cuzco to Chuqui-apu [modern La Paz] in Bolivia". Just beyond Cuzco, the two streams that flow through the city join to become the Hautenay river, and the land is water-logged. The road here was therefore paved, walled and terraced, fern-like leafed Molle trees lining it on either side. One league (three miles) out of Cuzco, the wayfarer passed Surihaulla ("Ostrich Field"), where the Incas once kept and raised the three-toed rhea, the South American ostrich, for its feathers.

Next came the salt pits—Cachi-mayu—called Las Salinas by the Spaniards. At the time that Cieza arrived there, on his way south, the place was still fresh in Spanish memories as the site of the savage battle of Las Salinas, fought on 26th April 1538 between the forces of Pizarro and Almagro. This conflict became the subject of one of Cieza's histories (see *The War of Las Salinas*, Hakluyt Society, London 1929), though he stated that he "would rather escape from the narration of this battle and leave it buried in oblivion. I would wish indeed to be silent about their broiling conflict . . . but from it arose all the evils that afflict this land." Cieza gathered from the survivors all the pertinent information about this civil war between Spaniards fighting over the still-rich carcass of the Inca empire, and related "how the Indians . . . crowded on the ridges and hillsides, not caring that either side should be victorious, but that all should be killed . . .".

These battles and all the subsequent uprisings, the last being Gonzalo Pizarro's rebellion in 1546, did more to destroy the cities, *tampus*, bridges and roads of the empire than anything that occurred in the first few years of the conquest. The battle of Las Salinas ended with the judicial murder of Almagro by Hernando Pizarro, who as a result was imprisoned for fifty years in La Mota prison in Medina del Campo.

Two miles further along the road, the wayfarer came to Oma (now San Geronimo) and the "Narrows", where the salt marshes and a massive outcrop of the Andes restricted the width of the road. This place was long a source of contention between the tribe that originally held it and the invading Incas, who needed to control it if they were to be able to expand to the south, into the Colla section. Once the Incas had conquered it, their engineers directed the road over the rock (as high as that of Gibraltar) in order to avoid the marshes and the nearby lake, which often overflowed in the rainy season. On the summit of the rock they built a large community known as Tipon.

Cieza noted that "leaving Cuzco, one goes along the royal road . . . to the narrows of Mohina, the lodgings of Quispicanchis remaining on the left of the road, which is a wide paved causeway. At Mohina there were large buildings but now all are in ruins." This was so since the *tampu* had been burned "because of the disturbances of the civil wars".

In 1867, Squier, approaching the place from the south, noted, "We struck a well-graded road . . . leading to the great town of Muhyna [Mohina]", and the ruins there impressed him as being some of the oldest in Peru. Later, in 1912, Hiram Bingham surveyed the same ruins, and thought that "the whole valley invites careful systematic archaeological excavation".

This has yet to be carried out. However, in 1931, Robert Shippee, with Lt. Johnson as cameraman, flew over the area, and brought back a series of splendid aerial photographs of the whole Hautenay valley. The camera lens caught that which all else had missed: a large archaeological complex just beyond where the road crossed the river.

In 1953, the von Hagen expedition, using the aerial photographs as a guide, followed the Inca road from Mohina down into the valley, and found where the road had crossed the narrow but deep-flowing river. From here the road continued between huge walls thirty-three feet high to Piquillacta ("Flea-town"), one of the greatest storage areas in the whole Inca empire. Scattered about a relatively flat plain are the remains of over 300 ruined storehouses, many once roofed with straw. The area was neatly laid-out, and the royal road, which was wide, paved, and walled as described, ran through the plaza. Directly in front of Piquillacta is Lucre, and, between the edge of this lake and the top of the ridge above it, the ancient Inca engineers had constructed terraces so as to create more land in a sheltered area.

Strangely enough, Pedro de Cieza, who "turned aside everywhere", does not mention this immense storage area, and other sources are silent about it too. But, though no one spoke of Piquillacta, everyone commented on the gateway of Rumi Colca. Cieza observed that there is a "large and very strong wall. . . . In this great wall, there is a wide gate in which guards were stationed to take tribute and tolls, and in addition they apprehended anyone trying to take gold or other valuables from Cuzco. Here also were found their quarries." Two roads, the lower one running from the boundary of the lake, and the upper one running between the storage bins, converged at the gateway. It was doubtless a toll-gate—a check-point. Cieza commented on the twenty-foot-wide road, "very large and broad". Squier, who wished to make the first accurate measurements of everything, wrote that the wall across the valley was 750 feet long, thirty-four feet wide, and, at its base, thirty-six feet thick. He too thought that the gateway was a toll-gate, since beside it were the remains of a barracks, while above it—hardly perceptible from below, but clear in aerial photographs—was a large structure, a halting station.

Near the gateway, and twenty-one miles from Cuzco, were the quarries of Rumi Colca, from which the Incas prised large blocks of brownish andesite. From these they obtained the ashlars used to build the massive walls of Cuzco.

The royal road then proceeded to Lake Urcos, a small, round, deep lake that has the appearance of being the ancient crater of a volcano; its waters, reflecting the sky, are an intense blue. There was a *tampu* here, and all agree that it was an important one. The official list of *tampus* calls it the Tampu de Urcos, and names those who held it in fief.

Lake Urcos was also famous for the golden chain of Huascar, which was presumed to have been thrown into the lake to keep it from the conquistadors. It had been made to celebrate the birth of Huascar, the unfortunate son of Huayna Capac. Although none of the Spaniards ever saw the chain, they were told by the Indians that "each of the golden links was as big as a man's fist, that the chain was so heavy that 200 Indians had difficulty in holding it". The tale of the chain has been passed on to us by Garcilaso de la Vega, the first native-born *littérateur*, who died the same year as Cervantes and Shakespeare (1616). It is believed that the chain was really a thick hawser, resembling the rope-cables used to hang suspension bridges, and that it was plated with sheet-gold and had red tassels at the ends. It was used in a dance in which men alone took part. Huascar's name (he was born Inti Cusi, "Huascar" being his throne name) means "rope", a reference to the so-called chain. In Cieza's time, the Spaniards had already made plans to drain the lake in order to find the chain, but it remains unfound to this day.

Beyond Urcos, the royal road made its way up the valley of the Vilcanota. This river of three names—"Vilcanota", "Yucay", and, where it flows below Machu Picchu, "Urubamba"—has here carved for itself a broad valley, from the towering sides of which tumble brawling mountain streams that feed and widen the river. To the east rises Ausangate, with its many glaciers and snow-covered peak, which reaches an altitude of 20,181 feet. The valley floor, the level of which rises only gradually, is here about 9,800 feet above sea level, which means, in the Andes, almost hot days and cold nights. The whole length of the Vilcanota valley from here to the lofty pass of La Raya, 120 miles to the south, is one vast stretch of cultivated plants: tasselled corn (*sara*), purple-blossomed potatoes (*moraya*), and wheat, which was introduced shortly after the conquest.

Urcos also was a junction: the road south-west to Arequipa, then of minor importance, but now the second largest city in Peru, began there. This route was over 350 miles long, and the land it crossed was so rugged and sparsely populated that even the Incas used it but rarely. It is mentioned here only to emphasise that even this vast, bleak area, with all the enormous problems it posed for the engineer, did not deter the Incas from building a road through it, all in the cause of good communications.

Just before the next *tampu*, at Quiquijahna (pronounced "key-key-hah-nah"), the road bridged the Vilcanota for the first time. Cieza accurately gave the distance from Urcos to the bridge as three leagues (nine miles). The village of Quiquijahna was built on both sides of the river, the people living on the west bank having the responsibility of keeping the bridge in good repair.

The bridge was mentioned by most travellers along the royal road, and remained in use till 1877; thereafter it was replaced by a modern bridge with three arches. Huamán Poma confirms that it was originally a rope-cable suspension bridge.

Quiquijahna itself was inhabited mainly by the Cavinas tribe, "whose custom it is to use large ear plugs. The Cavinas go about dressed in woollen ponchos with a black fillet twisted about their heads. Their city, Quiquijahna —'Crystal House'—has, on the edge of the hills, fine houses built of stone. . . ."

"In ancient times they venerated a temple called Ausangate", the highest peak in the nearby range of mountains, and visible from as far away as Cuzco. Quiquijahna was also well known in Inca times as "the goal of runners, who raced to it during the August festivals of Coya-rayni and bathed in the waters of the river at this village . . .".

The next stop on the royal road was Cusipata, one of those *tampus* built where had been no settlement. Cusipata ("Pleasant Region") well deserved its name, for it lay in the river valley at the comfortable altitude of 10,500 feet, and the surrounding area was extensively cultivated. Here, long stretches of the royal road, fifteen feet wide, bounded by stone walls, and paved where it passes over a damp area, are still clearly visible and, in many places, in a good state of preservation. The old road runs parallel to the modern dirt road through the area, often running very close to it. Just before the modern village of Cusipata is reached, the remains of the small *tampu* built here can be seen.

Next to this *tampu*, situated halfway between two principal halting stations, was a *topo*, attached to the stone wall on one side of the road. As mentioned earlier, *topos* were used to measure distance, being spaced about four and a half miles, or, as one chronicler recorded, 6,000 paces apart. As Inca, like Spanish distances, were based on the most convenient pace, this would make the Inca pace about four feet and the standard road gauge of twenty-four feet—observed where conditions permitted, as they generally did where the coastal road was concerned—equivalent to six paces.

Further on, at Combapata, a royal *tampu*, represented in Huamán Poma's itinerary by a house symbol, the royal road was built on the lower slopes of the mountain. Combapata was also important as a village, for it protected a suspension bridge across the river and was connected with the Urcos–Arequipa road.

The whole of this area and its people belonged to the *repartimiento* of the famous Alonso de Mesa. Mesa had shared in Atahuallpa's ransom, receiving 135 marcos of silver and 3,330 pesos of gold, and had fought in the battles of 1534. In these he "performed marvellously, for he was young and robust, had a good horse and fine arms". With his wealth he acquired a veritable harem of Inca *pallas*. He took part in the defence of Cuzco during Manco

Capac's siege of it, and, in 1572, as an aged conquistador, acted as an "adviser" to the younger and more agile Spaniards assailing the neo-Inca state in Vilcabamba.

Coming to the great Temple of Viracocha, Cieza found himself in the territory of another tribe, the Canas. "They wear ponchos like the others and they have large, round, high woollen caps on their heads . . . in the village of Cacha there were great edifices . . . built in memory of their god Viracocha."

Just before the temple, the wall-lined road passes through an area covered with lava from the Haratché volcano. The lumps of lava, which look like massive coals just pulled from a furnace, are heaped about in the wildest confusion. Out of this residue of hell-fires pours a stream which the Inca engineers dammed with finely laid stones, diverting the water into various conduits, which irrigated terraces built among the lava heaps. The residual water passed into an artificial pond or lake, beyond which stands the Temple of Viracocha.

Aware that the temple was built in a style unique in Peru, Squier, who passed this way in 1867, put to use his surveying apparatus and measuring tapes, and made a ground plan of the temple. He found the median wall to be thirty-two feet long and forty feet high, with a base of well-worked stone eight feet high and featuring the familiar Inca niche; the rest of the wall was constructed of adobe. At various points the remains of wooden beams are still embedded in the walls, and some immense circular columns, six feet in diameter, still stand.

These columns, twelve apiece on either side of the median wall, rightly suggested to Squier that these supported beams resting on the wall. The roof was grass-thatched. All such public buildings were constructed by a central organisation according to the directions of professional architects and master-masons, who were exempt from the *mita* and were employed full time in designing public buildings, dams, bridges, roads and terraces. Since paper and its substitutes were not known to the Incas, the architects made models (some of which still exist).

Garcilaso de la Vega saw the Temple of Viracocha's destruction: "The Spaniards destroyed it despite the fact that it was unique of its kind . . . they ought to have preserved it and, at their own expense, kept up all these marvellous things, which would have borne witness to the grandeur of the empire they had succeeded in conquering. . . ." Garcilaso insisted that they destroyed the whole edifice, but, as can still be seen, they did not demolish it entirely. Many of the buildings that surrounded it are still sufficiently well preserved for a well-grounded architect–archaeologist to be able to restore them.

The language, as all who travelled the royal road noted, changed about here. Aymara, which is also the name given to the dominant tribes of the

region, was spoken. For centuries these tribes resisted the Incas' imperialistic designs, the Colla tribe, after whom the entire third quarter of the
empire (Colla-suyu) was named, being the first barrier the invaders had to
overcome on their way south. After 1430, however, Pachacutic undertook a
campaign to conquer all the tribes about Lake Titicaca, and one by one they
were incorporated into the empire.

The first main Aymara-speaking settlement that the traveller came to on
his way along the royal road was Sicuani, where there was a *tampu*. Huamán
Poma gives the name, perhaps more correctly, as "Ciquyani", and listed it
as a royal *tampu*. The town is in a ravine.

The Vilcanota valley begins to narrow here; night arrives earlier, and the
cold at night is more intense than further down the valley. "They have," said
Cieza, "many flocks of llamas; vicuñas, and equally wild huanacos range over
the higher slopes. There is much maize and wheat and plenty of partridges
and condors. They also catch excellent fish in the rivers." A bridge had been
placed across the narrowing river here to connect with the road to Arequipa.

For the next twenty miles the level of the land rises, until, at La Raya, it
reaches an altitude of 14,150 feet; this marks the great continental divide.
The wind here is ice-laden, and Squier remembered that when he approached
the narrow pass he saw a "frosty stream curdled with floating snow and ice
crystals fretting between the rocks". An enormous *apacheta*, fifteen feet high,
still stands here, and there was once also a temple of the sun (called in
Aymara *Huil canota*—hence the name "Vilcanota").

Near the pass are the remains of a stone wall, five or six feet high. It
seems more like a boundary line than a defensive wall, but this is what one
chronicler described it as, saying that it was "to prevent the Incas from
conquering the Collas, and the Collas from encroaching on Inca territory".
Close by are the remains of guard stations, where tolls were collected and
people's movements checked; for the Indians had few desires, and the ruling
Incas had a genius for ensuring that they stayed that way.

In this same area there is a freezing lake, surrounded by ruins of several
large Inca *tampus*. Despite the biting cold, Squier "made a plan of one of
these *tampus* (under the crumbling walls of which we found protection for
the night)". This *tampu*, he said, could "be taken as a type of this kind of
structure in general, although no two are precisely alike". The building was
180 feet long and divided into three rooms, each sixty feet in length. The
walls were built to the edge of the lake. There were large courtyards for
llamas, resembling those into which camels were herded at night in caravanserais throughout Asia.

Two rivers flowed out of this lake: the one flowing north became the
Vilcanota, the course of which has already been described; the one flowing
south was the Pucará, which continued to Lake Titicaca.

The *Ordenanzas de Tambos* (1543) spoke of this area as being "*despoblado muchos dias*"—depopulated for a long time; only sixty Indians lived here, and these were placed under the supervision of Francisco de Villacastín, who controlled Ayaviri, the next large *tampu*.

Ayaviri, situated in a broad valley close to river Pucará, "was", says Pedro de Cieza, "in ancient times a grand thing to see . . . and the place is now [1549] still worthy of note, especially the great tombs, which are so numerous that they occupy more space than the habitations of the living. . . . The people are of the same descent and lineage as those of the Canas . . . that is, they dress in long woollen ponchos that reach to the ground, and wear black fillets around their heads." Their principal weapon was the bolas.

"As Ayaviri is a large district through which a good river [the Pucará] flows, Topa Inca ordered [in about 1450] that a great palace should be built there . . . together with many buildings where tribute was stored. A temple of the sun was also built there . . . and Topa Inca settled in the province Indians known as *mitimaes*, with their wives. . . ."

These *mitimaes* (the hispanicised form of *Mitima-coma*) were, as mentioned earlier, loyal Quechua-speaking tribesmen moved into a newly-conquered area or one of doubtful loyalty. They acted both as a garrison, in order to prevent any uprisings, and as purveyors of the Inca way of life, including the sun cult. As population transfers were on a gigantic scale, this practice would (had not the Spanish conquest interrupted it) have produced a thoroughly heterogeneous population. Quechua was used for all official business, although local dialects were permitted, and native dress was approved and encouraged. However, in Ayaviri Pedro de Cieza noticed that "There are few original natives left and the *mitimaes* have become lords of the soil."

Nothing of the former greatness of Ayaviri remained above ground. Indeed, no one who passed by after Cieza even mentions the ruins, although the von Hagen expedition did locate the Inca road (together with a *tampu*) nearby.

Ayaviri was also an important junction, for near here the royal road divided, the two branches running on opposite sides of Lake Titicaca. The *Ordenanzas* observes, "Here separate the two roads that encircle the lake. They are called Oma-suyu [the eastern branch] and Hurcos-suyu [the western branch]." This was confirmed in 1613 by Vásquez de Espinosa, who also mentioned another road, "which branches off to the east at the village of Asillo and goes to the Carabaya".

Pedro de Cieza gave great emphasis to this lateral, since "Toward the forests of the Andes is the famous and very rich river of Carabaya . . . they took from it more than 1,700,000 pesos of gold, of such fineness that it exceeded the standard. Gold is still found in the river. . . ."

The main function of the lateral in question was to provide access to the "rich gold area". The road ran close to the edge of the deep and swift-flowing Carabaya river, which runs through a sheer-sided canyon. The land here is somewhere in the region of 13,000 feet above sea level, and takes the form of an undulating treeless plain broken by fantastic upthrusts of limestone and granite with wide veins of quartz. With good fortune and great physical effort, gold may be won from this rock. On the peaks of these crags are numerous burial *chullpas*—the stone-built, generally cylindrical houses of the dead.

The whole region is distinctly barren and inhospitable, and few living creatures are at home there. In the stunted sedge around one of the small, ice-fringed tarns a pair of Andean snow-geese (*huachuas*) may perhaps be seen, while on the grass tufted higher hills watchful vicuñas may be sighted.

The high altitude, isolated situation and lack of people made this part of the Carabaya province ideal for the vicuña. This creature, which is half the size of the llama and has a long graceful neck, was highly prized for the long, light chestnut-brown wool covering its chest and protecting it from the freezing cold of Andean nights. This wool was sheared by the Inca's hunters, under the strictest rules of conservation. A wool of unsurpassed softness, it is the finest known, with 2,500 hairs to the inch. Pedro de Cieza was the first to illustrate it (remarkably accurately) and describe it. One male dominates a herd or fifteen or more females, and the battles between contending males may last for days, until one or many die of exhaustion.

After a hunt, such as that in which Manco Capac invited the Spaniards to take part, the vicuñas that had been captured were shorn and released. The Incas, Garcilasco de la Vega informs us, "kept an accurate account, on their *quipus*, of the number killed and the number released. The coarse wool of the huanaco was given to the people; that of the vicuña, as fine as silk, was reserved for the Inca's service." To the same family of cameloids belong the alpaca and llama.

The alpaca, small, and looking much like "a Peruvian sheep", as one Spaniard called it, was thought by Pedro de Cieza to be "very ugly and woolly". It is the same shape as the llamas, but smaller. According to another chronicler, Pedro Blas Valera, whose complete historical work was destroyed when Sir Walter Raleigh raided and burned Cadíz, alpacas "are not reared for burden-carrying but for the sake of their wool, which is excellent and very long".

The huanaco, an animal found from Ecuador to Patagonia, where it was the Indians' principal source of meat and skin, is undomesticated. It is as tall as the llama and, unlike the vicuña, which travels in immense herds, tends to be solitary. Its "wool is short and rough, its flesh good and gamy". When Cieza was in Bolivia, he "ate a dinner off one of these fat huanucos . . . and it seemed to me to be the best thing I ever ate in my life. . . ."

The llama was the Incas' beast of burden. It furnished transport, wool, and meat, and its dung (*taquia*) was used for fuel. It is a very adaptable creature, able to survive at an altitude of as much as 17,000 feet, as well as travel in the hot deserts along the coast. Mochica pottery shows that, in desert regions, the Indians provided the llama with a woollen fringe, to protect its eyes from the hot sands. A llama loaded with half its own weight, 200 pounds, will normally travel between six and twelve miles a day; if pressed, longer. Its wool, too greasy for fine weaving, was used mostly for heavy blankets—coverings for doors, to keep out draughts at night— woollen sacks, and cordage. Its meat, as described earlier, was cut into long strips, which, when dried, became *charqui*. Then, since llamas tend to use a common voiding place, their dung, which looks like sheep pellets, could be gathered and used for fuel. Finally, the llama's lungs, liver and stomach were consulted by soothsayers for omens, recalling the Roman custom of consulting chicken livers before embarking on an important war. The llama herdsman thus had a responsible and honourable place in society.

Llama herds were an integral part of the Inca economy. As the principal pack animals, they carried goods during peace time, and weapons in war time. Each *ayllu* had its own herds of llamas, and the *quipu-camayoc* kept a record of the numbers involved, so that, at any given time, the governors knew the precise number of llamas in the realm. If one believes the first Spanish chroniclers, the figure ran into hundreds of thousands. Llamas, naturally, were the animals used to carry goods into the Carabaya, and to bring out the gold won from it.

"Carabaya" is the hispanicised form of the Quechua *Kara-waya*, "wound". The word is expressive, for the Carabaya river has carved out a terrifyingly deep canyon, from the bottom of which comes its roar, reverberating against the vertical walls. The road here is so narrow that two llamas can scarcely pass one another; yet it has been well engineered to negotiate the rugged, treeless terrain. Continuing on its way, it begins to zigzag down to the gold regions. This is the Carabaya, alternately cold and hot, rainy and unhealthy, a forbidding land entered by Indians only because it was the Inca's wish that they obtain the high-quality gold to be had there. "In this place in Peru," wrote a seventeenth-century lawyer to his Viceroy, "there are many gold mines . . . as for instance in the Carabaya. The Indians' labour there is harder than in most places, because the air temperature is so harmful, and they are in the water all the time washing ore. . . ." There were many gold mining villages in the region.

Since the hard labour of obtaining the gold was disliked at all times, the Inca officials took care to provide some relief. Duties were rotated, and only married Indians were selected to work there, their wives having to accompany them in order to cook for them and prepare their *chicha*. Their fields in the *ayllus* were cultivated for them in their absence and, when ill, they were sent home. There were rest periods, festivals and, says Cieza, "pleasure".

Gold was obtained mainly from the rivers, and extracted by means of the placer mining process. Since gold is heavier than iron and sinks, sand and rock had to be lifted out of the river bed and sifted by panning. The Incas' method was to construct a series of stone riffles—grooves or slats designed to catch and retain the gold carried downstream during the rains. The nuggets were held there due to their weight, and were collected in the dry season. Crude but effective hydraulic mining operations were also attempted —for example, by undercutting cliffs and directing rivers against their bases of gold-yielding quartz.

Gold was the "sweat of the sun", and, since the Inca was thought to be descended from the sun, all metal was State property. According to the learned Pedro Bernabe Cobo, certain rituals were attached to gold-mining operations: ". . . those who went to the mines worshipped the hills containing the gold, which they called *curi*. During the festival they were up all night drinking and chanting, entreating the hills to yield their gold easily . . . nuggets, grains of gold, and gold in powder form were worshipped under the name of *llimpi*." But, worshipped or not, the gold obtained was recorded on the *quipus* and sent, as one form of tribute, to the governors. Later it was smelted and cast into bars, in which form it was delivered to the goldsmiths, who fashioned such ornaments as were ordered.

No sooner had the conquistadors obtained, by means of ransom and plunder, all the gold and silver available above ground, than they asked to be led to the sources of these metals. The Indians willingly obliged, hoping in this way to rid themselves of their uninvited guests, among whom was a certain Pedro de Candia.

About Candia's bravery there was no dispute, but, with regard to his brain, Cieza states over and over again "that he was a man of little understanding". A Greek, called after his native Candia in Crete, Don Pedro arrived in South America in the early days of the conquest. He was one of the thirteen who stood by Francisco Pizarro on the isle of Gallo, was the first of the conquistadors to go ashore at Tumbes in 1527, and won a great share of Atahuallpa's ransom. He managed to stay on the right—that is, the winning side—during the civil wars, and, after the battle of Las Salinas, settled in Cuzco. He was one of 1,600 soldiers to do so—all of them so full of bravado and mischief, with plenty of money to gratify their desires, that the governor of the city was only too delighted to see some of them chase off after some *ignis fatuus* promising hidden gold and empires.

"It was only necessary for an Indian girl in his service to make him believe that on the other side of the cordilleras, to the east, was a very rich and populous region", and Pedro de Candia, having nothing to do but spend time and his money, gathered together 300 men and set off along the Antisuyu road. After crossing the Vilcanota and passing through the great fortress of Pisac, the expedition reached Paucartambo, one of the last great fortress *tampus* before the land fell away to the valleys, pampas and jungles of the upper Amazon region. Pedro de Cieza wrote a whole chapter on "How Pedro de Candia and those who went with him into the forests suffered incredible hardships, and how they found no way forward and had to return to the Colla-suyu".

Following the coca-leaf and the gold trails, through jungles and across rivers, the party emerged above the Carabaya. Unmindful of all the suffering his force had endured, of the loss of men, equipment, horses and Indians, Pedro de Candia asked permission to occupy the valley. The Governor, knowing that Candia "was not a man of sufficient ability for the post", gave it to another; but it mattered little who obtained it: "7,000 natives perished, and they were reduced to such straits that they had to eat each other."

Carabaya—the "wound"—certainly was well named.

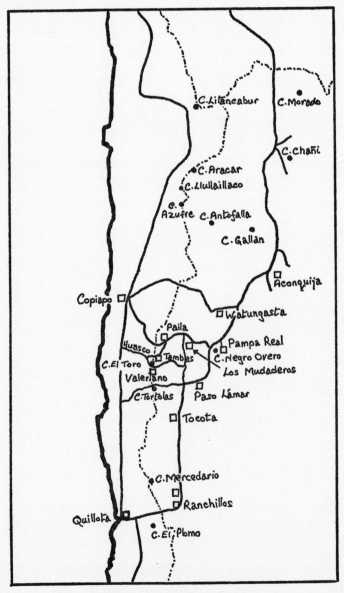

The Road to the End of the Earth.

## CHAPTER ELEVEN

## Lake Titicaca and the Silver Mines of Potosí

The royal road divided at Azángaro, not far from Ayaviri and about ten miles north-east of the great rock of Pucará, which is reached by the Hurcos-suyu branch. At about this point begins the Lake Titicaca Basin, which here, at its northern rim, is filled with marshes and swamps, where the high tortora sedge (used in the making of boats) grows. In addition, the area is the nesting place of great flocks of birds.

Although the area is for the most part perpetually under water, there is a limited amount of dry ground around the mouths of the river Ramis, which drains much of the north-western part of Titicaca Basin. Some tribesmen found this land suitable for their dwellings, and constructed vaulted turf houses there. Their descendants still build in the same style.

The Oma-suyu section of the royal road runs round the edge of these swamps and continues along the east side of Lake Titicaca to Tiahuanacu. On its way it passes through Huancano, Chico, and Moho, known for its traditional market and its many *chulpas*, or stone tombs.

Most of the *tampus* along this route belonged to either the Pizarros or Francisco de Carbajal, the chief lieutenant and adviser of Gonzalo Pizarro in his ill-fated rebellion. Had it succeeded, Carbajal would have become the Marquis of the Cañari, who, since they hated the Incas, had served through-out the conquest as Spanish allies. He would also have become prime minister of the new state that he had advised Gonzalo Pizarro to create.

On 21st October 1547, a great battle was fought near the *tampu* of Huarina, on marshy ground close to the shores of the great lake. Diego Centeño, fighting for President La Gasca, came onto the field with 1,000 men. Regarding Centeño, Pedro de Cieza said, "He was a gentleman, not very tall, with a pleasant countenance and a red beard . . . he was not very liberal as regards his own money, but expended the King's fifth with largesse." He had been pursued by Carbajal for years, over the length and breadth of the Andes, and, now that he had the larger body of troops, thought he would settle accounts with this Lucifer. On the rebels' side, Gonzalo Pizarro commanded the cavalry, and Carbajal the infantry, who, like their leader, wore surcoats of greenish cloth to blend in well with the ground. Each of Carbajal's 400 arquebusiers carried two or three loaded and primed blunderbusses.

Diego Centeño waited; but Carbajal goaded him into action by crossing and recrossing the royal road, thereby exposing himself to enemy fire. Despite the danger, he advised his own men, "Hold your fire, my lads. Wait it out." When their enemies were within a hundred yards, he gave the order to fire. Before Centeño's men could recover from the shock, the second barrage came, and then the third: more than half of them were killed and Centeño himself was wounded, though able to escape.

When Gonzalo Pizarro rode out among the dead and dying, he gazed down in wonder, crossing himself as he rode: "Jesus! What a victory."

It was his last.

Turning now to the Hurcos-suyu branch of the royal road, the first *tampu* reached after the place at which the road divided was Pucará, which means "fortress". The mountains of reddish sandstone tower 1,000 feet above the modern village, and there are still some remains of the fortress and other buildings that Cieza found "in ruin and decay". In addition, many stone statues representing human figures survive, as do other noteworthy things. The *tampu* of Pucará was held by Francisco Maldonado, who went to court in 1545 to explain Gonzalo Pizarro's position *vis-à-vis* the New Laws; loyal to Pizarro to the end, he died in the battle that ended the rebellion in 1548.

Vásquez de Espinosa, who came to Pucará in the following century, named it as "one of the marvellous works of the Incas" and spoke of the "great, proud building there, and the fortress called Inca-cancha". Pedro de Cieza, when he came, was told by some of the older inhabitants about the great siege that Topa Inca raised against the fort sometime before 1460. This came about because the people here belonged to the Colla league, which for centuries had effectively blocked Inca expansion.

The inhabitants of Pucará were famous for their pottery, and the tradition is kept alive today by the modern hand-made ceramics known as "Bulls of Pucará". These pieces are widely esteemed and collected.

Further on, the royal road came to the *tampu* of Nicasio, where Cieza "saw weeping Indians walking ahead of a funeral cortège and singing sad and dolorous words". The village was, and still is, important for its boats made of tortora and its fisheries, for large fish—*suchi* and *boga*—are caught nearby.

Two years before Cieza's arrival there, the Spanish overlord of Nicasio, Hernando Bachicao, had been strangled on the orders of Carbajal. A rogue of high degree, Bachicao was born in San Lucar de Barrameda (the port serving Seville), from which ships sailed to the Americas. He arrived in

South America some while after the beginning of the conquest, but took part in the battle of Las Salinas, and later, in 1541, became an official in Cuzco, where he worked with Vaca de Castro, who prepared the first guide to the Inca road system. Siding with Gonzalo Pizarro in his revolt against the New Laws, Bachicao was one of those who pursued the Viceroy, who eventually was killed near Quito. His character, however, was gauged by one of Pizarro's men, who warned his leader, "So far from Bachicao being, as he states, a disciple of yours, he and Carbajal are more like your teachers and you are their disciple." At the battle of Huarina, Bachicao, seeing the odds against Pizarro, defected to the other side; but, when defeat came, he tried to slip back undetected into the Pizarro lines. This did not escape Carbajal, who instantly had him put to death.

The royal road now ran beside the great lake. The first Spaniards to see it were Diego de Agüero and Pedro Martínez de Moguer, who arrived there in 1533 and took back reports of the "greatest lake in the Indies". Cieza, however, provided the first written description. Geographically, Lake Titicaca (or, more correctly, "Chucuito") is situated in a basin between two massive ranges belonging to the Andes chain. The lake is eighty miles long by forty wide and lies on the *altiplano* at an altitude of 12,500 feet, making it the highest navigable body of water in the world. Numerous rivers, large and small, enter the lake, but only one flows out of it, which accounts for its brackishness. The surrounding land alternates between arid pampas and more cultivable areas. The altitude prevents maize from being cultivated successfully, except in sheltered places, but potatoes, quinoa, wheat and barley grow well.

The whole area was densely populated in Inca times, and still is. Numerous distinct tribes settled around the lake, the dominant ones being the Lupaca and the Colla, "who warred against each other". Cieza describes them as wearing "woollen garments . . . On their heads, the women wear a bonnet shaped like a mortar and made of wool. This they call a *chullo*."

Juliaca was the next stop along the road. Here there was the usual large *tampu*, with walled areas for llamas, and smaller quarters for wayfarers. It seems to have become quite important, as Huamán Poma calls it a royal *tampu*, but all evidence of larger buildings has since disappeared.

Passing through Caracoto, a tribute-paying community, the road reached Hatun-colla, "which was a grand thing, for *hatun* means great. Now [1549] all has disappeared and most of the natives gone, having been destroyed by war." Cieza also tells us that Hatun-colla "was the most important place in the country of the Colla. After the Incas came, they added to the town, erecting many buildings and storage houses, to which tribute was brought from the outlying towns. A number of *mamaconas* [sun virgins], priests, and quantities of *mitimaes* were imported. There was also a temple of the sun. . . ." Almost everything vanished, but what did survive were the *chullpas*, stone towers for the dead, "for, in this province of the Collas, they erect them in rows in fields; they are as big as towers . . . handsomely constructed of matched stones, with doorways opening to the rising sun".

The *chullpas*, together with what remains of the other buildings of Hatun-colla, are mostly concentrated about Umayo, just a few miles west of the lake. The burial towers are either round or square, usually placed on hilltops, and tend to be scattered rather than built in rows. The style and form of the masonry is as fine as anything in and about Cuzco; some of the stones are decorated with sculpted animals—lizards, viscachas or pumas—and others elaborately carved. They are pre-Inca, and probably represent an offshoot, or even a development, of the older, Tiahuanacu culture.

Squier, who came upon them in the winter of 1867, was fascinated by their size and structure, and, though there were already drawings of them in existence, took daguerrotypes of a goodly number of them. One elaborately carved stele so impressed him that a representation of it was stamped in gold leaf on the cover of his book on Peru ( *Peru: Incidents of Travel and Exploration in the Land of the Incas*, Harper, New York 1877). Squier thought that "architecturally considered, these *chullpas* are among the most remarkable monuments of America".

Continuing along the road, one comes to Paucar-colla, which Huamán Poma lists as a royal *tampu*. After the conquest, it was given in fief to Gómez Mazuela. Seventy years later, in 1613, Vásquez de Espinosa appeared there counting his Christians, and recorded a total of 1,003 *tributarios*.

Chucuito, our next stop, butts onto a ridge that slopes gently down to the shore of Lake Titicaca, and was thought by Cieza to be "the principal and most complete settlement to be found in most of this great kingdom". Before its conquest by Topa Inca in 1450, it was the administration centre of the Aymara-speaking Lupaca tribes, and survived the conquest as an Inca administrative centre. Remains of the Ica-uyu and Kurin-uyu, buildings that housed the officials, are still extant, and Cieza spoke of the "great lodgings" there. Chucuito was deemed so important that it, together with several villages and *tampus* lying to the south of it, were given as a *repartimiento* (an allotment of tribute-paying Indians) to the King of Spain himself.

The next few *tampus* along the royal road occurred at intervals of approximately twelve miles. The first one reached after leaving Chucuito was Ancora, where there were many *chullpas*; then came Llave, Juli (notable for its four churches built in the mestizo-style, and the printing press set up there as early as 1590), Pomata, and Zepita. When Cieza passed through this region, "the governor was an Indian called Don Gaspar, very wise and of goodly reason". He further informs us that "near Zepita runs the Desa-guadero".

No one can be sure of its original name. To the Spaniards, who soon noted that it was the only river that drained Lake Titicaca, it instantly became the Desaguadero, or "drainage" river. The river, which, at 150 feet wide and thirty feet deep, is unfordable, was crossed in two different places by a pontoon bridge made of *balsas* (explained below).

Hernando Pizarro, when he arrived here in 1537 to bring the rebelling Lupacas "to justice", found, to his discomfort, that the bridge he should have crossed (the other was some fifty miles away) had been cut adrift. "Many of Pizarro's men pushed their horses into the stream; four of them were drowned; and the one that did get over was captured and sacrificed." The site was thus a place of some strategic importance.

Cieza had nothing to say about this bridge except that "there used to be guards to collect toll from those who crossed it". Garcilaso de la Vega, who must have seen a great deal of his native land before leaving it forever at the age of nineteen, reported that "the bridge is thirteen to fourteen feet wide, more than three feet high [above the surface of the water], and a hundred feet long. Every six months it has to be entirely remade."

It is to Squier, once again, that we owe the only authentic illustration of this famous pontoon bridge. In 1867, when he explored this area, there were two such bridges. The principal one was at Nasacara, fifty miles down river, and consisted of twenty large pontoons (boats made of *balsas*) held in place by massive cables of twisted cabuya fibre. These passed through each *balsa* and were in turn firmly attached to two massive stone towers. Tortora sedge, used to make the pontoons, was also used to fill them, thereby providing a continuous, hardened pathway. The second pontoon bridge, also illustrated by Squier, was on the royal road, "at the point where the river debouches from the lake". The pontoons were renewed every six months as part of the *mita* of the local inhabitants.

It should be noted here that the word *balsa* is Spanish for a light floating log, which may or may not be of balsa wood. The latter material is derived from a tree native to areas of heavy rainfall and belonging to the *Ochroma* species; the pre-Inca tribes of the far north of Peru used it to make rafts for coastal cruising, and it was one of these that Bartolomé Ruiz, the conquistadors' navigator, encountered on an exploratory voyage prior to the conquest. However, the *balsas* used in the construction of the pontoon bridges described above were made of tortora sedge, cut, dried and fashioned into cigar-shaped bundles. Four such bundles, bound together by cabuya rope, would be used to make one pontoon or boat, two forming the hull and two the sides. The Indians still construct boats of this type, which, depending on the length of the bundles, are generally eight to twelve feet long, though occasionally boats as long as forty feet are made. They are equipped with a simple sail and in shallow water are punted. Sailing techniques are rudimentary.

Continuing along the south side of Lake Titicaca, the road passes through

Huaqui and then proceeds to Tiahuanacu, which lies on the treeless *altiplano* twelve miles south of the extreme southern end of the lake. There is little grass here, winds are constant, and temperatures—especially at night and dawn—are arctic; yet here a people of whom we know nothing built a massive ceremonial city—"The most elaborate", wrote Wendell Bennett, "and the purest manifestation of culture yet to be found."

On arriving here, Cieza (who wrote the first and, until the nineteenth century, the best description of the ruins) noted that "it is not a very large town. . . . But it is famous for its great buildings. . . . Near the main dwellings is a man-made hill laid on great stone foundations. . . ."

This was the Acapana—an immense (650 by 540 foot) hill, a partially artificial, stepped pyramid, once entirely stone-faced, with house foundations and a large stone reservoir. The Acapana has every appearance of having been a fortified *pucará* such as that of Sacsahuamán, used for refuge during a siege. North-west of this structure is a larger rectangular unit, the Calasa-saya, which presumably was a temple enclosure; and to the west is another large structure, generally known as the "palace".

Who were the Tiahuancans? "I asked the natives," wrote Pedro de Cieza during his visit in 1549, "in the presence of Juan Vargas [famed for his personal capture of Illa Tupac, one of the principal generals of Manco Capac]. who holds an *encomienda* among them, if these buildings had been built at the time of the Incas. They laughed at my question. They were built long before the Incas, but they themselves could not say by whom."

It is generally now held that Tiahuanacu never supported a large-scale population, that it was not a city-state but (until the advent of the Incas) a remote and isolated place, ruled by priests and supported and defended by soldiers. The impact of Tiahuanacu was widespread: designs and sculptural techniques similar to those used in the city are found all about Lake Titicaca and as far north as Huari (Viñaque), which is situated in the Andes, near Vilcas-huamán, some 400 miles away. It is a tribute to Cieza's superb powers of observation that when he saw the ruins of Huari he judged that "they were not Inca and by the state of ruin and decay into which they had fallen, must have been there for ages". So, by inference, Huari was either a Tiahuanacu colony or strongly Tiahuanacu-influenced.

What most struck Pedro de Cieza about Tiahuanacu was "the great gateways . . . tremendous things", the most magnificent of which is the famous monolithic Gateway of the Sun.

This was the great gateway Squier rode 500 miles to see. He found it to be thirteen feet five inches long, seven feet high and eighteen inches thick, and photographed it ("of some interest to me, as it was the first photograph it was ever my fortune to take"). In the centre of the gateway the sun god is depicted, the rays from his head terminating in puma heads, and the staffs in his hands being adorned with condor heads. Winged figures along the whole

46. Aymará Indians from the shores of Lake Titicaca playing their traditional pipes. The headdress is of bird feathers and paper flowers. The feathers and the pipes are of ancient origin. (*George Holton*)

47–48. The *aroya*, a basket on a pulley for crossing rivers when traffic did not demand a bridge: (*left*) de Bry's 16th-century drawing; (*right*) a modern *aroya* near Ayaviri north of Titicaca.

49–51. Boats made of sedge, a water reed which grows in Titicaca: (*centre*) the typical shape of the balsa reed boat here on Titicaca and on the Pacific coast; (*bottom left*) George Squire's drawing of a pontoon bridge made of boats over the Desaguadero, the sole outflow of Lake Titicaca; (*bottom right*) the author's reconstruction of a pontoon bridge at the same point on the Desaguadero.

52. The walls of the temple of Viracocha, an important religious centre in the fifteenth century. Colla-suyu road passes before it.

53. D'Orbigny's illustration of the round-roofed houses typical of the Aymará Indians, in the Cochabamba valley.

54–56. Llamas and the wild vicuñas in their Andean setting: (*top*) llamas on the repaved Huarochiri road; (*centre*) a silver statue of a llama of Inca design; (*bottom*) wild vicuñas in the Carabaya area herded for woolgathering – the wool of their lower necks were reserved for the Lords-Inca.

D'Orbigny's drawing of the early 19th-century dress of the Aymará Indians; Spanish influence is apparent.

Espanoles en el trage de Chile

Jorge Juan's mid-eighteenth-century drawing of Spanish dressed in the Chilean fashion; the ponchos show a clear Indian influence.

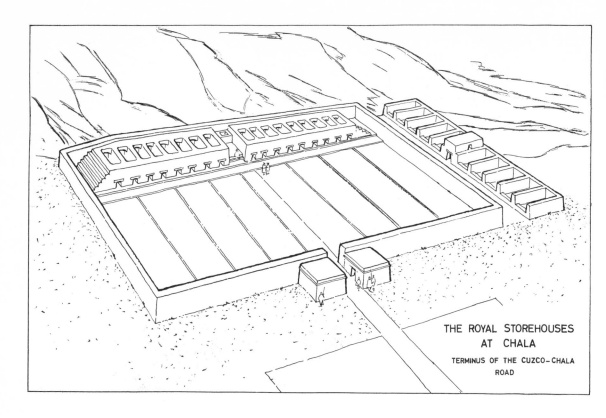

THE ROYAL STOREHOUSES
AT CHALA

TERMINUS OF THE CUZCO–CHALA
ROAD

59–61. The Royal Storehouses at Chala, where dried fish, seaweed and shellfish were lodged before being transported to Cuzco: (*bottom left*) the author on the coastal road north of Chala with a retaining wall to keep it level.

62. Cahuamarca ("view town") where the road climbs precipitously to avoid the impassable desert and then swoops back down to the sea.

63. A coastal inlet near Chala where the Indians harvested seaweed.

64. A bull of Pucará, a ceramic bull placed atop houses to ward off evil spirits.

frieze repeat this motif, which appears throughout Peru—on weavings, ceramics, and metalwork—and represents the Weeping God, weeping zoomorphic tears of puma heads and condors.

Near Tiahuanacu the two branches of the royal road (the Oma-suyu and Hurcos-suyu) coalesced, and in the same area a road branched off to La Paz, anciently Chiquiapu and now the capital of the modern state of Bolivia. This city was held "in high esteem" by the Incas, because of the quantities of gold found nearby.

The main highway, however, continued to the villages and *tampu* of Siquisaca, beyond which it left the area inhabited by the tribes of the Lake Titicaca region and entered the larger province of the Charcas, a widely settled area "highly prized by the Incas". At the place called "Acontina" by Huamán Poma the road divided again, a branch leading due east to Chiquisaca (later known as La Plata and today called Sucre) and Pocro, another city famed for its silver production. This belonged to Hernando Pizarro.

Under the Incas, Chuquisaca had been only a minor administration centre, and it was the Spaniards who brought it to prominence. The new town was founded as La Plata by Captain Pedro Anzures ("Peransures"), who, Cieza tells us, was an "old conquistador . . . well versed in the art of war, widely respected, well-liked and very liberal". In an effort to prevent the split between Almagro and Pizarro, he went to Spain in 1536 and obtained royal decrees defining—in vain—the territory belonging to each. Anzures fought on the winning side at the battle of Las Salinas, participated in the famous expedition into the Carabaya, and, after its failure, founded La Plata, in 1538.

Chuquisaca was, says Cieza, "very famous in the kingdoms of Peru because of its great treasures of silver. Land brings very high prices at the present time [1549] because of the wealth that has been discovered in the mines of Potosí."

Potosí fell within the jurisdiction of Diego Almagro's kingdom of "New Toledo", but it was not until after his time that the massive silver deposits in the area were discovered. "An Indian called Huanca," related the learned Jesuit José de Acosta, "going out one day to hunt deer, ran up against rocks, covered with certain trees called quinoa, whereupon, being forced to hold on to the branch, its roots came out; they were covered with silver from a vein of a silver-mine. Now he knew it to be good by the experience he had as a miner working the silver mines at Pocro. He brought the ore to Pocro and put it into a *huayra* [a primitive blasting oven heated by charcoal and fanned by the perennial high east winds to reach the temperature of 1006 degrees centigrade]. Having found a mine of great riches and his happy fortune, he secretly dug and drew ore out of this silver vein. One day he was discovered by a Spaniard named Diego Villaroel. Five famous veins were discovered and the mine was registered in both their names on 21st April 1545."

Potosí later came under the control of Gonzalo Pizarro, who used its riches to finance his rebellion against the Crown. The redoubtable Francisco de Carbajal, who was put in charge of the mines, thought them "more valuable than the whole kingdom of Castile", and by 1560 they had produced 58 million pesos weight of silver bullion. By 1600 the population of Potosí was 160,000, greater than that of any other place in America at the same time.

Pedro de Soría, who was in charge of the actual operation of the mines on Pizarro's behalf, was urged by Carbajal to "do what you can to extract the silver for His Excellency [that is, Gonzalo Pizarro], whose expenses are increasing." He brushed aside Soría's complaints: "I heard not from some mangy soldier but from distinguished knights that you have salted away 150,000 pesos in gold, so it would not be a bad idea to give it to some of those soldiers whom you say have complained to you." Beset, Soria begged for "agricultural and mining implements" and received permission to occupy Hernando Pizarro's house and use his servants. The demand for silver never stopped. "Send me," wrote Gonzalo Pizarro, "by those 7,000 Indian cargo-bearers all the silver you can find, Hernando Pizarro's share as well. At present I cannot sleep at night thinking of the many I have to clothe and feed and what I owe to those who follow me. . . ."

That had been in 1547. In 1549, when Cieza was on his way "to visit these provinces, carrying with me letters from President La Gasca for all the *alcaldes* asking them to assist me in discovering and learning all the important things . . .", matters had changed. Pizarro and Carbajal were dead, their holdings forfeit; and Pedro de Hinojosa had obtained possession of all Pizarro's property, which yielded an income of 100,000 castellanos a year. Hinojosa had shown that perfidy *can* pay. He had come to Peru in 1534 with Hernando Pizarro. In 1547 he was in command of Gonzalo Pizarro's armada, but this he turned over to President La Gasca, taking part in the final defeat of his friend and liege in 1548. And so, with the help of circumstances and equal parts of perfidy and guile, he was master of it all.

Balsa Bridge over the Rio Desaguadero.

## CHAPTER TWELVE

## The Road to the Ends of the Earth

At this point we part company with Pedro de Cieza, who tells us, "Beyond this province of Charcas lies the province of Chile. Now I have taken you over the Royal Road from Colombia to Potosí, which I estimate to have been a good 1,200 leagues. . . . Therefore I shall not proceed further."

Our guide, in a certain uncertain way, for the next 500 leagues (1,500 miles) is of a wholly different character from Cieza. Made up of primary stuff, a maker of history rather than a recorder of it, he is none other than Diego de Almagro, one of the original participants in the Spanish discovery and conquest of Peru.

In 1522, Almagro, Francisco Pizarro and the priest Fernando de Luque contracted "before God and Man" to find and conquer Peru and to share equally the spoils from the "Kingdom of Gold". However, in 1527, after two unsuccessful expeditions, and experiencing difficulty in obtaining support, Pizarro went to Spain and obtained a royal contract that appointed him Governor and Captain-General of Peru (though still unconquered) but allotted to Almagro the secondary post of Captain of Tumbes, the most northerly port of Peru and the point at which the conquest started. Further, Almagro was given the more pedestrian job of finding men and materials and transporting them to Peru, so that he was not present at the seizure of Atahuallpa. Thus from the very beginning there were disputes between Pizarro and Almagro, and these grew in intensity as their combined forces marched towards and conquered Cuzco.

There the quarrel was heightened, as Almagro received a lesser share of the spoils than Pizarro did; so, to forestall further bickering and avert the possibility of civil war, it was suggested that Almagro be made governor of all the lands south of where the territory of Pizarro ended. Royal approval was obtained for this, and the dividing point set at the rich coastal valley of Chincha, thirteen degrees south of the equator.

Now, although geography was then far from being an exact science, latitude could be determined fairly accurately, and Almagro was quick to note that Cuzco—the principal bone of contention—lay fractionally south of Chincha and thus in his territory. On 12th June 1535, however, a new agreement was drawn up in which it was stated that the geographers would return to Spain for "new instructions" and that in the meantime Almagro would set off to find what his new realms held. Thus, in this atmosphere of distrust, the first exploration of the royal road from Lake Titicaca "to the ends of the earth" began.

"Almagro was a man of short stature", wrote Pedro de Cieza (who, however, could not have known him personally), "with ugly, coarse features, but of great courage and endurance. He was liberal, but given to boasting: letting his tongue run on, however, he was well informed about the land and people and a great part of the discovery of these kingdoms was due to him. He was a foundling. He came out of such humble parentage that it could be said of him that his lineage began and ended with himself. . . ." This last sentence is something of an exaggeration, as the names of both his parents are known (Juan de Montenegro and Elvira Gutiérrez). However, he did not take either of their names but instead adopted the name of the village where he was born in 1479.

Almagro was illiterate and one-eyed; when the patch was removed from where his left eye should have been it revealed a glaring scar, the eye socket empty, with a jagged wound into the forehead. This eye had been claimed by an Indian arrow in the early days of the search for the "Kingdom of Gold", and the lack of it had earned him the nickname of "the Blinkard". But he was a natural leader of men, true to his word, doughty and well-liked.

For Almagro and all the other Spaniards Chile was a vast unknown. The Indians questioned about it told them that it was a land of deserts and high mountains, albeit rich in gold, and thus it became clear from the outset that careful planning was essential. Accordingly, Almagro ordered one of his captains to Lima, there to secure, fit out and fill with supplies three vessels. With these he was to sail south and eventually meet up with the main party, though where or when it was impossible to determine.

Meanwhile, Almagro assembled a force of 570 men, comprising both cavalry and foot soldiers. Hernando de Soto, immensely wealthy, offered a good portion of his money to come as second in command, but Almagro turned him down for Rodrigo Ordóñez, a Jew who had adopted Christianity and whose name also was adopted. A native of Oropesa, Spain, Ordóñez had won his spurs in the Italian wars and was decisive, knowing and spirited.

Aid also was sought from the newly installed Inca, Manco Capac, who gave it willingly, no doubt being only too glad to have so many troublesome Spaniards out of the way. He selected 12,000 tribesmen to act as cargo bearers and provided a whole train of llamas. Villac-Umu, the highest priest in the land, and Manco's half-brother Paullu were given charge of the

Indian faction. Paullu, then scarcely twenty years of age, was a man of curiously conflicting motives. He sided with the Spaniards against his own people, and, when Manco retreated to the fortresses of Vilcabamba, became puppet Inca in place of him.

When arrangements were sufficiently advanced, Almagro sent ahead 100 mounted soldiers and thousands of the Indians, in relays. These followed the royal road south of Lake Titicaca into the province of the Charcas and eventually all met up at the *tampu* of Paría. There, not very far from the highly saline lake of Aullaga (now Poopó), Captain Juan Saavedra set up camp and began organising stores. Under his orders, as transmitted through Paullu, the Indians slaughtered llamas and prepared *charqui* from their flesh; maize, beans and peppers were stored in twenty-five pound bags; and flour was prepared from *chuño* (dehydrated potatoes).

In August 1535, Almagro set out from Cuzco with the main force, which made good time and joined up with the advance party at Paría. The combined forces then proceeded south. Despite the presence of Paullu and Villac Umu, they soon encountered resistance, this being offered by natives from the *montaña* below Charcas. These Indians fought with bows and arrows (weapons never used by the Incas), and Almagro's horse was killed. In falling it almost crushed him.

At Tupiza on the upper San Francisco river (a tributary of the Río de la Plata), the army of conquest came to a halt as Paullu intercepted a messenger and a relay of Indians who were on their way north with tribute gold from Chile. One Spaniard estimated the treasure as worth "90,000 castellanos [one castellano being a sixth of an ounce or 4.55 grams] and others valued it as three times that amount". "The gold was a sight to see," one of them remembered, ". . . it acted on [the men] like a horse being pricked by a spur." This gold was assumed to be part of the ransom of Atahuallpa, delayed, by the immense distances involved, from reaching its destination. The Spaniards were particularly impressed by one gold nugget weighing 14 pounds and had high hopes for the success of their expedition.

Immediately after this incident Villac Umu disappeared and half the Indian carriers with him, though (mainly because Paullu remained behind) Almagro did not at first see any sinister connection between the two events. However, his anger was roused, and this was reflected in the manner in which he replaced the Indians who had taken off. "Any natives," wrote Padre Cristóbal de Molina, "who would not voluntarily accompany the expedition were taken along bound by ropes and chains. They imprisoned them at night and led them by day, loaded, dying of hunger. . . . When the mares of some Spanish horse foaled, these Indians were forced to carry them in litters. . . ."

Cristóbal de Molina (of Santiago—to distinguish him from a padre of the same name who came from Cuzco) was born in 1491 and travelled widely in

Europe before he arrived in Peru in 1532. His presence on the expedition was part of the ritual of conquest, for the Crown and Church desired spiritual benefits as well as material gain. Seeing it as their sacred duty to impose their religion on all Indians—by exhortation if possible, but by force if necessary—the Spaniards took their beliefs with them as they took their horses and their swords. Before any hostilities could be opened, it was necessary for the officiating priest or a royal notary to read the Requirement, which stated the Spanish Emperor's claim, as sanctioned by the Pope, to the whole land of the Americas, and urged the natives to cast off their evil beliefs and embrace Christianity. If an interpreter were available, the strange document was translated, but, if not, it was read in Spanish, leaving the Indians to absorb the meaning by some unfathomable means. If they accepted it and allowed the Spaniards to settle, there would be no hostilities, but, if they did not, blood and fire were sanctioned.

"I went," Cristóbal de Molina wrote to his King, "with Almagro in his discoveries to Chile." And he became one of its historians. Almagro himself was illiterate—which he admits; for a document dated 2 November 1537 bears only Almagro's *rubrica*, which was his official form of signature. It was countersigned by the notary: "*at Almagro's request, as he stated that he did not know how to write.*"

But "illiteracy" should not be regarded as perjorative or synonymous with "stupidity"; in fact, we are informed by this same *padre* "that as Almagro wished your Majesty to be well informed, he sent along one called *Henao, to delineate all the routes* he traversed and discovered, that is to say from Tumbés (in Perú) 3° south latitude to River Maulé, 35° south latitude, which by land is 1,024 leagues or (3,072 miles) *and draw as well the nations and tribes* with their dress rites and each one in the manner of living—as well as many other things." This last part of the report and *Henao's* drawings have not come to light. However, there is a well-known and often reproduced illustration of an Araucanian Indian of Chile—the earliest known illustration of an Indian wearing a poncho which appeared in a book listed in the bibliographies as "Marcgrav", but more correctly Georg, Markgrav de Leibstad (Markgraf being a title), 1648 *Historiae rerum naturalum Brasilia . . . et Chilensibus,* Ludgum, 1648 (reprinted São Paulo, 1942).

Molina describes how the native porters worked without rest all day long, ate only a little roasted maize and water. . . . "One Spaniard on this expedition locked twelve Indians in a chain and boasted that all twelve had died in it. When one Indian died, they cut off his head so as to terrify the others and to avoid undoing . . . the padlock on the chain."

This was precisely what Indians did to Indians in their wars. The Spaniard feared. He travelled in the unknown, he was a prisoner of space, and terror was a weapon.

Pedro de Cieza in an attempt to give balance to these outward acts of cruelty asked his readers to remember the "unheard of trials which such a small number of Spaniards underwent in so vast an area . . . the amazing episodes that have taken place in the wars and discovery of 1,600 leagues of territory and the hunger, thirst, death and fatigue." Then in moral judgment: "I would not condemn the employment of Indian carriers when it is done in moderation . . . but if four Indians were wanted, he took a dozen . . . and there were many Spaniards who made the poor Indians carry their whores in hammocks borne on their shoulders. Were one to enumerate the great evils . . . there would be no end of it for they thought no more of killing Indians than if they were useless beasts. I do not claim that these evil deeds were committed by all the Spaniards, for I know and saw many instances of good treatment the Indians received."

Thus they proceeded, death stalking them, to Jujuy (now in Argentina), where the main highway met the lateral to Tucumán. The road over which they travelled varied in width from ten to twenty feet and can still be clearly seen, as the scrub removed centuries ago has not returned, and the road surface is only the naturally hard sandy soil of the *puna*. At the usual intervals of twelve to fifteen miles are the remains of *tampus*, many of which have recently been rediscovered by a group of hardy Argentinian archaeologists. It was one of the marvels of the Inca communication system that roads and resting places, bridges, and the *topos* to mark distances could be erected in such isolated areas and maintained.

On the plains of Chuciana (modern-day Salta), Almagro and his men rested while waiting for the snow in the passes to melt. Throughout the spring of 1536 the Indians (referred to in the records as mere "pieces of service") prepared the stores for the next few months, while the smith set up his portable anvil and pounded out horseshoes from copper (there was no iron). Copper horseshoes were expendable, but horses were not.

The whole army began to move forward when scouts reported that the snows had melted. However, the thaw brought about a rise in the river Huachipas, in crossing which many Indians were drowned.

Arenal, a wide stretch of barren desert, was passed in six days of gruelling travel, at the end of which bald mountains were seen, and nestling between them a lake, which the Spaniards christened Laguna Blanca (though it was only in so far as its waters were highly saline and undrinkable). The road, still clearly marked, was unpaved, as the tortured earth had a residual mantle of pebbles, stone and sand that provided a hard enough surface anyway. The only vegetation thereabouts was provided by short, tough, miserably-leafed bushes that from the distance appeared to grow thickly, but close to were seen to be widely spaced. They proved useless as fodder for man and beast alike. The Inca engineers had to clear these bushes to make way for the road, which can still be seen crossing the *altiplano* in an unerring straight line.

*Tampus* in this desolate region were constructed of *pirca* (loose stone), cemented, where possible, with *llanac allpa* ("earth that sticks"). In certain favourably located areas, impressively large and well planned centres were erected, many of which have been excavated by archaeologists. Mummies, Inca footgear, headdresses, weavings, ceramics and metalwork (of copper, bronze, silver and even gold) have been found. In addition, on-the-spot investigation (no mean feat at these altitudes, where travel often must be undertaken on foot or by mule) has shown that, far from there being only one Inca road in these parts, there was a whole network of roads criss-crossing the Andes between Argentina and Chile. The achievement of the Incas in engineering such a road system is staggering enough when one considers how inhospitable and desolate this area is, but it is near incredible when one realises that they did not begin the conquest of this area until 1471, only about sixty-five years before Almagro arrived there.

Tupac Yupanqui, called Topa Inca, was installed as Inca in 1473. Before that, while he was still a field general, he had received embassies from tribes far to the south, in Tucma (later Tucumán), Argentina, and these tribes had been absorbed into the Inca empire. On acceding to the position of Inca, however, Topa Inca decided, wrote Garcilaso de la Vega, "on a greater undertaking . . . the conquest of Chile". Guides and scouts were sent out, precise intelligence gathered and transmitted. As water and basic food supplies were scarce, the army advanced in relays: after a reconnaissance in force, three armies of 10,000 advanced to the province of Cuquimpú (Coquimbo), where Chile actually begins. The tribal states of Atacama, then Copiapó, submitted, for seeing a host of 30,000 men "they immediately surrendered, which delighted the Inca, who saw the gates of the Kingdom of Chile open before him". Following this, the Inca armies pushed on to the Maulé river, 200 miles south of present-day Santiago and thirty-five degrees south of the equator. There, after meeting fierce resistance from the Purumacha tribe, the Inca called a halt to his army's progress, and the Maulé river became the southernmost frontier of the Inca empire. Inca rule was soon firmly established in the newly conquered area and an efficient communications network developed.

## CHAPTER THIRTEEN

## The Atacama Desert — and Beyond

In order to penetrate the province of Chile, it was necessary for Almagro and his men to cross the Andes, which they did by way of the pass they called "San Francisco". The mountains they saw as they climbed towards it were at first bare, then, beyond 13,200 feet, snow-capped; the pass itself, seventy miles long, was snow-bound, and hunger and cold waged continuous warfare against the tired army. Almagro, realising how exposed his forces would be in the claustrophobic pass, had feared ambush, but there was no need for it with nature itself so hostile.

Within the fifty years before the arrival of Diego Almagro, the Incas had set up a road network of simple, albeit efficient, communications—roads, bridges, *chasqui* system with tampus—with so complete a political domination that its structure withstood the civil wars between Atahualpa and Huascar, and withstood the psychological cultural shock of the arrival of the "bearded ones" and the death of Atahuallpa; now, in 1536 they had their actual presence.

Hunger, snow and cold appeared in continuous cacaphony. The Indian carriers were lightly sandled or barefoot with one woollen poncho, the Spaniards were not too heavily clothed under their steel corselets, although the King of Spain had sent Almagro a fur coat. The horses were fully vulnerable to the frigid winds, the freezing nights, the grassless earth.

Man at this altitude is subject to *"soroche"*; a lack of oxygen brings on severe headaches, dizziness, the sort of symptoms described by Juan de Acosta: "The air is so thin and penetrating that it goes through one's bowels". Then the glare of the reflecting sun on the snow brought on snow-blindness—the Indians called it *surumpi*, when as a side effect the inside of the eyelid developed sharpened tubercules that made it painful to close the eyes. Such was the passage of the Pass of San Francisco. The Indians, "the pieces of service", died by the thousands, the horses, a still more painful loss, died by the hundreds. These astronomical losses were not mere Spanish rodomontade, for when Juan de Herrada followed Almagro's spoor a few months later, the dead Indians were so many that the frozen bodies were piled like so many ashlars to construct barriers against wind and snow. As for the dead horses, in the deep freeze, they supplied the food for the myrmidons on the way to the new green pastures of Chile. The case of Jerónimo de Castilla is typical. His body was so stiff from frostbite he actually took off his toes with his boot one night and failed to discover their loss until the following morning.

Diego de Almagro, aware that succour must appear, chose the best twenty horses, placed the Inca Paullu on one and set off down to the coast, less than one hundred miles away.

No one recorded the reaction of the coast dwelling Diaguitas when suddenly out of the desert twenty horsemen appeared. The tribesmen living about the fringes of land bordering the River Copiapó were perhaps too startled to react and the Spaniards too hungry to worry. Whatever did occur must have been glossed over by the gentle words of Inca Paullu.

Aid was needed, the Inca's word was law and it was freely given. A long line of Indians carrying food and water followed a company to the pass of San Francisco.

Almagro took in quickly enough his strategic position. Copiapó, the principal centre of the coastal Diaguitas, was 50 miles back from the sea, located on both sides of a river, the fertile Copiapó, and under extensive agriculture (maize, beans, chile pepper, squash, yuca, potatoes). However, north and south was the Atacama Desert, the driest in the world, where rain never fell.

The tribe, which had filtered down through the passes of the towering Andes, were an offshoot of the more cultural Diaguitas who lived in what is now upper Andean Argentina, famous as pottery makers and artisans in casting massive copper and bronze objects.

Since it never rained, houses were made of sun-dried brick, adobe, or, as along the river, built of reeds plastered over with *llancac-allpa*, "sticky earth". Their material wealth, in Spanish eyes used to towering mounds of Inca gold and silver, was nothing: pottery was mostly utilitarian, fishing supplemented the farinaceous diet, copper pieces cast in the form of halberds, metal-tipped spears they had, gold and silver none. Each Indian had 4 to 8 llamas, the chieftains 12 to 20. Food was simple and monotonous, fresh maize was roasted or boiled; when dried and ground, it was made into a water-flour paste which was baked in the ashes. Stews made of dried meat or fish were extended by beans or corn and enlivened by fiercely sharp chile peppers. Salt leached from the sea was a trade item. Meals were taken twice daily just before high noon and again at dusk. This, too, was once the Spanish way before they adopted the midday meal: *almuerzo* ("lunch") was in word and action Arabian.

The loss in crossing the Andes was appalling: over five thousand Indians dead, 170 horses and seven Spaniards, although these had been killed before entering the Pass of San Francisco. Yet Almagro knew that three ships were sailing down the coast with supplies, three different groups of reinforcements were expected coming overland, and the Daguitas, even with his depleted cavalry, would offer little resistance. So certain was he of this that he ordered a festival and at its height seized thirty of their chieftains. Almagro wanted to know the fate of three Spanish scouts who, disobeying his orders, had gone ahead of him. There were means of extracting this information. The Spaniards had been killed, which must have been expected. On the basis of *lex talenis*—the law of retaliation—the chieftains, on the basis of ten for one, were burned alive.

Almagro had made his mark.

The march southward was carried on following the marked road, a pathway cleared of all stones or vegetation to the standard width of 25 feet. Water was carried. At first, because of the intense heat and the glare of the sun reflecting on the nitrate-covered sand-gravel, they moved at night, but then they found that the small rills pouring off the mountain did not run at night. Puzzled, they sought an answer: it was found that the warmth of the sun melted the glaciers and in full sun the small rills carried down water. At sundown this stopped. Those who knew the deserts of Perú to the north knew that rain did not fall on the desert coast. The sky was often overcast, rain hung in the clouds like unshed tears but did not fall. Why? The question interested them not in the abstract, for the reasons were a matter of life or death as was the manner in which their leader could prognosticate when and where water would be found.

More, three vessels despatched from Lima with life-sustaining supplies were far behind schedule because of the contrary winds. Everywhere along the 2,500-mile-long desert coast the wind blew fiercely northward; depending on its strength, it hindered or aided shipping. Often the arrival of the noon-breeze blowing across the nitrate pampas of Chile broke with a roar that heralded its coming.

The *conquistador* knew the sea to be very cold, that the northern current was strong, varying between 3–6 knots an hour. Did the current produce the winds? Jose de Acosta, the learned Jesuit who travelled on these coasts in 1590 and had such trouble with *soroche* found the winds ". . . troublesome and unwholesome. . . . The sky was clouded, yet it never rains . . . a wonder of nature, never to rain upon the coast and ever to have one wind . . ."

The movements of the sea and the reason of the Humboldt Current arising near the Antarctic and moving on an average of 100 miles width along the entire coast to the equator was due, of course, to the whirl of the spinning earth. The current striking the coast caused an upwelling of deep cold water, and the winds carried this colder water through what is essentially a tropical clime, filled with minute sealife called plankton. These attracted fish, which, in turn, attracted rich bird life. Almagro and his men were constantly surprised by overcast days contradicted by brilliant sunsets which were out of reach of the meteorological phenomena of the coast. The cold air of the current lowered the temperature that moved across the deserts.

Despite a definitive answer to the reasons why, Almagro was able as a good leader to move his men through a blazing heat at midday and rest during the sharp cold at night, for in a desert, refrigeration sets in as soon as the sun sets. By the time they had covered one hundred miles and reached the territory of the Picunches, "The North People", they had arrived at Coquimbo: there they had the welcome news that one of the three ships, the *Santiago*, had arrived.

Food, bacon, salt pork, bread, onions, garlic, sugar and wine, horses, pigs and cattle, iron horseshoes, saddles, clothing, new steel partisans, those kind whose foliated razorsharp edges can wreak havoc on human flesh—these brought their delights, gastronomical and tactical.

Coquimbo, watered by the Choapa River, had a bay and a natural harbour, fertile valleys, and, had Almagro been looking for it (which he was not), one of the largest deposits of copper in the Southern Hemisphere. Golden cities, "another Perú", were his object.

It was here that Almagro heard of Gonzalo Calvo.

The surprise when they met should not have surprised anyone. Somehow these things were always happening during the conquest. In Yucatan, Hernan Cortés found Gerónimo de Aguila who had been shipwrecked, captured by the Mayas, carted off to slavery and was there in 1519 to aid Cortés make the conquest of the Aztecs. In Colombia, Jiménez de Quesada, the Spanish commander was sent into exile and a knowable death for theft of Chibcha emeralds; yet he survived and met a company of El Dorado seekers who had climbed up the sides of the Andes and brought about one of the strangest confrontations. And now here was Gonzalo Calvo.

Who was Gonzalo Calvo? How had a Spaniard been able to make his way alone 2,000 miles from Perú, passing through one of the most desolate deserts in the world and through peoples understandably fiercely hostile to the Spanish, then find not a lone refuge but a position of considerable influence among the Piunches? He adopted Indian dress, learned the language well without forgetting his own, he had wives, a house and position. However, his long hair failed to hide his disfeatures: both his ears had been cut off. He had, he told Padre Cristóbal de Molina, been mutilated by the orders of Francisco Pizarro for some miscreant deed, and being unable to endure this disfigurement he deserted and moved down to Chile—precisely in what manner is not explained.

The tribe in which Gonzalo Calvo threw his lot lived in the fertile Aconcagua Valley, watered by a river of the same name, which came out of the snows of the melting glaciers of the heaven-towering peak of Aconcagua, the highest (23,000 feet) in the Western Hemisphere. Under it was another pass—the Uspallata—used by the Incas and through which an Inca road with *tampus* had been constructed. Although the valley offered much in the way of permanent settlement, fertile valleys of subtropical temperature, rich mineral sources of iron, copper, lead, silver, gold, manganese, none of these earth-riches could be converted immediately into usable loot.

The army, now swelled to over seven hundred men—for it had been joined by reinforcements brought by Ruy Diaz, a group which included Almagro's young son Diego, aged fifteen—made the passage southward in good order, with, at first, no difficulties.

Then suddenly they were attacked. Almagro had kept strict discipline and did not allow his men to provoke or pillage. They had the good will of Gonzalo Calvo and his tribe, so why the attack? Then it occurred to him that the interpreter Felipillo was missing. A determined manhunt found him with numbers of *Yana-Kona*, Indian carriers who were planning to decamp.

Felipillo's turn had come. Although his original native name is unrecorded, his personal history is well known. When in 1527 Francisco Pizarro with his slender forces made the first Peruvian contact at Tumbez, the large most northern Inca coastal city, he decided to leave behind two of his company, Alonso Molina and Ginés, a manumitted negro slave. They were to learn the language and details of the country pending Pizarro's return. In turn Pizarro took two young men of the Tumbes tribe back to Spain, one of which was called by the diminutive "Felipillo".

Pizarro's arrival in Spain, with gold, incredibly beautiful weavings of vicuña fibres, silver beakers, three llamas and two Indians, and with high talk of finding the Kingdom of Gold excited, as was natural, great public curiosity. And so Felipillo—little Philip, was paraded about with the llamas, the feathered cloaks, the golden treasures so as to awe the king, from which a royal consent to capitulation-contract was expected and acquired. Felipillo slipped out of his Indian poncho, had his hair cut, purchased ballooning knee breeches and rough-skin leather shoes, a doublet of slashed sleeves, a linen neck ruff and a small sugar-loaf hat. In four years he learned to read and write Spanish.

When Francisco Pizarro returned to Tumbes in 1532 armed in body and soul for the conquest, Felipillo was the interpreter. The ruin of his native land suggested change and he found, through inquiry, that there had been in the interval of his absence, that is between 1527 and 1532, a civil war between Atahuallpa and Huascar, contenders for the empire, that Atahuallpa had killed many of his tribesmen, the Tumbes, doubtlessly some of his *ayllu*. The Tumbes had, in fact, only recently been conquered by the Incas (1465), and the Quechua they spoke was grafted on their own Yungas-speech.

As they travelled onwards and upwards, Felipillo became aware that he

was out of his element. He did not know the highlands, his Quechua speech
was impure and five years absence had not helped his vocabulary. Felipillo
was then the only Spanish interpreter. Because of Atahuallpa's treatment of
his own people, the Tumpiz, he was implacably hostile, constantly giving a
different "colouring" to Atahuallpa's retorts to Spanish accusations. Using
the advantage of his position, he tried to get to one of Atahuallpa's con-
cubines, a forwardness which, when it reached the ears of the imprisoned
Lord Inca, sent him in a towering rage: "That such an insult should have
been offered by so base a person as this Felipillo was an indignity," he said,
"more difficult to bear than his imprisonment," Under Inca Peruvian law
such a crime could only be expiated not merely by his death but by that of his
whole family and kindred.

However, it was the Lord-Inca Atahuallpa who was garrotted.

Now in the winter years of 1536 it came the turn of Little Philip. He had
been sent down with Almagro since neither the Inca Paullu or others could
understand Spanish. These tribes on the coast who did not speak Quechua had
to speak to one who spoke their speech and that of the Inca, which then was
translated to Felipillo and he in turn to end the triple cascade, gave it in
Spanish to Almagro.

A turn of the screws on his thumbs brought out all that Almagro needed
to know: he was briefly tried, briefly hanged and forever buried.

After this hiatus of deception and death, Almagro broke up his army in
three sections: one under Gomez de Alvarado in July 1536, moved southward through a landscape which was heavily forested and scantily populated,
almost without opposition, until he came to the River Maulé which a crude
reading of their astrolabe told to be 35° south latitude.

There was an Inca garrison. When the Spaniards tried to go beyond it,
they ran into the fierce Araucanians. The resistance of the Araucanians, the
weather (it rained and it was cold) and the lack of loot brought him to a full
stop. "Even", as Padre Cristóbal de Molina wrote, "though there was
strong evidence of earth-riches he did not remain. Since the land was not
teeming with gold he found no good in it."

Almagro himself, meanwhile, had led his party around the fertile lands of
Aconcagua. The Spaniards scoured the land like a moving throng of army
ants, but found no impressive architecture, no indications of wealth even
though there were mines being worked, as the histographer Oviedo said,
"as well as if the Spaniards had been engaged in them and so worked that the
best pan produced a bare twelve grains of gold."

The disillusionment was complete. Chile-in-Fancy became Chile-in-Fact.
Almagro wanted another Peru and there was but one Peru. He now knew
that the gold they had been given on the way in Charcas-Bolivia, impressive
and glittering with golden nuggets, had been a lure to lead him and his men
to Chile and destruction. This deception Diego Almagro at first suspected

had been instigated by Francisco Pizarro. The suspicion was right, the suspect person was wrong: it was Manco Inca.

There was only one Peru and that was Peru.

His men who had followed him without plaint now loudly clamoured to be led back to Peru, to Cuzco which they, as well as Almagro, believed lay in his province. For if you remain here and die here, they reminded Almagro, "you will have nothing to leave to your son but the name of Don Diego".

Extrasensory perception or even lower in the realms of perception, the ability of foresight, is not often granted human beings: certainly not to the here-and-now attitudes of one such as Diego Almagro. For had Peru not been so great an *idée fixe*, to him would have fallen Potosí, the greatest silver mine in the world, the tin mines of Bolivia, the only such in the New World, the copper lodes of Chile, the continent's largest reserve, the nitrate fields of Atacama and some of the most salubrious earth on the American continent; and more, it would have saved his life, that of his son and regiment of his followers, instead of which . . .

INSTEAD of which within five years it would fall—at least the Chilean portion of it—into the hands of Pedro de Valdivia. He was born, it is believed, in 1502, and most definitely at the district of La Serena (in the province of Estremadura in south-west Spain), although fourteen villages claim the honour. His father was an *hidalgo* but his mother "of very noble descent": so he took her name. In his own *probanzas de servicios* written in order to obtain awards he averred that from "the age of 19 he served as a soldier, in imitation of my forebears who were and still are employed in this same career of arms. . . . I served His Majesty in Italy in the time of Prospero Colonna . . . was present at the taking of Milano . . . served in Flanders and was with His Majesty in Valencia when the King of France came against it. . . . I came to the Indies in 1535. . . ."

He fought at the Battle of Las Salinas in 1538 where all of the "Men of Chile", as they became known, were mostly killed and Diego Almagro captured. Valdivia witnessed the will and testament of Almagro. For his services to the Pizarros he was given the vast estate of La Canela which would have been Almagro's fief including a silver mine at Porco, whose veins made him at 37, after the Pizarros', the richest man in Peru.

In his correspondence with friends he questioned his own sanity, when he asked and was given by Hernando Pizarro permission to go to Chile and settle the country. There were still about many veterans of Diego Almagro's trek whose bodies maimed from festering veldt sores physically told of the hazards. Still he went.

Five years later, in 1545, he addressed a letter-manuscript to the *High-Placed Lord Hernando Pizarro*, telling at first hand the whole of his trip thither and the settlement of Chile. Having had no news from Peru, he did not know that his "High-Placed Lord" in September 1545 resided in La Mota prison in Medina del Campo, awaiting his King's displeasure (he emerged twenty-six years later).

Valdivia explained that he raised 15,000 pesos worth of horses and arms and set off, "about January in the year 1540", following the spoor of Almagro's trail "equipped, not so much with necessities as with the will to overcome all obstacles. . . ."

It took him eleven months to arrive at Aconcagua, "which Almagro had called the Vale of Chile", and once there, tried to impress on the Indians that he had come to settle "and colonize the land", that the Indians could serve the Christians as the Incas and *Caciques* did at Cuzco. Valdivia had maize, wheat and vegetables planted and "on the 20th of February 1541, I founded the city which I called Santiago".*

Despite the disruption of the Inca empire, the death of its principals, the breakdown of its system, *still* Manco Inca, who set up his neo-Inca realm in Vilcapampa one hundred miles north-east in the *montaña* from Macchu Picchu, was able to send messages all over the land, including Chile. He ordered the Indians to destroy Valdivia's settlement of Santiago. They did so. "And so faithfully," Valdivia wrote, "did they carry out the Manco Inca's instructions that they even destroyed our sheep and burned the wool." Santiago City was razed. However, with the help of the Yanaconas (who sided with the Spaniards) they rebuilt the incipient settlement.

"We had a little maize left which we were able to find, this we sowed. We saved two little pigs and a hog, one hen and one chicken, that was all. In the first year we were able to gather twelve *fanegas* of wheat which we had sown."

Then there was mutiny. By an overlapping of consents and agreements, capitulations or contracts, privileges and rights, and Crown and its Council of the Indies—in a *lapsus* for which they were famous—had given sprightly little Pedro Sancho de la Hoz a similar contract for the settlement of Chile, not precisely but so vaguely worded that as Pedro Sancho de la Hoz was so well placed through marriage at court, Valdivia did not think it prudent to oppose him.

IN October 1536, however, Almagro did not know any of this. He had

---

* The author, by the courtesy of the Huntington Library in Pasadena, California, has microfilmed the whole collection of 3,000 pages of manuscripts (1,646 folios) that form the Pizarro-La Gasca collection (years 1544–48), one of the most valuable of such outside of Spain. Although some of the La Gasca papers have been printed in Spain *very few of Pizarro-La Gasca papers have been published*. The author intends and has been granted permission to edit the whole of this collection provided that life, money and happiness and *el tiempo por gastarlos*—that is—the time to spend them, is provided by the right sources.

decided to go "back to Peru". But how . . . and which way? Not one among them desired to return through the frigidly vertiginous passes of the Andes and as an alternative before them lay the desolation of the Atacama Desert. It was by dead reckoning 1,300 miles back to Arequipa, their first destination in Peru.

Beyond Copiapó, no one had knowledge of the conditions or the presence of water. Almagro, as usual, exhibited his capacity as leader. One of his *capitanos*, Ruy Diaz, who was soon to spend some uncomfortable moments in the ensuing months as a captive-hostage of Manco Inca at Vilcapampa, was given charge of the ship *Santiago*. It carried water and food and eighty passengers even though the vessel was less than fifty feet in length. Its programme was to keep pace with the land army and as well move ahead to see that wells were dug at the space of each day's *jornada*, that is, twenty kilometres.

Men were to be sent forward at intervals six at a time. In this way each waterhole was sufficient to supply the small group, horses and Indians, and would refill itself by the time the next group arrived.

In this manner they went forward. Past the Point of the Flamingos, where salt ponds held hundreds of nesting birds, then to Cachinal where a waterhole was prepared, next over the reddish rock outburst of Llano Colorado, then to El Pozo, where there was a prepared well of sweet water—*agua dulce*.

At Copiapó, the valley which they had first encountered when they crossed the Andes, they met a new party who had followed them. Juan de Herrada, with his group of eighty mounted men, had just come down from the Andean crossing, suffering as Almagro had, expecting that they had the benefit of eating the flesh of dead horses left behind by the first party.

Juan de Herrada brought with him official documents from Spain wherein he found that while Almagro was confirmed in his governship of Chile, yet the wily Hernando Pizarro had argued the Council of the Indies to "push"— that is, to "extend"—the territory of Francisco Pizarro southward by 70 leagues. This made certain that Cuzco lay within his boundary.

All else was overshadowed by the fact that all Peru was in revolt; led by the young Manco Inca, Cuzco was under siege. To Peru! but which way, desert or cordillera? In a building they had erected as church, mass was said—it was the first time that little Cristóbal de Molina had a chance to perform a matter of this divine sort—and he asked God's guidance. A hand vote after services was unanimous for the desert crossing.

At a place called Botija at 25° they prepared to turn inward. The sea, cold, wind-bound, with tremendous thundering waves, was alive with birds and through night and day with the bark of sea lions. It was their habitat. The coastal Indians hunted them for their skins and from these sewed and inflated large pontoons, two fixed together in the manner of a catamaran, with a light platform on which one, or at most two, could go into the sea to fish with harpoon, net or hook.

At Botija below 24° south the Almagro forces regrouped and prepared for their assault on another aspect of nature. The Andean rock spine lay like an unbroken wall 2,000 or more feet (600m) high. To reach it at this point they were to cross 60 leagues, that is, 180 miles of sheer desolation with only one known waterhole—Aguas Blancas—between them and the next water source in higher climes.

It was here that Almagro made the sort of gesture that made all his followers beholden. He called them together and before them destroyed all of his loans to them for equipment. All these details are furnished by many who accompanied Almagro, those veterans writing to the Crown, in material letters known as *Probanza de Servicios*, proofs of service. One of them, Diego de Pantoja, declared that "I returned to Peru with Almagro by way of the coastal deserts," conquering and pacifying many lands and provinces and passing many despoblados, from Atacama to Arequipa.

The Men of Chile were amazed by the fidelity of Inca Paullu. He suffered as all others, even more so, for he had been born and bred in the Andes. He gave invaluable assistance by his mere presence, the local tribal groups all supplying water, food, aid. On the grim trek along the Atacama Desert it was the Inca Paullu's men who guided the expedition, dug and cleaned the wells before each arrival of the next contingent. Without this aid Almagro would never have lived those eighteen months which was as a small journey in hell. A *conquistador* admitted, writing in 1540, that Inca Paullu "could have easily done them serious damage had he wished, for he knows much about warfare and because so many men obey him".

At length the expedition reached the sixty-mile-long Salar de Atacama, a high desert with a large salt lake. Around the lake's margin, at an altitude of 7,580 feet, were small, compact villages of Indians, whom the Spaniards referred to under the general name of "Atacameño". They spoke a language called Kunsa, which was quite different from either the Aymara of Bolivia or the Quechua of Peru. They herded llamas and alpacas, of which they have left realistic rock drawings, and tilled the soil, tapping the outflow from the glaciers high in the mountains surrounding them to obtain water for irrigation and so extend the area under cultivation. They also had contact with the sea, which they reached by following the valley created by the river Loa (which made an oasis in the desert at Calamar) down to Cobija, where the coastal Indians kept their fleet of boats made from inflated sealskins.

The Atacameños, were the middlemen of the region, trading goods from the mountains (that is, copper and bronze tools, alpaca wool, tanned llama leather, and various Andean food products) for fish, shellfish, seaweed, seal leather, whalebone and other things drawn from the abundant sea. Both the coastal and mountain dwellers obtained what they needed, and the Atacameños drew a profit from the transaction.

The Spaniards found nothing to loot: little gold, some copper, ordinary ceramic wares, large amounts of skilfully carved wooden objects, but nothing to arouse their acquisitive instincts. The Atacameño way of life illustrated a formula for survival: if one is defenceless the best thing is to be poor.

The Atacameños had only recently (about 1460) been brought under the Inca yoke, which rested lightly on them. The roads they had built for the Incas are still to be seen: ten feet wide, unpaved, with the usual resting places. At the northern end of the brackish lake a road leading through the high sierras to Bolivia met the road running due north over the desert. On the advice of Paullu, Almagro decided to continue along the desert road, which he was told was the quickest way to Cuzco; following this route, the army passed the towering active volcano of Atacama, paused at the fresh-water lake of Chiu-chiu, and then proceeded for 200 miles over the high, uninhabited wasteland to Tarapacá. Sixty miles from the sea and less than 2,000 feet above sea level, Tarapacá is a valley "poor in water" and suffering extremes of temperature. The ground there seemed irretrievably sterile, but where it had been irrigated and guano (the nitrogen-rich droppings of sea birds) used as fertiliser, agriculture flourished. "This guano", wrote Pedro de Cieza, "is gathered from the bird-islands off the coast. The natives go to them in their inflated sealskin rafts and bring back the guano . . . [which] greatly enriches the ground and increases the yield even if the soil was once barren."

One hundred miles over the same general type of terrain separated Almagro's army from Tacna, and although the letters of "the Men of Chile", as they were henceforth known, groan with the words "poor in water," the region of the *puquios* appeared. Puquios were huge artificial underground water reserves—much like Roman *cisternas*. If it lay on a water course, water was gathered from infrequent rains or trickling rills and held. Tacna was an oasis at an altitude of 1,800 feet a few miles from the sea, with "a grand population of *Indios* and dotted with great tombs for the dead", none of which at this moment interested the Men of Chile. Since they now travelled a well-organised Inca road, twenty-four feet wide, often with dry stone walls, they were "in these valleys *tambo*-lodgings and storehouses like those in other plains and sand wastes". The Inca road went north to the River Moquegua, turned north, followed near its bank an Indian village which one day would have the same name, Moquegua. Then following the route over gradually rising high country, Garumas, Omata, Puquina, the army came into sight of the high valley of volcanos. One of them, snow-crowned El Misti was actively belching out fumes and ash.

There were many rivers to cross. Just before reaching Arequipa their long-sought goal, Almagro lost his first soldier: death by drowning came upon Francisco de Valdés, age 27, and the son of Gonzalo Fernández de Oviedo y Valdés the royal histographer of the Indies.

OVIEDO, as he is generally known in the bibliographies, has appeared again and again in the variegated history of the Royal Road. Noble as his name suggests, Oviedo had been born in Madrid in 1478, served in the usual ways in Spain and Naples and went out to America in 1513, where he acted in an official capacity in Panamá. He returned to the New World and to the island of Santo Domingo which was the nerve centre of America. Here all ships out of Spain first touched; here all ships bound home from America had their clearance. Oviedo was made royal histographer and subsequently spent thirty-feur of his long seventy-nine years of life in the Americas. Every soldier, *capitán* or governor was interviewed by him, from which he acquired first-hand information of all discoveries. Francisco Pizarro on his way back to Spain in 1527, after the first contact with Peru, gave him his impressions; Hernando Pizarro six years later wrote and then told him of the conquest of Peru. His *Historia de los Indias* was the greatest contemporary account of the opening or closing (depending on ones ethnic point of view) of the Americas. It was because of his eagerness to have first-hand knowledge of the new lands of Chile that he suggested that his own son Francisco accompany Almagro.

"He was," wrote William Prescott, "a man at once a scholar and a man of the world. His curiosity was indefatigable extending to every department . . . He was at once the America's Pliny and their Tacitus. His works abound in portraitures of character, sketched with freedom and animation, his reflections piquant and often rise to a philosophical tone . . . and varied by a multiplicity of personal anecdotes that give a rapid insight into the characters of the parties." Oviedo was the principal historian of Almagro's great expedition into Chile but when relating his son's drowning at the river crossing near Arequipa, he suddenly interjected a personal note. "On the road they crossed a river so deep and furious that it was a miracle that men were not overwhelmed. But here the unfortunate Francisco de Valdés drowned.

"He was the son of *capitán* Gonzalo Fernández de Oviedo y Valdés the chronicler of this history. His death means that I can feel and grieve more intimately with others (who were the Men of Chile) and can be more closely concerned in these adventures." No sooner had he learned of the death of his son, then came the news of the death of his five-year-old grandson. "So although being a reasonable man, my loss cannot but make me sad . . ."


AT Arequipa, which had been founded by Francisco Pizarro the year before, they were welcomed by the handful of Spaniards who had already taken root in this superbly placed city. A little over 7,000 feet altitude, a mere fifty miles from the sea and a good port (Mollendo), warm in the day, cool, even cold, at night, it had been well organised by the Incas. Widely cultivated, irrigated with streams of mountain water, the only problem until the arrival of Almagro was the volcanic action of El Misti, which rose Fujiyama-like to a perfect cone 5,800 metres high. It remained eternally snow-topped even while it threw up flames, fumes and ash.

Diego Almagro would not rest. The whole 3,000 miles of horrendous travel through Andes and desert did not seem then to have made any physical impression on his body, now over sixty. But time had become Diego Almagro's numbering clock so that he need take the shortest route from Arequipa to Cuzco. It was also the most dreaded. From the moment the advance guard of Almagro's army left Arequipa, the Inca road began its climb.

In a straight condor's flight to the first station Quiquijana on the royal road, it is over three hundred kilometres, but a road that scales peaks must appease and appeasement adds hours and distance to a journey. The road never descended below an altitude of 13,800 feet. At such a height there is permafrost, snow, winds and a frigidity that goes through furs, clothes, skins to the very bone marrow. *Hatun-cuna*, midway or about 10 travelling days, has vast ruins, there are remains of *tambos*, and *apacheta*, rock cairns on which Indians in travelling tossed on a propitiary stone to lighten the load or protect the traveller. It is the origin place of rivers, which here are ice-fringed rills. The great River Apurimac has its beginnings here.

The *Ordenanzas, Tampus*, that itinerary of Inca roads and the *tampus* with a list of those Spaniards who held them in fief in 1543, will be remembered, by the first Peruvian governor, Vaca de Castro, as *"the road that goes to the Villa de Arequipa"*. One goes from Quiquijana (which is on the royal road) to Pomacancha, which is located on a lake . . . then to the *tambo* of *Yanaoca*, where the Indians are held by Juan Figueroa and next to Cora, also owned by him . . ."

Then follows the *despoblado* until the road reaches Hatuncana and so on to Arequipa. The *Ordenanzas* warns that the land is *"very cold and very poor"* there is a great scarcity of wood and no food. This is the Inca road, the lateral taken by Almagro and a few years later by another ageless *picaro*, none other than the redoubtable Francisco de Carvajal who wrote to his liege Gonzalo Pizarro on 22 January 1547, "I intend to leave directly for . . . Yanaoca, Quiquijana and Urcos en route to Cuzco . . ."

So disappeared Diego Almagro into the nothingness of *Hatuncana*. And in another year, 1538, into oblivion. He will appear again and again as the royal road makes its way along the desert coast of Peru, 1,000 miles north to Tumbes where it all began, but time will be running out on him. For on April 25, 1538, as Cieza de León recorded in his *Battle of Salinas*, many of the Men of Chile would die. Diego Almagro with the troubled weariness of old age would be legally tried by Hernando Pizarro "as a disturber of these realms," sentenced to be first garrotted, then "taken to the gallows where his head was cut off and then his corpse removed to the house of Ponce de León where it was placed in a shroud".

The discoverer of the whole skein of Inca roads that made up the third quarter, the Colla-suyu, was, as Cieza de León wrote of him, ". . . a man of short stature, with ugly feature but of great courage and endurance. He was liberal but given to boasting . . . he was well informed. A great part of the discovery of these kingdoms was due to him. He was a native of (Almagro) in the Aldea del Rey and born of such humble parentage that it may be said of him that his lineage began and ended with himself . . ."

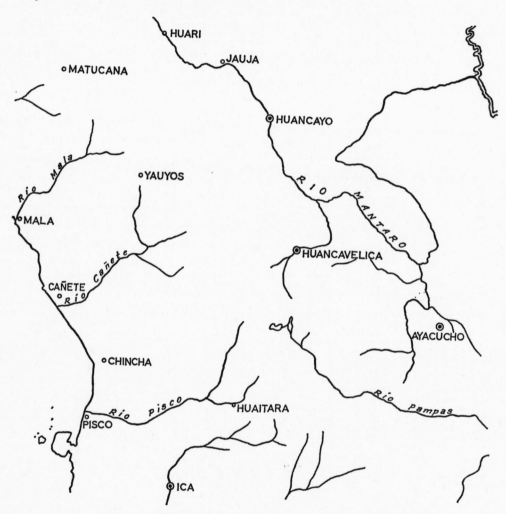

The cities of the coast from Ica and Pisco to Mala and Matucana.

## CHAPTER FOURTEEN

## Chala: The Seaweed Route

The moment that the traveller along the Inca coastal highway leaves
Arequipa on his way north-west, he notices an abrupt change in the landscape: vividly green fields give way to charred, uninhabitable desert. This
marks his entry into Conti-suyu, the western quarter of the Inca empire.

This area includes, said a chronicler, "the regions and provinces neighbouring the Southern Sea [the Pacific], and many of those of the highlands".
The coastal regions (roughly corresponding to the coast of modern Peru)
are desert, punctuated, every thirty miles or so, by fertile river valleys. A
short distance inland, the land rises sharply to the Andes, and the greater
part of the highland area between the coast and Cuzco came within the
jurisdiction of Conti-suyu, though it is impossible to be precise about its
boundaries. What is certain is that this mountainous area was sparsely
populated, inhabited mainly by the hardy Sora and Rucanas tribes.

The life style of the Andean peoples was naturally completely different
from that of the coastal tribesmen; however, from the earliest times the two
groups traded with each other, and were able to supply each other's needs.
The coastal peoples needed a constant supply of llama breeding stocks, for,
while the llama had been successfully acclimatised to the coast, it bred
poorly in the desert. Alpaca wool, the main type used for weaving, was
needed for blankets to keep out the cold at night, and, since the alpaca lives
only at the highest altitudes and does not adapt to the coast, its wool had to
be imported. The same applied to vicuña wool, which was particularly
highly prized, and to copper, gold and silver, metal sources on the coast
being few. In exchange, the coastal tribes provided the Andeans with corn,
potatoes, yuca, chillis, ground-nuts, sweet potatoes and the produce of other
warmth-loving plants. Seaweed, collected in huge quantities at various key
points on the coast, was much sought after in the Andes, since it is nutritious
and has a high iodine content, helping to keep down the incidence of goitre.
Salt, also produced along the coast, was vital to the Andean tribes, since their

diet was based on grain and grain-eaters need salt. In addition, the coastal peoples traded the *potuto* (the large conch shell *Spondylus princeps*), which when bored with a single hole and blown emits a full, awesome sound that the Indians used to "call down the upstairs gods".

Before the whole area came under Inca domination, the coastal and mountain peoples occasionally raided each other's territories, but the differences in climate were too great for either of them to occupy the other's lands for long. However, during the eleventh century a religio-military invasion from the highlands sought to establish the cult of the Weeping God (associated with Tiahuanacu); and, though the occupation proved relatively short-lived, the motif of the cult is found on pottery and weaving in much of the coastal region. Only with the advent of the Incas did a mountain people attempt a full-scale occupation of the coast.

According to Garcilaso de la Vega, who drew the information from memories handed down verbally from his Inca ancestors (on his mother's side of the family), it was the fourth Inca, Mayta Capac, who first took an acquisitive interest in the numerous rich lands that lay west of Cuzco in the Conti-suyu quarter. Since Mayta Capac flourished some time before 1300, this would put the beginnings of the conquest about a century and a half earlier than is generally accepted. Garcilaso also stresses that, in order to reach the people of the Conti-suyu, the Inca was obliged to cross the upper reaches of the Apurimac river by a bridge that "was the first of its kind in the history of the Incas". This bridge, the foundations of which can still be seen, would be the one at Accha, and would have been built about fifty years before the Huaca-chaca if this chronology can be trusted.

The mountain areas to which the Inca first turned his attention were occupied by the Soras and Rucanas, small, but ruggedly built people able to withstand the rigours of living at high altitudes and to carry, for a considerable length of time, a cargo equal to their own body weight. When they submitted to the Incas in about 1400, they were given the task of carrying the litter of the Inca. These blue-clad litter-bearers retained their function well into colonial times.

During the period 1438–71, the Inca conquest of Conti-suyu was completed and the road network extended throughout the area. By 1463 the direct route from Cuzco to the coast was open. However, although the later Incas did use this road to obtain fresh fish from the sea, it (and the region generally) became far less important economically than religiously, since along it lay the site of Pacarictambo, the "Origin *tampu*". According to Inca mythology it was from there that the Incas emerged after the Universal Flood. Conti-suyu was also seen to have some strategic importance, since in 1437 the Inca Pachacutic had received help from the inhabitants of the area in saving Cuzco from the Chancas. No one can be sure where the administrative centre of Conti-suyu was established, though, after the conquest of the coast, the Incas founded in the Cañete valley a huge city (so large it was called "New Cuzco") that may have become the capital of the quarter.

Beginning in Cuzco, the Conti-suyu road ran first to the Chunchul river, where it passed over the Chaquil-chaca or "seaweed bridge" and then proceeded along the north side of Mount Anahuarque. In about 1300, the fifth Inca, Capac Yupanqui, extended the road over the first high divide, past the village of Yuarisque. There the road descended a gorge and bridged the narrow Cusibambamayu, so reaching Pacarictambo and coming within striking distance of the Apurimac canyon. By 1350, the Incas had enough control of the great gorge to bridge it.

Once across the Apurimac barrier the Incas proceeded, says one chronicler, "into that Conti-suyu quarter where there is a place called Pomatambo— midway between Cuzco and the sea. There they fought a series of battles with the redoubtable Sora and Rucanas tribes from which the Inca emerged victorious." By 1450 or before, the Inca armies had advanced as far as the great shallow lake of Parinacochas, which lies at an altitude of 12,000 feet, equidistant (about 110 miles) from Cuzco and the coast. In its mirror-like surface are reflected the snow-covered pinnacle of Cora Cora (the dominant peak of the area), and the thousands of pink-winged flamingoes (parinas) that nest there. The lake is ringed with ruins, the most notable being Incahuasi, which commemorate the success of the Inca conquest. By some time after 1450, the Incas had gained control over all the land between Cuzco and Chala, the coastal terminus of the Conti-suyu road, and from there they extended their dominion over the whole of the desert quarter.

West of Arequipa and about 180 miles east of Chala are the pampas of Vitor, a dry, desolate area lying at an elevation of about 5,000 feet and sparsely clad with sturdy xerophytic plants. The ground there is hard and stony, and offered a natural roadbed to the Inca coastal highway, which passed through the region. The first tampu out of Arequipa was that of Vitor, which was built beside the upper Sihuas river about fifty miles from the coast and about twelve miles from the next tampu, called Sihuas. Both these tampus were given in encomienda to Miguel Cornejo, "a virtuous and generous knight" who shared in the ransom of Atahuallpa and befriended Francisco de Carbajal on his arrival in Peru. Despite the generally hostile terrain, vines were established in some parts, taking advantage of the considerable deposits of volcanic ash.

From Sihuas the road ran along the river valley of the same name on its way towards the sea. Though the seaward slope here is gentle, the area as a whole has a deeply troubled character: the nearby volcanoes, many of which are still active and threatening, have caused enormous rifts and broken up the pampas into deep, transverse valleys. Fertile soil is restricted to narrow bands of riverine land, in between which spurs of the troubled land tumble down and into the sea. In each valley lived a distinct tribe, bound to its neighbours by a common agriculture, but divided from them by space and often by differences in language. The royal road united all these valleys.

On its way to the sea the road crossed the valley of the Majes river, which is fed by the glaciers of the Nudo de Coropuna (21,696 feet high) and in its upper reaches is known as the Colca. There, amid volcanic peaks 10,000–20,000 feet high, Robert Shippee and his photographer, Lt Johnson, found a "forgotten valley of Peru" (see the *National Georgraphic* of January 1934).

Padre Antonio Vásquez de Espinosa, who travelled widely in Peru in the early seventeenth century, and braved hazards that other Spaniards were careful to avoid, reported that the valley belonged to the province of Collaguas (inhabited by the Colcas) and "was highly populated with many villages and well-governed". Yet no one followed up this hint until 1931, when the Shippee–Johnson expedition filmed the valley from the air and found it to be highly cultivated, containing broad, flat table lands, all under cultivation, a network of roads and the most extensive agricultural terraces in the Andes. Many of the roads and terraces had been constructed, with incredible engineering skill, up the face of perpendicular cliffs, and some of the terraces, which were still maintained, had been extended to the very rim of now-extinct volcanoes.

Philip Ainsworth Means, one of the best archaeological historians so far, was prompted by it to undertake a thorough study of the Colcas. He found that they were related to the Soras and Rucanas, and believed themselves to have originated from the volcanoes that so often disrupted their existence. Because of this belief, it was once their practice to bind the heads of their children so that they would look conical like a volcano. Their territory was rich, containing silver mines, salt deposits and many hot springs, and, since the Colca river was too deep to be tapped for irrigation, they constructed conduits to catch the water from melting glaciers. They traded their salt, through middlemen in Cuzco, for coca leaves and dried llama flesh.

After entering the Majes valley, the royal road proceeded to Camaná, one of the most fertile places on the coast. There the Majes flows into the sea— with difficulty, since a high surging surf hinders its outflow; and the surrounding land is low and marshy. The *tampu* of Camaná was originally built right by the sea, but after an earthquake in 1599 it was rebuilt further inland. Camaná has long been famous for its freshwater shrimps, as large as small lobsters; and the houses of the area are unusual in that they are built of a wickerwork of woven sedge canes, plastered all over with greyish adobe.

The next *tampu* along the coast was Uncona, also situated in a verdant river valley. In Inca times the local inhabitants had responsibility for the upkeep of the *tampu*, for supplying the troops stationed there, and for conveying people across the river when it could not be forded. The name "Uncona" recalled to the Spaniards "Ocaña", a town in Toledo, and was changed accordingly.

observed at places going past Pacaritambo, Tantar, Yuarique, then crossing the small contained river over a stone-laid passage called Chaquill-chaca, the seaweed bridge, since this was the principal route over which Chaquill—seaweed—was transported to the upper realms. Along the entire coast, but highly concentrated about the coves and inlets of Chala, the giant kelp *Macrocystis*, grew into wonderful submarine forests of gigantic algae. When waves receded, the algae looked like waving banners, submarine forests, where strips of seaweed grow 70–80 feet long with ribbon-like branches. As it still is to Chinese and Japanese, seaweed was an important item in the otherwise farinaceous diet of the Andean dweller. It was an iodine source which kept down the incidence of goiter, and a source of nutriment and minerals. The kelp was pulled out, dried, packed and carried by llamas or man-pack. Five men over a five-day period could gather five tons of kelp which when dried was reduced to one-fifth of its original weight.

Fishing too was important in and around Chala. The fact that the Conti-suyu road was the most direct route from Cuzco to the coast meant that it was from Chala that the Incas in the capital obtained their fresh fish, which was delivered post-haste by *chasquis*. Like the *tampu* and storage area, the roads, bridges and *chasqui* stations used by these runners are still well preserved in the Chala area.

Just a few miles out of Chala, on the way north-west along the coastal highway, the influence of the hills of Atiquipa becomes apparent. Here the desert is terraced down to the very sea—the only such place in 2,500 miles of coastline. Time has dealt kindly with the curved terrace walls, which even now could be replenished with soil and used successfully.

At Atiquipa a mountain rises abruptly to the height of 4,700 feet and the road just as abruptly turns inland and upward. Though riverless, the valley through which it passes is green and fertile, with many trees. This small area provides the one exception to the rule that it never rains along the coast, one reason being that the highlands, where rain does fall, here stretch right to the sea. Little is known of the original inhabitants of the region, though their numbers must have been considerable. The Incas took full advantage of the favourable conditions and made Atiquipa into a centre of agriculture.

From Atiquipa the Inca road climbed to Cahua-marca ("View Town") the administrative centre of the area. This is a large settlement of stone-roofed, solid although rustic structures, situated at an altitude of 4,000 feet. The views from here are indeed extensive: beyond Atiquipa can be seen the fierce desert known as Arenal de Tanaca, where the constant south-east winds, which approach the desert at an angle of forty-five degrees, keep the immense sand dunes in continuous movement. The modern Pan-American Highway penetrates this area, but it is only by employing a crew of men to maintain the road twenty-four hours a day that it can be kept clear and free for traffic.

The Inca part of Cahua-marca is indicated by the ruins of a sun temple built in the late Inca coastal style, and numerous *colcas*, underground cisterns (*puquios*) and *chullpas* (burial towers). Cahua-marca served as a reconditioning centre for llamas, and was perhaps used also for mating and rearing them, since, while they had been adapted to the coast and were extensively employed there, they failed to breed in the lower lying desert regions. Cahua-marca's altitude and nearness to the coast would have made it an ideal breeding ground.

After continuing through the hills for some distance, the road then descended along the edge of the sand dunes to the valley of the Yauca river, straddling which lay the large *tampu* of Jaqui. At ground level the remains of this *tampu* appear amorphous, but an aerial view reveals a clear pattern of dwellings, a large plaza, a circular defensive wall and the traces of a cultivated area by the river. There are boiling hot springs nearby, and fragments of pottery may be found strewn over the ground. The available evidence suggests that Jaqui was a centre of pilgrimage.

Fifteen miles further on (and a good day's or a full night's ride away) is Acari. The high-placed road there, through country that is freezing by night but terrifyingly hot by day, keeps as straight as the terrain will allow it to; but in places its course is hidden by sand dunes, caused by the wind blowing across from the Arenal de Tanaca.

Acari, located on a bluff overlooking the river of the same name, is reached by a descending stone-laid step road and caught the interest of Vásquez de Epinosa: "Two miles back from the sea, there are groves of trees in the valley and many remarkable constructions of the ancient people, which have lasted to the present time [1617] and will stand forever, as it does not rain."

Acari appears originally to have been a Nasca settlement, but after the Incas gained control of the area (some time after 1350) it was refounded, and became an administrative centre of some importance and prosperity. Where possible, the Incas adapted older structures to suit their needs, rebuilding only where necessary. Locally available building materials were utilised: large pebbles taken from the river were set with adobe; roof beams were wooden, flat and thatched with cane. A large, walled rectangular plaza (160 by 110 feet) was constructed.

At this point the main coastal highway met one of the feeder roads leading to Lake Parinacochas. This road ran due north-east and reached an altitude of about 12,000 feet at Puquio; Hernando Pizarro travelled along it in 1538 on his way to fight Diego Almagro, who soon afterwards met his doom.

65–67. Pre-Inca Chimu engineering: (*top left*) the Great wall of Peru snakes up from the Pacific sea coast into the interior for 100 miles, built by the Chimu to prevent incursions of southern tribes; (*top right*) a circular fortress built to defend the wall; (*bottom*) the Chimu sun temple at Paramonga close to the sea. (*Shippee-Johnson*)

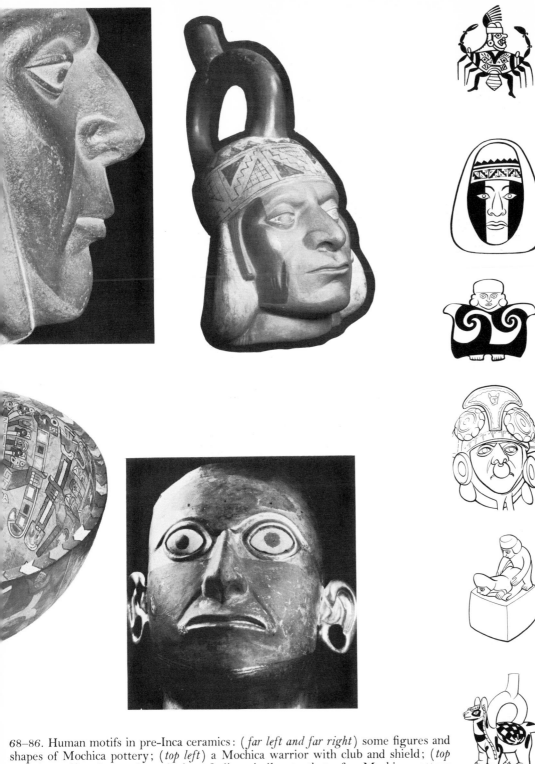

68–86. Human motifs in pre-Inca ceramics: (*far left and far right*) some figures and shapes of Mochica pottery; (*top left*) a Mochica warrior with club and shield; (*top centre*) profile of a modern Andean Indian similar to that of a Mochica pottery portrait; (*top right*) a Mochica "stirrup" vase, a portrait in ceramic usually placed in graves; (*bottom left*) an Inca vase showing ear-spools and headdress; (*bottom centre*) a Nazca cup showing the influence of the Tihuanacan sun god, called "the weeping god"; (*bottom right*) a painted silver head found at Mochi at the pyramid of the sun.

87–95. Mochica and Chimu architecture from the Conti-suyu coast: (*top left*) the remains of the Mochica pyramid of the sun at the foot of a pyramidal mountain; (*left centre*) a ceramic model of a Mochica pyramidal temple; (*centre left*) an example of polychromatic Mochica wall decoration found near Casa Grande; (*centre bottom*)

...aroque eighteenth-century façade modelled by Indians with Indian motifs; (*bottom ...ft*) the restored adobe decorations from one of the palaces at Chan-chan (Chimu ...lture); (*top right*) two Chimu friezes, made of mud, from Chan-chan; (*bottom right*) ...tail of the Inca ruins at Tambo Colorado showing the influence of coastal architecture on Inca building.

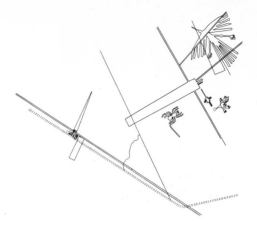

96–100. A desert landscape with figures: (*top left*) the mysterious tree of life, 600 feet high, etched in the sand (8th century?) facing the harbour of Pisco; (*top right*) the fantastic Nazca lines, possibly astronomical symbols, etched (13th century) in the desert north of Nazca; (*centre*) a Nazca figure of a man playing a flute carved in the iron-hard huaranga wood; (*bottom left*) the unwrapped mummy of a Paracas man, still with its woollen headdress; (*bottom right*) a deserted wind-swept landscape north of Lima through which the Inca coastal road ran.

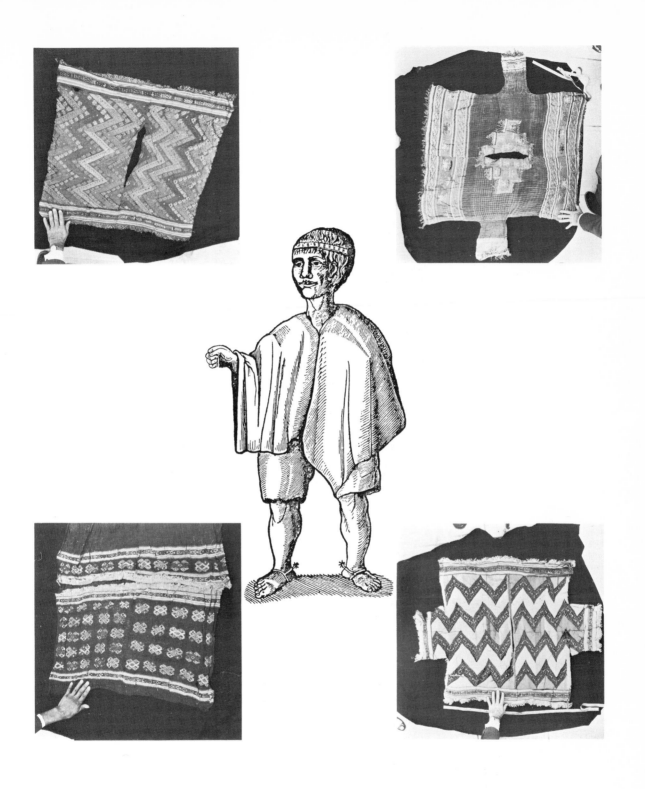

101–105. (*centre*) The earliest known European illustration of a poncho from an Araucanian Indian of Chile; surrounded by twelfth and thirteenth-century woollen ponchos recovered from graves at Chancay.

106. The author on the stone-laid Cañete-Jauja road which overlooks the modern road and watercourse.

CHAPTER FIFTEEN


The Marked Desert: Nasca, Pisco and Chincha


From Acari the Inca coastal highway (still clearly marked) proceeded alongside the Acari river and then north along the Cerros de Chocavento. The first *tampu* was at Apoloma-Poroma, after which the road continued to Nasca, which in Inca times was a large administrative centre.

"In the main valley [that is, the valley of the río Blanco, where the modern city of Nasca is located] are the great buildings of Caxamalca", wrote Pedro de Cieza, "and many storehouses erected by order of the Incas." Nearby, the fortress of Paredones guarded the lateral road joining the coastal to the Andean highway. This lateral, parts of which can still be seen, climbed up and over the cordilleras, then kept to the north bank of the Pachachaca river as far as the *tampu* of Cocha-cajas, where it met the royal road of the Andes.

The Nasca valleys, as they became known to the *conquistadores*, were five: Santa Cruz, Palpa, Ingenio, Nasca and Apoloma. Linked by a tangled web of rivers, both perennial and seasonal, they appear on the map like the splayed fingers of a hand.

These verdant valleys, compressed between deserts that are as dry as old bones and have known no rain of consequence in 5,000 years, were the arena of the famed Nasca culture, known for its pottery painted with highly stylised representations of birds, mice, llamas, bats and fruits, and with the figures of a veritable pantheon of anthropomorphic monsters (among which the cat god is the most dominant). This type of pottery dates from about A.D. 500. After A.D. 1000 Nasca was subjected to the influence of the Tiahuanacan culture, centred on the mysterious city near Lake Titicaca; and from then on motif of the Weeping God was a common feature of Nasca pottery and weavings. Most of our evidence of the Nasca culture has been provided by excavation of the deep graves in the area, there being few surface remains and little evidence of building sites or settlements. However, the Nascas are credited with the so-called "Nasca lines"—a maze of lines, rectangles,

circles, and representations of such animals as whales, fish, birds and spiders
—which are etched into the desert soil within Nasca territory. These are
generally presumed to have had some horological or astronomical significance, but in the absence of written records (or, indeed, of relevant folk
memories from those far-off days) it is impossible to be certain.

From Nasca, the Inca road (which passed right through the mysterious
"lines") proceeded to El Ingenio, the next *tampu* along the route. "El
Ingenio", which early on replaced the original Indian name for the place, is
Spanish for "sugar mill", one having been built there "in the early days of
the conquest", according to Vásquez de Espinosa. The *tampu* there was
large and built of adobe, but, in imitation of the best Inca stonework,
trapezoidal windows and niches had been constructed. It had the usual large
plaza with a raised platform from which troops were reviewed and the
people harangued.

North of El Ingenio the land is a tangle of verdureless mountainsides and
desolate canyons, in one of which—the narrow Quebrada de Santa Cruz—is
an immense ruin that stretches from end to end of the canyon, the remains of
numerous houses being mounted on the various escarpments. From above,
the outline of the remains is clear, but at ground level all is amorphous. The
royal road passed this way, eventually to emerge on the pampa of Huayuri.

Huayuri is a fertile oasis. Although without a discernible water supply, it
was clearly a place of some importance, as Huamán Poma pronounces it
"Huayuri . . . Town and Royal *Tampu*". Alongside a pallid greensward
lie the remains of this *tampu*, which included a corral (presumably for
llamas), two large plazas, and perhaps a sun temple, though the structure in
question has been badly eroded by the scouring winds.

All wayfarers who passed this way and left records of their treks agree
that the journey from the river oases (forty-two miles to the north-west)
was hellish. "*Muchissima arena*" ("overwhelming sand"), wrote Vásquez;
"one must travel at night because the day heat is so intense that it will kill
the animals. . . . There are so many sand dunes and the wind is so strong
that in that year of 1617 I almost lost my life . . . since I was deserted by
my guides." Only the tall wooden poles that the Indians had placed along the
road as markers saved him.

After Ocucaje, which, though located on the Ica river, has only poor
sources of water, "there were then", Cieza states, "great stands of carob
trees". Vásquez de Espinosa adds that "One finds them so extensive that
they are at places impenetrable. On the Nasca–Ica road there are five
leagues of these woods, so thick that the Royal Road is the only way to get
through them and one sees nothing but wood and sky."

The tree in question was not in fact the carob but a related species called
by the coastal Indians "huarango". Forests of these trees, which often grow
gnarled and twisted and are supported by a massive network of roots that

penetrate to great depths in order to find moisture, were once frequent on the hot sandy coast. The coastal people used the wood of the tree to build fires, to cover graves, to provide beams for houses and to carve elaborate ceremonial digging sticks. Their principal idols were carved from it.

One of the principal features of what Cieza calls "the cool valley of Ica" was the Chirana, a large canal that Garcilaso de la Vega tells us "very artfully collected water and diverted it to Ica . . . so that the acreage of the land considerably increased". As the Ica river, from which the water was drawn, does not run its full course all the year round, the diversion point was located upstream, at Trapiche. Garcilasco insists that the canal was built "by the Inca lords", but, as the coastal tribes were masters at irrigation, it may well have been pre-Inca. By Cieza's time it had been destroyed.

Ica is situated about forty miles from the coast, and between A.D. 400 and 1000 was the centre of an Ica–Nasca tribal unit. Its culture was quite distinctive, as its pottery and the elaborate digging sticks carved from huarango wood show, and it managed to hold its own even when the Tiahuanacan culture penetrated the area. However, it is certain that the inhabitants of Ica had contact with and were influenced by the mysterious Paracas people, of whom little more is known than can be learned from their art forms.

The original city (of which there are extensive remains) was sited on the now deserted Pampa de Tate. When the Incas arrived, in about 1470, they set up their own administration centre and "ordered palaces and storehouses to be built there"; the chieftain of Ica at the time was called Aranbilca. The records also reveal that Ica was one of the first places of which the Spaniards took possession following the death of Atahuallpa. Juan de Barrios was given all Ica as his fief in 1534 and confirmed in it in 1544 by the *Ordenanzas de Tambos*: "Xapana, chief of the *yungas* in the land called Ica, turned over 1,300 Incian vassals to the new Spanish overlord." The area had been thickly settled but, as Pedro de Cieza rightly bemoans, was soon to be depopulated "by the cruelty of the civil wars, which consumed all these poor Indians . . . who suffered great harm as a result of the contention between Pizarro and Almagro . . .".

Ica was also an important road junction. One road led seaward to Huaca China, which had evil-smelling but highly medicinal sulphur baths and is still frequented as a spa today. A second route, which is now visible only from the air, ran to Paracas, situated on the peninsula overlooking the bay of Pisco from the south. This area is described in detail later. A third route led to Humanío, on the upper reaches of the Ica river, and from there climbed forty miles to Huaytara, where it converged with the main lateral to Vilcashuamán (see Chapter 6 above).

From Ica, the main coastal highway crossed twenty-two miles of desert —in the course of which there was only one water source, that of the Villacuri

—before reaching "the famous river and valley of Pisco". The river is perennial, rising in the high mountains of Cholochaca, and along its valley ran the main lateral to Vilcas-huamán. This route has been followed since the earliest times and is believed to have been used by the Tiahuanacu-influenced colony of Viñaque-Huari for an early pre-Inca invasion of the coast.

The *tampu* of the Pisco valley was located at Umay. Up to 1931 its layout and that of the nearby remains of terracing (which give clear evidence of the natives' irrigation methods) were still clearly visible. Above the *tampu*, running along the lower escarpments of the Andes on its way to the next valley, can be seen the walled royal road.

A few miles up the Pisco valley is the site of the Inca fortress, checkpoint and administrative centre called Tambo Colorado. Though obviously once of importance, it is not mentioned by any of the chroniclers. Air and ground surveys show it to have been a group of buildings centred on a trapezoidal plaza. Though constructed of adobe, the buildings are dressed in the style of classical Inca stone construction and recall, in some respects, structures found in the Cuzco area. The walls were painted yellow and red (hence the name "Colorado"—"coloured") and around the tops of some buildings are interesting decorative friezes.

The Inca road, in keeping with their basic native custom of not allowing either houses, buildings or roads to stand on or traverse cultivable land, ran above the centre which is on the sharp slopes of the protruding escarpment. It moves without compromise, through terrain, and if it must, through all or any features. It moves right through pre-Inca graves of Mt. Sierpe. These circular, stone-lined although unused graves lay in rows, seven to nine, and marched up the 50° angle to the slope called Mt. Sierpe, that is the "shaking" line of graves reminding the one who named it of a serpent. There are over 5,000 such graves; empty, graves in so far as they are circular and stone-lined, and of the same construction of those graves which are found with mummies, weavings and pottery. For years, ever since 1931 they appeared on the photographic plates of the aerial surveys of the Shippee-Johnson expedition, they were the "strange and mysterious pockmarks", but when discovered and surveyed by the von Hagen expedition in 1953 and found to be unused graves, the mystery was compounded. The Inca engineers would have seen the same phenomena but as in the case of the the equally mysterious Nasca lines, they filled in those which interfered with the road and ran it over and through them.

THE lateral to the Andes goes forward and upward. The first to survey it was the renowned Dr. Max Uhle, who walked and rode over it in 1901. The road, he reported in a letter, was often no more than 5 feet in width if the precipices were unmovable, but when a patch could be made, it widens to

15–18 feet, "wide enough for llamas and passing Indians and wide enough for those carrying a litter . . . perhaps an Indian may have felt less horror in passing in such a manner above steep precipices." The whole valley showed Inca occupation and dominance. At Huaytara, 80 kilometres from *Tambo Colorado*, commanding the valley and the two laterals (the other one coming up from Ica), was the fortress of Huaytara, 4,000 metres in altitude. "Huaytara," commented Max Uhle, "contains . . . fine remains of the Incaic period of Peru . . . baths [which I have cleaned] and an ancient stone wall which forms now mostly part of the Christian church . . . containing about 10 high niches of marvellously worked (stone) marvellously preserved."

Max Uhle's letters of that period were addressed to Mrs. Phoebe Hearst, the mother of the publishing magnate William Randolph Hearst, who, as one of her many aids to archaeology, financed a part of Dr. Uhle's Peruvian researches. Born in Dresden in 1856, after the then usual classical education and the usual Ph.D. degree, he began his interest in archaeology in 1888. The rest of his life was spent in the Americas, particularly in the land of the Incas, and so he is universally known as "the father of Peruvian archaeology". "Uhle," so states his biographer, "did more field work in western South America than anyone else who ever lived." He also wrote extensively and sent back to the University of California so massive an amount of pottery and other study material that it has nurtured four generations of archaeologists. In 1936, on his eightieth birthday, numerous governments honoured him with recognition in form of decorations and declared him "bene merito". When World War II began, Dr. Uhle was 83. "He was," said his biographer, "in this crisis put under the protection of the Peruvian Government" (*Max Uhle, 1856–1944* by J. H. Rowe, University of California Press, 1954).

Without pension or annuities, he bought and maintained a small house in Lima in which archaeologists lived. In January 1942 he was arrested by the orders of the F.B.I. There was Dr. Harry Tschopik, since deceased, who worked on the archaeology of the Chullpas about Lake Titicaca. Isolated, cold and monotonous, Tschopik went often to lower-placed Arequipa, where, since they were so numerous between the years 1936–41, he was often the guest of and entertained by German residents. Beer flowed and since Germany was the focal point, the Germans talked. When American draft laws went into effect, Harry Tschopik of Peabody Museum, Harvard, had an alternative: enter the services or be engaged as the fingerman for the F.B.I. Tschopik prepared the lists, the Rio de Janeiro Agreement in 1941 did the rest. Dr. Uhle, 88 years of age, forgetful, senile, was high on the list. He and all the Germans living in Peru, some born there, some of long residence, were arrested by Peruvian police acting under F.B.I. orders: no warrants, no hearing, no trial, no evidence. But there was a choice: return to Germany in mid-war or go to the concentration camps in North America.

Those that chose America went there for six years, lost all their property; those like Dr. Uhle chose Germany. May it be recorded that Dr. Gordon Willey of Harvard University alone protested "about Dr. Uhle being treated in this manner". Uhle died five months later. Dr. Hermann Beyer, a resident for over a half-century in America and Yucatan, one of the foremost authorities on the deciphering of Maya glyphs, was likewise betrayed at the age of 70 by his archaeological colleagues, arrested in the same manner under the same pretext. He died in a Texas concentration camp. And to bring evidence in the first person singular, the author of this book, a third-generation American, born in St. Louis, Missouri, in 1908, who did intelligence for the American Navy and first brought in 1936 the names of those high officials who were planning a revolt against Hitler, was arrested in the same manner on the night of the bombing of Pearl Harbour. He was arrested by the F.B.I. as a "dangerous German alien." and also lodged in a concentration camp: no warrant, no trial, no explanation, no apology. He was released to join his regiment. There are thousands of such *islets* in America's own Gulag Archipelago.

PARACAS, on the peninsula to the south of the bay, is a large necropolis, famed for the exquisitely woven and embroidered fabrics that have been recovered from it. The graves date from A.D. 200 onward; in them were buried mummies wrapped in trappings of vicuña wool, alpaca wool or spun cotton, complete with sashes and headgear. The sand and the hot, dry south-westerly wind have kept all this in a remarkably good state of preservation, but in so doing have compounded the mystery of who the Paracas people were, since there is no trace of any settlement in this wind-blown, uninhabitable area. A road ran from here to Ica, and the early Ica pottery shows a Paracas influence, but these are only indecipherable clues.

Nearby is Tres Cruces, another mysterious survival from the past. Cut into a high sandy bluff looking out to sea, it is a huge engraving 640 feet long. Examined minutely by the von Hagen expedition in 1953, it was found to be cut into the sand to a depth of at least one yard and at an angle of fifty degrees. It can be seen distinctly only from out at sea. Thanks to the fact that a hard crust has formed on the sand surface, it has been preserved and the sand blows across it without blurring any of the original pattern.

What did it mean? It certainly predates the Incas. No Spaniard mentioned it, even though in 1534 Francisco Pizarro planned to establish his capital at Pisco rather than at Lima. Were the bodies of those buried at Paracas brought by sea and guided there by the Tres Cruces? But this is ruled out, since balsa-wood rafts were not used below latitude five degrees south, and tortora balsas can accommodate only two people. Whatever Tres Cruces may be, it is definitely a very American symbol, a tree of life. It recalls the "foliated cross" of the Maya culture.

From Umay, the main coastal highway passed through a rocky defile and then continued across the lower spurs of the Andes north-east to "the beautiful valley of Chincha". A lateral left the principal route, which kept to foothills and went straight for Chincha. And there on hand in 1546 was Pedro de Cieza, informative as usual.

"The large beautiful valley of Chincha is famous throughout Peru because its warriors were feared by the rest of the inhabitants." It must have been so. Early in the conquest the name *Chincha* was known and appears in the contract of Francisco Pizarro for his conquest. During the march to search out the Inca in September 1532 they were told that the coastal Inca road "leads by the way of all the valleys to Chincha" and "from Chincha it leads to Cuzco", which is precisely true for it is on the same degree of latitude, as will be subsequently seen.

Chincha is a compact, rectangular valley with a base of twenty miles on the coast and one of the most fertile and prosperous on the coast. The centre is called *Tambo de Mora*, evidently a stepped pyramid around which was built a formal court. It was the sanctuary of the god called Chinchay-camac by its Inca conquerors who left it undisturbed, albeit subordinate to its own cult-of-the-Sun. The early Spaniards learned that the great Lord Chincha was called Huaba-rucana "whose house [in 1558] is still extant".

The inclusion of the title *Rucana* is confirmation of Chibcha oral history which relates that they moved *en masse* into the highlands and conquered the Rucanas and brought back much booty. Cieza indeed says the same, that the Chinchas "wrought great damage to the Soras and Rucanas . . . thereafter winning much booty and returned to their valley".

When the Topa Inca appeared in 1450 with his armed hosts they judged that they were dwarfed by the mere numbers of troops and so made their accommodation with the people of the Sun. The chieftains following Inca policy held their rank only that there was an Inca overseer, *mitakoma*, that is Quechua-speaking people, to aid in their rapid absorption into the empire with the requirement that the Chincha Lords reside in Cuzco for stated periods. Cieza knew such a Lord as late as 1547 "still alive and a man of great intelligence and good understanding (that is for an Indian)".

There were more than 25,000 Indians in the valley when the Spaniards arrived; but in the following ten years their numbers were seriously depleted due to the civil wars. For a few brief months, Chincha was called "Almagro". When the Men of Chile took over this part of the coast in the belief that it lay within Almagro's realm of New Toledo, their leader made the town of Chincha his capital and renamed it after himself. However, the town soon reverted to its original name and—such was its importance—was given in *encomienda* to no less a person than the King of Spain himself.

## CHAPTER SIXTEEN

## Cañete to Paramonga

Continuing north from Chincha, the royal road transversed a thirty-mile stretch of silent, treeless desert to reach the valley of Huarco (or, as the Spaniards renamed it, Cañete, after the viceroy of that name). Between the two valleys there was only one *tampu*, that of Topará, which was watered by a shallow and inconstant stream.

After easily gaining the submission of the fierce Chinchas, Topa Inca assumed that Huarco would do nothing to interrupt his victorious progress: "The Inca advanced along the hot desert with his troops in orderly fashion, sent Chuquimancu [the overlord of Huarco] his emissaries, at times with gifts, at times with threats and menaces. . . ."

In answer, however, the Lord of Huarco sent away the women, the very old and the very young and prepared for battle. This Topa Inca had not expected, and, as the summer was coming on and the invaders were not used to fighting in the intense heat of coastal summers, he returned with his armies to Cuzco and in 1460 or thereabouts prepared to assault Huarco from another direction. This resulted in one of the most astonishing pieces of road engineering in the annals of man: the road leading from near Huancayo, a large market town in the Andes, to the coast at Huarco. The road began with enormously wide stone steps (still extant and in good condition) leading off the royal Andean road at Chango Bajo, and then proceeded by way of Huamachuco, Cupapata and Hatunhuasi ("Big House", suggesting the immense size of the stone-built *tampu* there) to Haqui, where it came to the upper reaches of the Cañete river. This river had dug a deep canyon out of the Andes, and the Huarco road passed along it. Built into the sheer rockface, with retaining walls reaching down twenty to thirty feet to find a firm base, it was skilfully engineered to keep twenty-five to thirty-five feet above the river, the level of which can change with frightening ease. Below the road ran a large stone-lined irrigation ditch that was built by the coastal peoples and later enlarged and improved by the Incas; this irrigated the valley of Huarco.

Chuquimancu, remembered as "fierce, proud and powerful", the lord of three valleys (Chilca, Coayllo and Runahuanca, all contiguous), "was treated as a king . . . who exacted homage even from those tribes which were not his vassals", but still he could not (though he must have tried to) prevent the building of that road. Each day it inched further down the valley. As a commercial artery, it was superfluous, since there was a parallel route a few miles to the north, linking Pachacamac (near Lima) to Jauja; the new road was primarily a route of conquest. The immense labour that went into its construction—for it was over 125 miles long and for the most part ran over land 13,000 and more feet high—suggests just how important the Incas considered it to be.

Where the valley begins to flatten out, the Incas met the first serious resistance. Cieza's informants—the official rememberers—stated that the struggle continued for four years "in spite of the fact that the Lord Inca returned to Cuzco during the summers because of the heat, while his troops [perhaps auxiliary troops drawn from the hot desert coast] continued the war". Eventually Topa Inca determined to bring the affair to an end. He came down to the Cañete valley with a retinue of nobles and had a new city built there that was given the name "New Cuzco" (not to be confused Manco Capac's "New Cuzco" at Vilcabamba).

This city, now known as Incahuasi, is an immense complex of official residences, administrative buildings and so on, situated fifteen miles from the coast and a quarter of a mile from the Cañete river in a wide, dry valley. It is the largest Inca site along the coast and with all of its peripheral buildings covers at least five square miles. Houses of the Chosen Women (ñustas) were as at Ollantaytambo, perched high on a hill above the main city, which was built in a flattened valley and modelled on the usual orderly Inca plan. At the centre of it is a keystone-shaped plaza 600 feet long and featuring a raised altar with stairs on two sides and, an imperial reviewing platform. Roofs were supported by immense round columns built of wedge-shaped stones cemented by adobe—an architectural feature only otherwise found at the Temple of Viracocha in the Andes. However, the most out-standing feature is the storage chambers, 248 large cubicles arranged, with the precision of beehive cells, around a large number of drying platforms.

Since the site has been completely neglected by archaeologists, it is not known how long it remained occupied—whether it was deserted before or after the Spanish conquest. All that is certain is that the building of the city ensured Inca mastery of the Cañete valley. Chuquimancu retired to a fortress built on an isolated hill in the centre of the valley, there to make his last stand; but the Incas did not storm the fortress, being already sufficiently in control of the area. Soon, taking advantage of roads that Chuquimancu him-self had had built, they were able to forge north to Pachacamac.

The coast immediately north of the Cañete valley alternates between marsh and cultivated fields; thus, the royal road kept to the desert strip between this area and the highlands, running about twelve miles back from the coast. The next stop along the road was Uquira, situated on the river Coayllo and within the valley of that name, twenty-eight miles from Cañete. It survives as a particularly fine example of a small, compact Inca administration centre and *tampu*.

About twelve miles further on, the road came to Mala (originally Malaque), which, though of no great importance as a *tampu*, looms large in the history of Peru as the place where the war between Almagro and Pizarro began. Being situated halfway between Almagro's capital, Chincha, and Pizarro's capital, Lima, it was chosen as neutral ground for a "peace" conference between the two factions. However, Pizarro did not intend that Almagro and his Men of Chile should leave Mala alive, and to this end Gonzalo Pizarro and his men "hid in the cane brakes near the *tampu*" awaiting the signal—a trumpet blast—to ambush the party.

One of Almagro's fellows sensed trouble and began to sing part of an old ballad—

> *Tiempo es el Caballero,*
> *Tiempo es de andar de aqui.*

("Time it is, Cavalier, time it is to flee from here")—so alerting his comrades to the danger. Immediately Almagro and his men took to their horses and rode off, with the business of reaching an amicable arrangement about the division of the Inca realms left unconcluded. It was then 10th November 1537, and soon the chain of events was to lead to the complete, though transitory, victory of the Pizarro faction.

Beyond Mala, the road passed through the green hills of Chilca, of which Pedro de Cieza observed, "Very strange . . . no rain falls in Chilca, there is neither river nor brook, yet the Chilca valley is covered with cornfields and plantations of tubers and fruit trees . . . only watered by dew and dampness . . . in deep holes they place the seed corn and with each the head of a small sardine . . . in this way the corn comes up and bears abundantly. Truly it is a remarkable thing. In this area of the sea they catch so many fish that they supply these Indians with food and all they have from their gardens. There were storehouses here and lodgings for the Incas where they would stop when they were visiting the provinces of their kingdom."

This small riverless valley was allotted to Pedro Alchonel, famous for his trumpet. In the advance on Cuzco in 1534, the Spanish vanguard, led by Hernando de Soto, passed the famous hanging bridge over the Apurimac river and came upon the pass of Vilcaconga. There they were ambushed. It was night, their losses were grievous and they were beset by weariness and wounds. Then out of the night came the blast of a trumpet signalling the

in Ecuador, come to serve this mosque and offer tribute every year. There were houses and superintendents to receive the tribute . . . The town of Pachacamac is very large. Adjoining the mosque (the Temple of Pachamaca, the Creator God) is a house of the sun, well built and situated on a hill with five surrounding walls. There are houses with terrace roofs as in Spain. The town appears to be very old, judging from the ruined houses it contains: and the greater part of the wall has fallen."

The principal Lord was called Taurichumbi.

Our friend Pedro de Cieza, who saw it in 1546, thirteen years later, thought Pachacamac to be "one of the most sumptuous temples to be found in these realms. It is built of man-made adobes . . . and on its summit the temple with many gates, which like the walls, was adorned with the figures of wild animals. . . . Beside the temple there were many spacious lodgings for those who came there in pilgrimage.

"When the Incas made themselves masters of these kingdoms . . . and saw the splendor of this temple and how old it was and the sway it had over all the people, it was agreed that Pachacamac should remain with the authority of the cult it possessed provided that they built a Temple of the Sun. . . ." All of which is verified by the ruins themselves.

ARMATAMBO, which lies at the base of Molar Solar, an isolated mountain outcrop (in that suburb of modern Lima known as Las Palmas) was the official stop in the Rimac valley, close upon Pachacamac. It was an enormous place of houses, compounds and rectangular plazas above where the royal road went through the valley. A small rivulet called Surco was directed from the main river and was brought to the Halting Station: "*Arma*", meant bath in Quechua, so this was the Purification *Tambo*, where pilgrims bathed and purified themselves before proceeding.

As in the south, so in the north, the valleys were dominated by a Great Lord. He was called Cuis-mancu. Pachacamac may have stood on neutral ground since it was their Mecca. But the wide and fertile valleys of the Rimac, thought to have been peopled by the Huanchos, was thickly populated, as evidenced by the irrigation systems and the massive ruins.

The Incas divided the valley into three administrative centres: Carahuayllo to the north, Maranga in the centre, and Surco to the south. Each administrative centre had 10,000 families, so writes Padre Bernabé Cobo, who at a young age came to Lima in 1599, where he trained to be a Jesuit. "This valley (of Lima) and territory was once very thickly populated as can be seen from the ruins of their towns. Innumerable small communities situated in the limits of their governance obeyed them. . . ." Such was the small centre of Puruchuco, eleven kilometres from today's Lima, which has been lovingly restored and gives echoes of what all this once was: "You can still see," wrote Bernabé Cobo in 1600, "the houses of their *caciques*, the walls painted with various figures . . ."

When Lima was selected for the Spanish colonial capital, with its one side on the Rimac River, three Spaniards had been sent out to explore the possibilities of this site for his capital. They found, the report read, "the region very good: it has fine water and firewood and land for cultivation".

The Inca Lord was then called Tauli Chusco.

Since the coastal Indians and their latter-day Inca lords did not look to the sea, other than to supply them with fish, mollusks, and seaweed, sea harbours were of no importance. But they were to the Spanish. They found such a harbour at Callao, 25 kilometres from Lima. It was at this chosen site that Lima was founded on the 6th of January 1535, the streets ruled out like a chequerboard, the main plaza having on its four corners the church, the Cabildo, the Governor's palace and what would one day be the Mint.

Within ten years Pedro de Cieza found the valley . . . "thickly populated until the lands of the Indians were taken from them. There are some good houses there and some of them very handsome with their turrets and terraces". In Lima lived at this time over 380 Spaniards with only fourteen Spanish women being present. Juana Hernández was the first; she came with the expedition in 1532. Doña Iñes Muñoz claims to have been the first white woman to be married in Peru.

In one of these "handsome houses", Francisco Pizarro, on the night of 26th of July, 1541, was murdered with some of his followers by the desperate "Men of Chile", which continued the strife that brought Gonzalo Pizarro in direct confrontation to with his King and Sire.

In recording all this Pedro de Cieza said, "I should be well pleased were I not to have to write about such sad events but in order that the coming generations may understand the mad proceedings of all these people and although my mind grows callous about it, I promise to trim my quill well to relate them." Which he did.

It also was to wreak more destruction on the Indians, their persons, possessions, land, *tampus* and roads than all the proceeding years of conquest.

The royal road to the north crossed the Rimac by a ford (there was also a bridge) and the first Spaniard in 1533 "marched along the road with a high wall on either side".

This is the same road that Hernando Pizarro took on his return in March 1534 in his gold-gathering trek. "Altogether," he wrote to his King, "I collected 85,000 *castellanos* of gold and 3000 *marcos* of silver."

Soon after leaving the environs of Rimac-Lima and crossing over the small perennial river, the Chillon, the royal road again turned inward and upward to avoid the desert at Ancon (famed for the graves that yielded so many pre-Inca mummy bundles). It climbed to 800 metres behind the Cerro Pasamayo to avoid an uncontrollable mountain of sand which tumbled into the sea. The present-day Pan American Highway, failing to take a leaf out of the Inca's

notebook, engineered its road through the massive sand deposits of Pasamayo and requires continuous maintenance in order to remain open.

The Inca road, however, climbed to Pasamayo, which lies at about 3,000
feet above sea level. There lived a small group of Aucayma Indians, who in
1690 numbered 370, in 1810 170, and today have disappeared entirely. Some
way further on, just above the Chancay valley, lay the first large *tampu* north
of the Rimac.

This *tampu* has been known by a variety of names. Hernando Pizarro
referred to it as Suculacumbi (perhaps the name of the chieftain) and noted
that the "Lord of the village . . . and his Indians were friendly"; other
sources refer to it as Tambo Pintado ("painted *tampu*"), presumably
because it was vividly painted; and it is now known as Baños de Boza, on
account of the natural sulphur baths in the area. These were much frequented
by coastal Indians suffering from rheums brought on by dampness, since the
coast is overhung with fog for five months of the year.

Though once well populated (as the extensive ruins show), its population
was much reduced through the civil wars. In 1617 it contained only "22
tribute-paying Indians, 10 elders, 18 children, 31 women". The graves found
there have yielded unusual woven and painted fabrics and curious pottery,
which, though crudely modelled and painted, is very striking. The strangest
thing about this pottery is that it dates from a time when all other places
along the coast were producing highly-finished work. "If," says one archaeologist, "the crudeness is in reality an artistic mannerism for the sake of
achieving an aspect of bold originality, then it certainly accomplished its
purpose."

Some thirty miles further on was the village of Llachu (Huacho), which
Hernando Pizarro renamed Tambo de los Perdizes, "Place of the partridges,
because the Indians kept so many there in cages". This in turn was only a
short distance from Huara, a town with "large lodging houses along a clear
rolled road". Here it was that Hernando Pizarro and his men, on their way
back from Pachacamac, turned off the coastal highway and followed the
lateral leading by way of the Oyon canyon to Jauja (see Chapter 4).

Huara also features in the history of war between Gonzalo Pizarro and the
wily bishop Pedro de la Gasca, who came to Peru to enforce the New Laws
rejected by Pizarro and his followers. In keeping with the scorched earth
policy that he was urging on his followers, Pizarro ordered that the chieftains
of the Huara area be sent elsewhere. Anton Sánchez, writing from Huara on
7th April 1547, begged Pizarro to rescind this order, " for if they go, there
is not an Indian who will remain and this Huara is the very key to the land
and the sea".

In 1819 William Stevenson, who had served as secretary to the British
Admiral Lord Cochrane and was a very observant traveller, noted that
"Huara consists of one long street, 2,000 inhabitants, with a sugar mill,
operated by water power, the first in the land, a church built by the Jesuits

and a handsome brick bridge of one arch—needless to say not Inca—which crossed the Huara river."

Eighteen miles further on, the road, after making its majestic way across the pampas of Tutumo, keeping well back from the coast, came to the Supe river, the bed of which is often dry and thus no obstacle to the traveller. Shortly after this it reached the more formidable Huamánmayu (*mayu* being Quechua for "river"). Hernando Pizarro was punted across it in a tortora-balsa boat kept for that purpose, the horses swimming. "They have," said the scrivener, "no bridges across the coast rivers, because they become very wide when they are swollen. The lord of Huamánmayu [now called La Barranca] had his Indians ferry across our loads. . . ."

The next river, the Patavilca, was crossed at a place called Cochas. William Stevenson related that eighteen miles back from the main road at Cochas there was a suspension bridge made of rope hawsers. This was thirty-eight yards across and had a mean width of five feet. On one side of the river at this point is the *hacienda* of Huayto; on the other, Vinto. There, on a dry hill almost 700 feet above sea level, Huayna Capac had an enormous public granary built. Stevenson found there some maize and beans that, though over 450 years of age, were still edible and, when planted, proved still to be fertile.

There is no mistaking the next landmark—the "fortress", as Cieza and many others thought it to be, of Paramonga. The building in question was in fact a temple, similar in structure to the great temple of Pachacamac, and placed on the highest hill in the area, close to the narrow but fast-flowing river Fortaleza. Described as "a strong building with seven encircling walls painted in many devices, both inside and out, with portals built like those of Spain", it was a tiered edifice constructed from the usual sun-dried adobe and culminating in a series of small rooms. Robert Proctor, an English traveller who visited Paramonga in 1820, spoke of the "painted rooms . . . with uncouth drawings of birds and beasts", as Cieza had done nearly 300 years before. On the surrounding hills are the remains of numerous other buildings, and through the upper Fortaleza valley runs the lateral road that Hernando Pizarro followed on his way from Cajamarca.

The greyish-brown, verdureless hills of Paramonga marked the beginning of Chimú territory, which at its greatest extent stretched from here to the end of Peru, "where the trees begin". The origins of the Chimú empire lie further back than do those of its Inca counterpart, into which it was eventually absorbed; and, due to alliances with various Andean tribal groups, its sphere of influence extended well beyond the arid coastal region on which it was based. Topa Inca is said to have conducted his invasion of the Chimú realms "in the most orderly fashion", but despite this the conquest proved a long-drawn-out affair, beginning in about 1460 and continuing till about 1480.

CHAPTER SEVENTEEN

# The Land of the Chimú

The Chimú kingdom was an impressive realm 620 miles in length and with dominion over eighteen valley-oases. Its inhabitants were by no means mere savages till the Incas came on the scene, but in many respects were as advanced as, if not more advanced than, the invaders. However, this did not prevent them from coming under the Inca yoke. One of the principal weaknesses of the Chimú empire was the isolation of the various oases comprising it.

This becomes clear as one follows the course of the Inca road north from Paramonga. It is about forty-five miles from there to Huarmey, in the next river valley, and it is hot sandy desert all the way; the road, no longer the unerringly straight road it was further south, winds through verdureless hills of pink and metallic green and blue rock, and through wind-blown sand dunes that the now-eroded walls of the road once held back. In places it is forced close to the shore and runs within earshot of the frantic cries of birds and the roar of sealions.

Yet, even in what is now utter desolation, and despite the absence of any sign of surface water (the sea apart), there are indications that this area was once not quite so devoid of human habitation. At a place called Pampa Bermejo the ruins of a massive Inca structure can be seen; and at Las Zorras ("the foxes") are the remains of ancient buildings, irrigation ditches and cemeteries. "The thing that struck me most", said Cieza, "when I crossed this valley [in 1547] was the multitude of graves to be seen . . . all covered with bones of the dead. . . ." This whole area, in fact, is one mammoth ossuary, the bones discarded by the *huaqueros* (tomb robbers) littering the land.

Huarmey itself was, wrote Stevenson, "only a small village noted for its strong *chicha*, a fermented beer made from corn". Robert Proctor described the village as "one long wide street" and found the way there by muleback "long and toilsome".

The Huarmey river and the rivers feeding four other valleys in the region all have their source in the immense bulk of the Cordillera Negra. However, the source is not very reliable, and as a result the five valleys suffer from annual water shortages. The Huarmey valley is narrow, and seems too small to have yielded any noteworthy archaeological treasures; yet from here have been recovered a breastplate covered with hundreds of golden sequins; gold bangles; and wooden spear-throwers with gold sheeting.

The valley was given in *encomienda* to Don Martín "El Indio", who was one of the two Indians of Tumbes whom Pizarro took to Spain with him in 1527 and who later served as interpreters. Martín's name is absent from the major early reports on the conquest, so it is impossible to be sure what part he played at the time; by contrast, the other Indian interpreter, Felipillo, features frequently.

Martín was the only Indian who became really fluent in Spanish, both written and oral, and the only one (apart from Paullu Inca) whom Pizarro gave an allotment of land and Indians. Pizarro's fondness for him is evident from the fact that he gave him the name Martín and the gift of a horse; and it is said that the Indian fought as a cavalryman. Later he received a knighthood and a coat of arms. He became a Christian, wore Spanish dress, and became the first Indian to marry a Spanish woman, Luisa de Medina.

A faithful follower of the Pizarros, Martín demonstrated his loyalty to them in a number of ways. When in Spain on one occasion, he was forbidden, by royal decree, to leave Seville; but he somehow eluded the vigilance of the port authorities and returned to Peru, "to my *tampu*", which was Huarmey. Later, after Gonzalo Pizarro's armada had capitulated to President La Gasca and many of Pizarro's followers in the north had deserted to the royalist side, Martín held firm. On 28th April 1547 he wrote to Pizarro asking for instructions and stating that he had posted Indian spies all along the coastal road. By June, the Royal Armada was nearing his valley, but instead of deserting he joined the loyal Pizarro supporter Juan de Acosta. In the redistribution of *encomiendas* following the defeat and execution of Gonzalo Pizarro, Martín was deprived of Huarmey but permitted to go to Spain to protest to the King; whereupon he died.

A further thirty-six miles of desert seperates Huarmey from the Casma river valley. Halfway along this stretch of road is the intermittent Culebras river, where the traveller can slake his burning thirst if he is lucky and there is water in the river bed. A few *tampus*, maintained by people who had been obliged to settle there by the Incas and who had no other function than to provide sustenance for travellers, were established along this road.

As one approaches Casma, abundant evidence of the Chimú past of the area may be observed. A number of hills are crowned with fortifications, of which the most notable are those on top of Chancaillo. These E. G. Squier described as "consisting of an irregular oval . . . a mile in circuit, occupying the summit of a steep rocky hill . . . three walls, the outer one twenty-four feet thick and twenty-six feet high . . .". After turning inland from the

sand-bound coast, the Inca road, twenty-four feet wide and bordered by low
stone walls, ran directly below the fortress, then, after passing through a
large *tampu*, forded the river Moxeke and proceeded to the large Chimú
urban centre now known as El Purgatorio. From there, passing over country
studded with Chimú temples, all adobe-built, it continued to the river Casma,
which it crossed just above its confluence with the Moxeke. There there was
another *tampu*.

There is no mention of the Casma valley in the history handed down from
the Incas, who took great care to stamp out tribal memories of other cultures.
However, Casma harbours the remains of one of the oldest of the many and
varied coastal civilisations. This, the Sechín culture, is notable for a ceremonial
centre built of carved stone pillars and blocks, many of which feature sculp-
tured faces that are openly humorous. The Sechín is distantly related to the
Andea area culture known as Chavín, which flourished in 1200–400 B.C.

From Casma the Inca road ran straight to the *tampu* of Huambacho, about
which Pedro de Cieza remarks that "all I have to say of it is that it is of the
same sort and manner of those we have seen and had lodging for the Lord-
Inca, and that from the river [Nepeña] that runs through it, they drew
water in ditches to irrigate the fields they had planted." Yet there is far more
to Huambacho than this, for here one encounters the first obvious signs of
the Mochica culture, which was an antecedent of the Chimú. Remains of tall
adobe pillars that once supported light reed roofs are frequent, and display
highly imaginative designs—step designs and representations of birds and
gods all feature.

Across the upper valley of the Nepeña the pre-Inca engineers built a stone
dyke 3,936 feet long and proportionately wide and high. This is one of the
few such works known and is a wonderful piece of hydraulic engineering;
the water held behind the dam was distributed by conduits and used to
irrigate the land. Further up the valley, at Moros, there are a number of
other remarkable stone structures, pyramidal in shape. The tallest of these
is Pañamarca, the walls of which feature a polychrome frieze thirty feet long,
portraying valets attending elaborately dressed and painted ruler–warriors.

From the top of Pañamarca can be seen the straight line of the Inca road
from Casma, and, just beyond Huambacho, the deep oval bay of Samancó,
which provides one of the few really protected harbours on the Peruvian coast.
From there the Indies sailed out to sea in their tortora-balsa boats, "the
little horses of the sea", as the Spaniards called them.

After the Spanish conquest, Huambacho developed from *tampu* to village.
As it controlled the bay of Samancó, it was in 1685 the object of an attack
by the English pirate Edward Davis, and because of its heroic defence was
designated a city by the King of Spain. However, in 1820, when Stevenson
passed through on his way north, he found it "only a small hamlet . . . with
thirty ill-built houses, but the oldest part that stood near the sea was much

larger . . .''. Its day of glory was past.

North of Huambacho the royal road snaked its way forward through the outcrops of rock thrusting through the sand and so reached the first Chimú defensive wall, part of the outer defences of the great wall of Peru. The Inca engineers demolished part of the wall to make way for the road, which thence proceeded to Chimbote. However, the way there was not easy: as soon the road passed beyond the rocky outcrops and the protection they afforded, it ran into overwhelming sand, which the fierce south-easterly winds keep forever shifting. These build up and then obliterate immense sand dunes called *médanos*, which are crescent-shaped and often beautifully symmetrical. The road here is now mostly invisible; sometimes the winds will expose a section of wall, then cover it again.

Halfway up an exposed rocky slope, and near where the road emerges from the sand are the remains of Tambo Real ("Royal *tampu*"), which lies just above a seepage of brackish water. From here the road can be traced as it proceeds, gaining altitude, towards the Santa river and valley. At Cambio puente ("Exchange Bridge") the road can be seen (as it was by a scientific traveller in 1890) "running by the rail-line; on the left side is the Inca road, bound by high adobe walls".

The Santa is the largest river on the Peruvian coast; at its mouth it is just over a mile wide. In the rainy season in the mountains, the water of this river has a force of more than 5 miles an hour: but, because the coast is narrow here, only a small fraction of the water that passes through the Andean gorge known as the Callejón de Huaylas can be utilised. Nevertheless the coastal tribes took the best advantage of the river they could, diverting water to irrigate the agricultural terraces they fashioned from the valley slopes.

"In bygone days," said Pedro de Cieza, "the valley of Santa [its original name seems to have been lost] was very heavily populated. There were great warriors and native lords [Chimú]. They dared to measure their strength against the Incas'. . . . The Incas ordered great lodgings [at Tambo Real] and many storehouses [at Cantagallo] to be erected there, for this valley is one of the largest. There is a large and turbulent river and it is crossed by Indians on balsa-wood rafts. There used to be many thousands of Indians here, but now [1547] there are not more than 400 left, a sad thing to consider. . . . They used to dig great irrigation ditches filled with water taken from the river with which they watered most of the valley. The natives go dressed in blankets and a sort of shirt, the women the same; on their heads they wear a band or insignia. . . . The ships travelling along the coast always take on water here from this river."

At the mouth of the Santa, near the *tampu* of Chimbote, is one of the finest natural harbours on the coast of Peru, though this was not of any great interest to the land-based Incas. However, the Indians ventured out into the coastal waters to fish, to search for seals, and to collect guano from the nearby islands.

On the north side of the Santa lay the *tampu* of Gallinazo ("buzzard"), as it is now called. It is well preserved and built in the normal style, of sun-dried adobe; the road through here is equally well preserved.

Gallinazo served as an administration centre for salt gathering, since in the riverless valley just beyond it there are salt-water springs. From very early on, the coastal people took advantage of this quirk of nature, constructing rectangular stone-lined basins into which the salt water was fed and left to evaporate. Thanks to the pitilessly hot sun and the lack of rain, this happened quickly, leaving a deposit of salt. The salt was then piled in high white pyramids (which are still a feature of the landscape, here as the salt-pans are still in use) before being loaded for distribution.

After Salinas (as this place appropriately is known), the royal road headed for the coast at Chao. Since there were no geographical obstacles in its path, it ran straight across the pampas, which provided a naturally hard road surface.

Then came the wall! No one in four centuries had mentioned or even suspected it, and it was not until one day in August 1931, when Robert Shippee and Lt. Johnson saw it from the air, that it re-entered the pages of history. "While we were operating from the base [at Trujillo] we made a flight . . . followed the valley of the Santa river to the coast . . . then we noticed what appeared to be a wall flowing up and down the ridges. . . . We wondered for a moment as to the purpose of such a structure, decided that it was worthwhile and made a number of photographs. . . ." A few days later they returned: "turning inland we picked up the wall . . . and we followed it for at least forty miles . . .". On their next flight they noticed and filmed "at irregular intervals on both sides of the walls . . . some circular, some rectangular forts . . . we finally lost sight of it at Corongo." Corongo! That was in the sierra, ninety miles from the sea! Shippee and Johnson had found and traced from end to end "the great wall of Peru" (see R. Shippee, "The Great Wall of Peru", *Geographical Review*, vol. XXII, no. 1 January 1932).

What was it, who built it, and for what purpose? Clearly the wall was for defence; but who the original defenders were, and who their enemies, are questions that cannot be answered on the evidence currently available. The most that can be said with certainty is that the wall is pre-Chimú (the ceramics found allow approximate dating), though the Chimú reoccupied and improved it and may have constructed the parts of adobe.

The greater part of the wall is of *pirca* rock construction and over ten feet high. It winds its way from the sea, over the low mountain spurs parallel to the Santa, and up into the sierra. In the higher areas, where rain does occasionally fall, terraces were fashioned from the near-perpendicular mountainsides, and earth and fertiliser transported there over considerable distances.

These terraces were then used as a readily available source of food supply for the wall's defenders, who occupied the many lookout posts and strategic-ally-placed, enormous fortresses, which were built of stone blocks carefully fitted together without mortar.

In about 1460, the Lord Chimú began to receive ambassadors from the Inca, who, after successful invasions of the south coast, now turned his eyes towards the Chimú realms. The Lord Chimú told the ambassadors that his people worshipped Pachacamac, the creator-god, and Mamacocha, the ocean-mother, who fed them with her fish, and that they had no wish to worship the sun, who gave them only pitiless, excessive heat. "The great Chimú", said Garcilaso de La Vega, "replied that he would defend his kingdom . . . he wanted neither new laws nor new gods."

Following this, "The inhabitants of Santa [that is, the defenders of the great wall and the fortresses] . . . fought with such ardour . . . that the great Chimú was hopeful that the Incas would grow weary"—instead of which the final clash came in a way that neither empire had planned.

In about 1461, the Inca general Capac Yupanqui led out a huge raiding party to test the defences of the northern tribes. He had the Inca's orders to turn back at the Yanamayu ("Black river"), which then lay outside Inca control; but when he reached there he experienced a mass desertion by the recently conquered Chancas. In order to redeem himself in the eyes of Inca Pachacutic, the general thrust on to Cajamarca, which was then an indepen-dent tribal centre and had a defence treaty with the Chimú, whose water sources it controlled.

Fighting was severe, but though aided by the Chimú, the Cajamarcans were defeated. Capac Yupanqui established an Inca garrison, then prepared to return in what he supposed would be triumph. *Chasquis*, running in relays, brought the news to Cuzco, but when Pachacutic heard it he was enraged at his half-brother's disobedience—particularly as he saw that it would require a lightning invasion to gain control of all the land between the last Inca outposts and Cajamarca—and ordered that the general be killed on the road. Within a year however, Topa Inca (Pachacutic's heir) set out with a massive army and conquered all the innumerable tribes between Cuzco and Cajamarca —500 miles of previously unsubdued territory.

As a result of Topa Inca's conquests, the royal road was extended and Cajamarca brought into direct contact with Cuzco. The Incas had turned the Chimú's Maginot Line and now were looking down on them from the heights. They also controlled the Chimú's water sources.

In this way the Incas assured themselves of victory over the Chimú empire, which had been born somewhere around the year 1000, at about the same time as the Inca empire. However, the Chimú may in many respects be considered the natural successor of the Mochica culture, which flourished along the coast from about A.D. 400.

The Mochicas, like all other tribal groups, were farmers. They were masters also of irrigation, as has already been seen. The food grown was much the same as anywhere else in Peru, with maize as the staple food, and numerous vegetables and fruits to supplement it. In addition, the sea supplied fish, shellfish and seaweed, and grass was collected from the offshore islands. Mochica society was stratified, as was the Inca. Each village had its lord, who was in turn subject to a greater lord. Everyday dress "consisted of a shirt-like poncho and a blanket: they also wore a head-dress which was a round affair made of wool and sometimes spangled with gold and silver beads known as *chaquira*; and both sexes wore a kind of apron to cover their privy parts".

Since it seldom rained and there was a permanent growing season on the coast, the Mochicas had ample leisure to engage in non-agricultural pursuits. They were superb metalworkers, fine weavers (of feathers, as well as cotton and wool), and their pottery is unexcelled in the Americas. With a penchant for realism, their potters left lifelike portraits of warriors, priests, the possessed and the unpossessed, the lame and the blind, along with almost clinical representations of people afflicted by disease (just about every type they knew is represented). In addition, all their foodstuffs, cultivated or obtained, were realistically depicted, as were the dry landscapes characteristic of the region. In these beautifully detailed miniatures one sees the sun glaring down upon the wasteland, various types of desert flora, the cultivated greenness of river valleys, and fields of maize swaying in the lee of an offshore breeze. Another feature of Mochica pottery is its realistic and engagingly candid portraiture of various love positions (including many sodomite positions). These the puritan Incas found so shocking that they ordered the complete annihilation of tribes who practised sodomy and fellatio. To the Inca mind such practices were a waste of human seed and deprived the empire of work-service taxation; homosexuals and bachelors alike were taboo.

This wealth of pottery has been recovered from deep graves, where the sand has preserved colours and forms, and is so realistically moulded and graphic that it almost serves in place of a written language. As with all other tribes in these regions, the Mochicas had no writing. Their histories were remembered.

Sometime after 1000, the Mochicas, who had lordship only over four of the northern coastal valleys, went into decline. All archaeological evidence points to the fact that their downfall was violent and abrupt. When they re-emerged after the year 1000, it was as the Kingdom of Chimor, Chan Chan as its capital.

The Chimú, like the Inca, developed a massive imperial appetite. They progressed from the temple city-state stage into the conquering stage and finally, like the Incas, into a tribute state wherein they changed "from a mechanical aggregate of persons . . . into an organic unit whose members perform complimentary functions"—in sum, into a highly centralised empire with a regulated caste system. By the year 1400 the Chimús had taken over all the valleys from Santá to Tumbes. Like the Incas, the Chimú were organisers: water conduction, soil extension, managers of population growth even while living under desert conditions. They widened the earth domain, terraced the bare hills, brought guano fertilizer and earth. Much was done on a large scale. Weaving was mass-produced, as was pottery. Metal workers were artisans, apart from working in copper, bronze, gold, silver. The dross of their manufactures is still to be seen piled hills-high around their quarters in Chan Chan.

Society was stratified. There were the ordinary people, the producers, the priests and the directing classes. "The Lords of these valleys were called Cie . . .," Pedro de Cieza explains. Before the Chimú were conquered by the Incas, "these lords were greatly feared and obeyed . . . served with great pomp . . . surrounding themselves with buffoons and dancers who entertained them. Each Lord in his valley had great dwellings constructed with pillars of adobe and great terraces and doorways. . . ."

Chan Chan was to them as Cuzco was to the Incas. The political and economic centre of the Kingdom of Chimor is metropolitan in concept. It was built on the sterile parts of the Moche valley at its north-west corner, a six-miles square complex of walls, buildings, houses, water reservoirs. It extended to the edge of the sea. Everything was large scale; immense walls forty feet high, an admixture of small rock and adobe pressed into forms, known as *tapia*; the walls separated clan from clan. Each unit was a complete entity: it had regular streets, houses, cells, gardens, irrigated by special spiralling canals. Water was conducted into Chan Chan by aqueducts from sources high up in the Moche River.

It was this vital water source that the Inca army, under their Topa Incas, proceeded to "re-direct". The Inca attack was three-pronged, one part of which descended to the coast from the north, where the Chimú had no great wall or line of fortifications. A people can fight, often without hope: but resistance without water cannot go on long. The great Chimú Lord Minchan-caman capitulated and was taken and kept in honoured exile in Cuzco. One of his sons was appointed to the rule of Chimor as an Inca puppet.

The Inca road engineers and those social architects who transplanted whole populations, the oft-mentioned *mitakona*, were not far behind the military operations. North of the Santá valley, the road was directed to Chao on the coast, into the Viru valley and past the giant Moche pyramid called *El Castillo*; then it moved directly on to the high plateau that overlooked the immediate sea. It runs parallel with the sea coast: every 5 kilometres there are remains of circular houses. It passes on to a seaport and place, "where," said Pedro Cieza, "one comes to the valley of Guañape."

The *tampu* of Guañape is perched near the Cerro Prieto de Guañape about 750 feet above the sea. A reasonably protected harbour lies nearby, and six miles out to sea are a number of guano-rich islets. Guañape exhibited its importance as a port in 1546–8, when La Gasca was massing his fleet for an invasion of that part of Peru held by Gonzalo Pizarro. One of La Gasca's minions wrote to him from Guañape that he had reached "this fortified port, stopped for wood and water and was proceeding by sea".

Utilising the Mochica–Chimú highways wherever possible, the Inca road planners had the coastal road extended from Guañape to the Moche valley. On its way there it passed the immense Pyramids of the Sun and the Moon, then, after crossing the Moche river, reached a royal *tampu* where, says Cieza, "the Incas built great storehouses and houses . . . the highway ran through it, with its walls".

By 1535 this *tampu* had been refounded as a Spanish city by Francisco Pizarro, who named it "Trujillo", after his birthplace in Spain. The valley in which the new city was situated was so large and bountiful, and so densely populated, that it and the adjoining river valley, Chicama, were divided up between six conquistador–encomienderos, the most prominent of whom was Diego de Mora.

When Cieza passed through in 1547, at the height of the civil war, he found that the Spanish residents had adopted Indian techniques in irrigating their flower and vegetable gardens, which were always green and in flower. "The site is healthy and surrounded on all sides by farms . . . planted with pomegranates, figs and other fruits of Spain, wheat and oranges, a wonderful sight . . . everywhere many vines have been planted." Diego de Mora wrote to Pizarro about "the wonderful quantity of grapes at Mabina".

Diego de Mora was the first to grow sugar cane in this area (which in time became the sugar bowl of all Peru), and also established the first *trapiche*, a mill turned by yoked oxen and used to crush sugar cane so as to extract the juice from which sugar and rum are prepared. Mora had a practical turn of mind and managed always to land on his feet; though originally a follower of Almagro, he eventually won for himself the larger share of the *tampu* that became Trujillo, now one of the largest cities of Peru.

However, Trujillo in 1545–7 was a troubled paradise. La Gasca was on the move southward and Gonzalo Pizarro's men were wavering. Mora tested the strength of the political winds and decided that the time was ripe to swop sides again. On 15th April 1547 Gonzalo Pizarro was informed by his men in Trujillo that Diego de Mora had sent for him "and requested me to join them and enlist under the King's banner . . . he, Diego de Mora, has turned against your lordship. He takes about sixty soldiers with him as well as His Majesty's gold."

There are six distinct and different highways in the valley between Huanchaco (*tampu* and port of Trujillo) and Chicama. One, which is 85 feet wide and bound by high walls, is definitely a Chimú ceremonial road; it makes an elaborate entrance into Chan Chan. By contrast, the Inca coastal road, which ran across what is now the airfield near Huanchaco, was strictly utilitarian, and much of it has been erased by sand drifts.

Moving over a pampa of coarse gravel, pumice and sand, the Inca road passed through Chiquitoy (where it can still be plainly seen running alongside a well-preserved truncated pyramid), and proceeded into the Chicama valley, where Diego de Mora had his sugar mill. This was fed by water from the great Chimú canal linking Chicama with the river Moche over a distance of forty miles. On leaving the Chicama valley, the Inca road proceeds in a northerly direction making for the pampas of Paijan.

In describing the coastal road, the royal treasurer Agustín de Zárate—who arrived in Peru in 1544 to make an inspection of the royal accounts, was caught up in the civil war, and left abruptly when Francisco de Carbajal threatened to hang him from the tallest tree in Peru if he caught him writing anything—complained that "owing to wars between Indians and Christians, its paving is broken in many places". However, he affirmed that "This Inca coastal road is still [1545] to be seen . . . the cool valleys through which the road passes have rivers [and the road] runs amidst trees and shrubs. . . . Yet across each valley they built the roads with stout mudbrick adobe walls from end to end . . . where these roads leave the valleys they continue over sandy deserts . . . the walls in the valleys for the most part stand complete to this day as evidence of the greatness of these works. . . ."

The very reality of this road angered Fernando de Armellones: "For we cannot conceal the great paradox that a barbarian [Huayna Capac] kept such excellent order . . . whereas today [1550] we see only infinite deserted villages on all the roads of the kingdoms. . . ."

Most of this had been caused on the orders of Gonzalo Pizarro, who reacted violently to the news that Diego de Mora and many others of his erstwhile followers had deserted to the King's banner. On 18th April 1547, a letter went out from Lima to all Pizarro's men posted on the coastal road: "Take all the food supplies, llamas, fowls, wheat . . . Induce all the Indians on the coast to rebel. . . . As for the chiefs, bring them with you when the enemy [that is, La Gasca] arrives. When they arrive, no llamas, no mules should be left behind and those that cannot be brought should be killed. . . ." His men complied. From San Miguel, in the far north of Peru, the faithful Villalobos replied, "I gave the alarm at once. I sent ten cavalrymen to Maycabilica [Poechas] to burn the *tampus* and wheatfields. . . . I have rounded up all the *caciques*, mostly youths, of Tumbes. I have sent for all the llamas and women. I intend to burn this *tampu* and leave it devastated. I have placed spies both Christian and Indian all along the coast. . . ."

All along the route to and beyond Cerro de Chocofán, the road had been disrupted and *tampus* ruined. However, where the highway crossed the

Pampa de Falco in the valley of Jequetepeque it needed neither paving nor steps, and thus was able to proceed relatively unscathed over the naturally hard surface of the rolling pampa. At Pacasmayu, it passed the massive Chimú structures called Pacatamú, which the civil wars left in ruins. Pedro de Cieza noted of this valley that "woven cotton material is made in quantity. Cattle do well here and swine and goats even better. I went through this Pacasmayu in the month of September 1547 to join the other soldiers . . . to support the King's cause . . . and this valley seemed very pleasant to me . . . with its freshness and its many groves of trees and thickets filled with thousands of birds."

As it moved on towards Saña, the road again ran into desert. At first sight this wasteland appears forbidding, utterly desolate and completely uninhabitable, but closer examination shows that the sands are marked with prints of small gray lizards. At night, foxes, which here are semi-herbivorous, come out to feed on the berries of the *lipe*, which grows in the dry valleys. The dunes are often capped with the short spikes of the *yuca del monte*, an edible tuber, and with low, twisted, scraggy trees that yield a fruit of sorts; on the sheltered side of the immense *médanos*, coarse vegetation flourishes. Signs of human ingenuity are also present: near a rocky outcrop known as Cerro Colorado runs what was once a functioning stone-lined canal, which in places runs close to and even beside the royal road.

At Saña, where the road widened perceptibly, there was a large *tampu*. This is still extant and may be seen to be divided into two rectangular sections, each 200 feet long and proportionately wide. In one section were kept llamas; in the other, which contained a number of distinct rooms, was the hostelry. So far it was perfectly ordinary *tampu* (indeed, Cieza said that it was "similar in every way to the others"), but its historical importance was such that in 1786 Charles III of Spain sponsored one of the first official archaeological investigations, specifically to find out more about it. The reason was that it was there, on 10th November 1532, that Pizarro and his band of conquistadors turned off the main coastal highway and began the long climb to Cajamarca.

All the details of that epic journey, which was to end in the capture, and eventually the death, of Atahuallpa, were written down by Pizarro's secretary, Francisco de Xeréz. He explained that, after Hernando de Soto's exploratory trip to Cajas (see Chapter 3), by which the Spaniards had learned that Atahuallpa was at Cajamarca, Pizarro decided against proceeding directly into the mountains and instead led his men south along the coastal highway for some distance. This road Xeréz described as "bound by walls wide enough for two carts to be driven abreast on it . . . and in many parts trees were planted on either side for shade". After some weeks they came to Saña, where, it had been explained to them, a road branched off the main highway and led directly to Cajamarca. This Pizarro decided to take, even though "there was a difficult mountain to traverse . . . and disaster might befall".

They marched to the foot of mountains and crossed the Cerro de la Viña to the canyon of Examen. Here "they rested for a day to arrange the order of ascent . . . and so, having made these arrangements, the Governor, that is Pizarro, commenced the ascent".

Following the step road (parts of which are still visible at Cerro de Culpon) through a little-used but highly fortified pass, the Spaniards climbed up the canyon to Sintupaya, then to what is now Hacienda de San José de Nancho, and then made the near perpendicular ascent to Cerro de San Gregorio to Paujal, where there are ruins. Continuing to Trigal, "where the road worsens", and passing through an *abra*, or "opening", where there are ruins everywhere, they emerged at what they named San Miguel. From there they marched across the high cordillera ("the cold is so great on these mountains . . . the horses were frost-bitten") until they reached the royal Andean road, which they took to Cajamarca.

Retracing in the opposite direction the road that the Spaniards took to the *tampu* of Saña, one passes first the river and highly cultivated valley of the same name, and then, after the usual interval of sand, comes to the next valley and river, where three immense aqueducts irrigated a vast tract of land. The *tampu* here was known as Cinto (modern Patapo), which Cieza tells us lay in a "beautiful valley". Cinto was a large urban centre, as the many ruins of houses and garrisons and the extensive walls show; remains both of Inca and of Chimú pottery have been found there. Before the Chimú came along, the valley was probably a large Mochica centre. "It was," reported Xeréz "a well-peopled valley through which a great and rapid river [the Lambeyeque] flowed." "Cinto" was actually the name of the "chief of the village and fortress where Pizarro lodged. He was then with Atabilba [Atahuallpa]".

After another twenty miles of desolation, the road came to Jayanca. Cieza asked that his readers "must realise that between one beautiful valley and another . . . lie sand wastes and arid stretches . . . and as the traveller trudges through all this and glimpses the next valley, his heart rejoices . . .".

Between Cinto and Jayanca, the road went first through a harsh desert with light stone covering, then came into a veritable forest of carob trees. Among the trees are great Mochica pyramids (occupied later by the Chimú), about which are many graves that have yielded superb golden ornaments to the tomb robbers. In the midst of the forest rises El Purgatorio, a massive stepped pyramid and an enormous complex of buildings, all created for the worship of the "upstairs gods". Through all this ran the royal road, complete with *chasqui* stations, *tampus*, temples, and storehouses, and still visible despite the destruction wrought by time and man.

## CHAPTER EIGHTEEN

# Tumbes

The *tampu* of Jayanca was built alongside one of the great irrigation ditches constructed by the coastal tribes. This channel passed through the lands of what is now La Viña Hacienda into what Cieza called "the lovely, cool valley of Jayanca. Through it flows the bonny river [Leche] from which they drew water to irrigate. In former times this valley was thickly settled and in it were great lodgings [still to be seen] and storehouses of their rulers. . . ."

Jayanca and four other *tampus* lying beyond it were given in *encomienda* to Francisco Lobo and Diego Gutiérrez, who must have done something really worthwhile to deserve all five; however only Lobo appears in the records, and we know little more of him than that he became a partisan of La Gasca. The remains of the original city of Jayanca, "the capital, the principal city of many valleys", are vast and partially hidden in a forest of carob trees; however, it is easy to see why the thirteenth Inca, Huayna Capac, took as one of his wives the daughter of the *curaca* of the valley.

The next *tampu* was that of Motu or Motupe, of which Cieza says that the road leading there was "wide and well-constructed. . . . The valley is broad and very fertile in spite of the fact that the good-size river disappears before it reaches the sea. Carob and other trees cover a large part of it." The reason why the river never reached the sea is that it ran into and was dried up by the hot sands of the immense Sechura desert, which borders the valley; the same happens to all the rivers that run from the sierra to the desert.

All travellers agree that the next phase of the journey northward was "long, wearying and hot", or, as Cieza succinctly put it, "all sand and hard-going". Eventually, however, the road reached the *tampu* of Serran, from where a road branched off to Cajas in the highlands. This was the lateral that Hernando de Soto and his forty horsemen took when, in 1532, at the very beginning of the conquest, Pizarro sent them to reconnoitre and to learn the whereabouts of Atahuallpa (see Chapter 3).

After Serran, the road continued northward through Tala (Ala) and

Morropón, and so entered a long appendix-shaped valley watered by the river Piura. "Here," said Cieza, "they plant corn, which yields two crops a year . . . yuca, which is used to make bread and a beverage [*chica*]. They raise many sweet potatoes, whose flavour reminds one of chestnuts. They also raise potatoes and a great variety of beans . . . and the usual fruits; the guava trees grow in profusion and cassia, avocados, squash, *caimitos*, pineapples, and since the Spaniards arrived, figs, grapes, quinces, lemons, limes. . . . All this makes it a pleasure to cross these valleys."

The original inhabitants of this area were the Tallanes. They submitted first to the Chimú, and then to the Incas; but the period between the Inca and the Spanish conquests was so short that when Cieza visited the region he found that "most of them had not yet learned the language of Cuzco [that is, Quechua]". They were, said Cieza, "more pleasure-loving than others. The chieftains were feared and obeyed . . . dancers entertained them with music and sang. They had many wives, selected from among the most beautiful . . . they had great dwellings, terraces, gateways, mud floors covered with mats. And when the Lord ate, a great multitude gathered, who drank of his beverage brewed from corn. . . . Although there were three or four different tribes among them, these *yungas*, [the name the Incas gave to all tribes inhabiting the *yungas*, or hot lands] they all had the same customs. They used to lodge the Spaniards who passed by their dwellings and treat them very kindly . . . they no longer do this . . ." (quoted from Pedro de Cieza de León, *The Incas*, translated by Harriet de Onis, edited with an introduction by Victor W. von Hagen, University of Oklahoma Press, Norman 1959).

The reason why the *yungas* no longer willingly played host was simply that, thanks to the Spaniards, there were hardly any of them left. Though the deaths directly caused by the Spanish conquest were relatively few, the diseases imported by the Spaniards—smallpox, measles and mumps—carried away vast multitudes. So too did the Spaniards' harsh treatment of their conquered subjects: "those sent to govern them", explained Cieza, "have done so with such acts of villainy . . . oppressive and troublesome, I myself grieve over the exhortations and harsh treatment and violent deaths the Spaniards have caused among the Indians . . .".

For in April 1547 Gonzalo Pizarro had as aforementioned, written to all of his minions—issued to all his Lieutenants and Municipal Authorities—"not a single sword, a single Indian . . . all their food supplies, llamas, fowls . . . so that when La Gasca and the King's men arrived nothing shall be left alive: no llamas, no mules and those that cannot be taken, killed. . . ."

From the northern headquarters at San Miguel de Piura, the first Spanish city formed in 1532, came a letter telling Pizarro that his instructions had been carried out. "I sent ten cavalrymen to Maycailica (the other name for the place called Poechos) to burn the *tampus* and wheatfields. I have the principal *caciques* of Tumbes here, but they are mostly youths . . . I intend to burn the towns and leave them devestated" (*Pizarro-La Gasca Papers*, II, 672–3, Huntingdon Library, unpublished).

Poechos, which was the next stop, thirty kilometres up the Chira River, was in those actions so destroyed that only three fragments of walls remain, yet when first seen by Pizarro and his men marching to find "Old Cuzco" on May 25, 1532, "he formed his camp in a large village called Poechos whereto all the chieftains came to make their peace". The Lord of the place was called "Maycaibilca", which name was often used for the *tampu* itself. Near it "at a distance of the shot of a crossbow (150 feet) there is a fortress surrounded by a wall with many rooms inside where the Spaniards were lodged . . . every day the Indians brought it all the supplies that were needed".

The final stages of the journey to Tumbes, the terminus of the coastal Inca Empire and the beginning-place of the Spanish conquest was through the tangled foothills of the Cerro de Amotape. It was along this route that the secretary of Pizarro made the first historical notations of an Inca highway: "The road is all made by hand, broad and well built and in some bad places [he meant inundated] it is paved with stone." It went through a place called Lacones, buried in the high dry-forest where Dr. Georg Petersen, a German engineer working in the district for many decades, found the *tampu* (Iglesia de Huacos) occupying a high narrow summit, with an accordingly long and narrow *tampu* over 310 feet in length by 30 in width, with its many rooms still mostly intact. The road zig-zagged over low verdured hills climbing up to 2,650 feet. There has been found and delineated a large administrative centre, *tampu* and fortress of Guineal. Further along in short distance was Huaquillas. All through this dry forest the *conquistadores* marched "along a road 15 feet wide with strong walls on both sides above the height of a man. All the way was very clean and shaded with Trees whose boughs in many places hung over heavy with Fruit and an Abundance of Parrots and other Birds . . . In each of these vales the Incas had stately apartments for themselves and mighty magazines. . . ."

This is the road Pizarro took in the spring of 1532. On the third day out of Tumbes, that is 16 May 1532, "he reached a village among the hills". That village is now called Rica Playa and as all the rest briefly mentioned here, the discovery of Dr Georg Petersen.

Dr. Georg Petersen, a professional engineer, long resident in Perú, and whose professional work over twenty years kept him in this area, kindly turned over to the author the results of a lifetime of labour. This was done after the author's book *Highway of the Sun* was published. This material with maps had now been published in one of those publications of limited circulation, hard to obtain, which causes discoveries such as this to slip by unnoticed until it is later found and usurped unacknowledged. The von

Hagen expedition found fragments of the road during 1952–56 of that which
Dr. Petersen had carefully found. Now for the first time, the precise route of
Pizarro's expedition in 1532 and the exact route of the Inca coastal route
from Poechos to its terminus at Tumbes is known. The author wishes to
acknowledge Dr. Petersen's pioneer work, his kindness in turning it all over
to him and his confidence that it would be used and—as it is now done—
gratefully acknowledged. On the basis of this the definitive map of the
direction of the Inca highway has been made.

Tumbes was the end, or if one started from it, the beginning.

Tumbes, or perhaps more correctly "Tumpiz" could be seen from the sea.
It stood then close to the sea-shore near where the River Tumbes debouches
into the sea. Tumpiz was once connected with the very shore itself by a
paved stone road. The site is not modern Tumbes, but the old site, now
called "San Pedro de los Incas". The shoreline has now changed, given over
to the cultivation of rice, but even then part of the stone causeway is visible
and on which rice grows stuntingly.

William Prescott has, since he worked from original documents, narrated
the story well: how after five harrowing years of search, Pizarro and his
men were conveyed—by following the shore traffic of balsa boats sailing
northward from Tumbes—to the shore of that fabled city.

The Spaniards first came to Tumbes in 1527—not, on that occasion, as
conquerors, but as men eager for hard evidence of the fabled wealth of Peru.
Pizarro captained the single ship that took them there.

Alonso de Molina and a negro sailor named Gines were selected to make
the first reconnaissance of the city. The report they brought back of temples
covered with gold seemed so exaggerated that Pedro de Candia was sent to
confirm it. Though more zealous than bright-witted, Candia could be relied
on in such matters; and not only did he confirm Molina's description but
also added to it, telling of the temples of the sun virgins, of the irrigated
valleys near the city, and of the many people, all of whom were well dressed
and had golden objects hanging from their lips and ears. Exactly how
Candia described the city itself is not known, but an idea of how it must have
appeared in its heyday can be gained from the description given by Alonso
Enríquez de Guzmán, who arrived in Tumbes in 1536. Though the city had,
in the meantime, been severely damaged in the civil wars between Huascar
and Atahuallpa, and had suffered neglect following the dismemberment of the
central governing system of the Inca empire, it was still "the great city of
Tumbes, a city inhabited by Indians close to the shore. There is a great house
[a temple, the ruins of which still extant] belonging to the lord of the country,
with walls built of adobe bricks beautifully painted with many colours and
varnished. I never saw anything more beautiful. The roof, although thatched
in straw is painted so that it looks like gold and silver. . . ."

Tumbes was once Tallanes country. This tribe, which occupied the